FRENCH
CHEESES

EYEWITNESS ◉ HANDBOOKS

FRENCH CHEESES

Foreword by **Joël Robuchon**

Written by
Kazuko Masui and Tomoko Yamada

Photography **Yohei Maruyama**

Wines recommended by **Robert and Isabelle Vifian**

Consultant **Randolph Hodgson**

A DK PUBLISHING BOOK

Produced for DK Publishing by PAGE*One*,
Cairn House, Elgiva Lane, Chesham, Buckinghamshire HP5 2JD
PROJECT DIRECTORS Bob Gordon, Helen Parker
EDITOR Anderley Moore

SENIOR MANAGING EDITOR Krystyna Mayer
SENIOR MANAGING ART EDITOR Lynne Brown
PRODUCTION CONTROLLER Meryl Silbert

First American Edition, 1996
2 4 6 8 10 9 7 5 3 1

Published in the United States by
DK Publishing, Inc., 95 Madison Avenue
New York, New York 10016
Visit us on the World Wide Web at http://www.dk.com

Library of Congress Cataloging-in-Publication Data
Masui, Kazuko.
    French cheeses / by Kazuko Masui, Tomoko Yamada. — 1st American ed.
      p.   cm.
    ISBN 0–7894–1070–2 (flexibinding)
    ISBN 0-7894-1437-6 (hardcover)
    1. Cheese—Varieties—France—Encyclopedias. 2. Cheese—Varieties—
Encyclopedias. 3. Cheese—Varieties—France—Pictorial works. 4. Cheese—
Varieties—Pictorial works. I. Yamada, Tomoko. II. Title.
SF274.F7M36   1996
637'.35'0944—dc20   96-14790
                                          CIP

Printed and bound in Singapore

Contents

Foreword 6

How to use this book 8

Foreword

At last – and what a pleasure for me to say so!

Because among all the cheese books published to date – including that admirable work by Pierre Androuët – none as far as I know is based on so many valuable photographs for the identification and choice of a cheese ripened to perfection.

This book is for people who care for the good things in life, for amateurs with a love of cheese and serious gourmets alike. It takes you on a journey through the many regions of France, teaching you all you ought to know about cheese, and helping you in your choice. Expert knowledge is the key to an appreciation of pure and authentic flavors. Here is a reliable handbook for those who wish to share those flavors with their friends, and a clear and easy-to-follow initiation into the secrets of cheesemaking. Connoisseurs may read it with interest and pleasure. Amateurs will give it pride of place among their books and profit whenever they consult it.

Writing this preface fills me with a sense of duty, so that others may share what I know. Yes, I love cheese! It's a marvelous product, inscribed in that great trinity of the table, which it forms with bread and wine.

Cheese is part of what we have been eating from the beginning of time. A national French food for as long as people recall, it reflects nature as much as their own history. A concentrate of that life-giving liquid, namely milk, it allows us to conserve its many qualities. The extent of our range of cheese, remarked on already by

Cheeses from every region
The 22 different regions of France produce more than 500 cheeses from ewe, goat, and cow's milk.

the Roman naturalist Pliny the Elder, mirrors the diversity of our land as well as the art of dairymen and women and of social and economic developments over the ages. The example of monastic cheesemakers or that of cheese such as *tommes* or *reblochons* given in lieu of tax demonstrate the point.

To conclude then, what could be more satisfactory than to know for oneself which cheese to choose in preference to another? It's an informed choice, which shows understanding and results in joy.

JOËL ROBUCHON

How to use this book

This book is the ideal quick-reference guide to selecting and identifying French cheeses at home, in your local cheese shop, or traveling in France. More than 350 cheeses are organized alphabetically. Similar cheeses of the same family or type are grouped. Details are given on where the cheeses are made, methods of production, appearance, smell, and taste. Special feature boxes that appear throughout the book give useful background information.

At the end of the book, useful terms are explained in a concise glossary, which is followed by a list of French shops and markets that specialize in cheese. The book concludes with a comprehensive index that also indicates where each cheese in the book was purchased.

IMPORTANT WORDS

AOC stands for Appellation d'Origine Contrôlée, a government body that controls the quality and production of important cheeses. Turn to p. 77 for a full explanation of AOC.

Fermier, *artisanal*, *coopérative*, and *industriel* refer to the method of production. Turn to p. 22 for a full explanation of these terms.

Affinage is a French word that means both the ripening and curing of a cheese

Pâte is a French word that refers to all that is within the rind or crust of a cheese.

RUNNING HEADS
A single letter or the name of a group of cheeses tells you which alphabetical section you are in.

COLORED CIRCLES
A colored circle (see key opposite) indicates the method of production. Where several cheeses of different production methods appear on the same page, a similar number of colored circles may be seen in a corresponding sequence.

MAPS
Each entry is accompanied by a map. A red dot marks the origin of the cheese.

DOTTED LINES
Most cheeses are separated by a solid line. A dotted line separates cheeses with common characteristics or belonging to the same family.

MILK TYPES
The type of milk (raw, pasteurized, or whole) is given below the animal head(s). "Not defined" indicates milk type is not stipulated. See page 135 for full information on milk.

REGIONS AND DEPARTMENTS
The region of production is given by the side of each map, followed by the number(s) of the department(s) in brackets. These refer to the map of the regions and departments on p. 16–17.

TRIANGLES
A solid line followed by a blue triangle signals the end of a group.

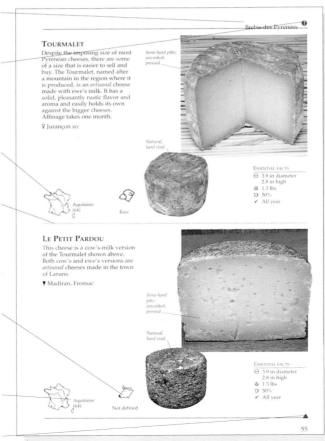

Brebis des Pyrénées

TOURMALET
Despite the imposing size of most Pyrénéan cheeses, there are some of a size that is easier to sell and buy. The Tourmalet, named after a mountain in the region where it is produced, is an *artisanal* cheese made with ewe's milk. It has a solid, pleasantly rustic flavor and aroma and easily holds its own against the bigger cheeses. Affinage takes one month.

♀ Jurançon *sec*

Semi-hard pâte; uncooked; pressed

Natural, hard rind

Aquitaine (64)

Raw

ESSENTIAL FACTS
⊖ 3.9 in diameter
  2.8 in high
⊕ 1.3 lbs
⊃ 50%
✓ All year

LE PETIT PARDOU
This cheese is a cow's-milk version of the Tourmalet shown above. Both cow's and ewe's versions are *artisanal* cheeses made in the town of Laruns.

♪ Madiran, Fronsac

Semi-hard pâte; uncooked; pressed

Natural, hard rind

Aquitaine (64)

Not defined

ESSENTIAL FACTS
⊖ 3.9 in diameter
  2.8 in high
⊕ 1.3 lbs
⊃ 50%
✓ All year

55

CAMEMBERT DE NORMANDIE (AOC)

To many people, the name of Camembert is synonymous with French cheese. Even before Camembert was granted its AOC in 1983, it was the most copied cheese in the world. You should always choose a Camembert by eye: the shape should be intact, and the rind covered in white mold, with reddish stripes and stains. The pâte should be creamy yellow, supple and give slightly to finger pressure. There should be a light smell of mold and the taste may be too salty at times. The locals prefer Camembert *moitié affiné* – half and half – when the *filet* or heart is still white and not yet creamy.

Coopérative and *industriel* versions of Camembert are produced, with an affinage of a minimum of 21 days from the date of manufacture within the AOC areas listed. Today, it is hard to find good Camembert: a young cheesemaker has taken up the production of Camembert *fermier* (p. 64) but his cheese has yet to be granted an AOC.

♥ St. Emilion, St. Estèphe

Rind of white mold pierced by red stains

AOC REGULATIONS: CAMEMBERT DE NORMANDIE

1. Concentrated or powdered milk, lactic proteins, or coloring may not be added to the milk.

2. The milk must not be heated above 98.6°F.

3. The uncut curd must be sliced vertically.

4. The curd must be cast with a ladle whose diameter corresponds to that of the mold; the operation is undertaken in stages, with a minimum of four successive fillings (pp. 64–65).

5. Salting is carried out with dry salt exclusively

6. After salting the cheeses are taken to the drying room, where the temperature is between 50°F and 57°F; they are left in wooden boxes. Before this, they may be placed on boards, in cellars at 46 or 48°F.

7. The words *Fabrication traditionnelle au lait cru avec moulage à la louche* may appear on the label of a cheese benefiting from the AOC. *Fabriqué en Normandie* indicates the place of production on the labels of cheeses not benefiting from the AOC.

AOC GRANTED 1983

ESSENTIAL FACTS
⊖ 4.1–4.3 in diameter 1.2 in high
🏋 8.8 oz min.
⁝ 4.1 oz per cheese
Ɗ 45% min.
✓ All year

Normandie (14, 50, 61, 27, 76)

Raw

66

MILK-TYPE SYMBOLS

A cow, sheep, or goat's head depicts the animal that produces the milk used in the production of the cheese. Where more than one type of milk is used, several heads are shown.

CHEESE NAMES
Where a cheese is given two or more names, the first is the local name used in the region of origin, followed by any other names by which the cheese is known.

MAIN ENTRIES
These give information on place of production, appearance, flavor, and smell. For some AOC or more important cheeses, details are also given on production methods.

ANNOTATIONS
These give information on appearance of each cheese.

ESSENTIAL FACTS
These give dimensions, shape, weight, fat content, dry matter, and season relevant to each cheese (see below for key to symbols).

AOC REGULATIONS BOXES
These boxes list some of the most important guidelines in the making of a cheese as outlined by the AOC (p. 77).

ESSENTIAL FACTS SYMBOLS

⊖ Shape
🏋 Weight
⁝ Dry matter – the residue after all the water in the cheese has been eliminated.
Ɗ Fat content – the amount of fat contained in the dry matter. "Not defined" indicates that the fat content is not stipulated.
✓ Season indicates when the cheese is usually eaten.

DRINKS SYMBOLS

Ⅱ Beer or cider
♀ Champagne
☕ Coffee
♥ Red wine
♀ White, or *rosé* wine
◻ Spirits (e.g. *marc*)

KEY TO COLORED CIRCLES IN RUNNING HEADS

The colored circles in the running heads give at-a-glance information on the methods of production used.

① Fresh, rindless cheese that is shaped and kneaded and has no affinage; e.g., *fromage frais* (fresh cheeses), p. 143–147

② Uncooked, unpressed, soft cheese with a white mold, e.g., Camembert, p. 66

③ Uncooked, unpressed, soft cheese with a washed rind, e.g,. Munster, p. 158

④ Uncooked, unpressed, soft cheese with a natural mold sometimes covered in ashes, e.g., *chèvre* (goat's cheeses), p. 78–111

⑤ Uncooked, unpressed, soft cheese with veins of blue mold, e.g., *bleu* (blue cheeses), p. 29–35

⑦ Uncooked, pressed, semi-hard cheese, with a natural mold, e.g., Saint-Nectaire, p. 184

⑧ Uncooked, pressed, semi-hard cheese with a washed, rubbed, and waxed rind, e.g., monastery cheeses such as Port-du-Salut, p. 173

⑨ Cooked, pressed, hard cheese, e.g., Beaufort, p. 26

⑩ Cheese started with whey, e.g., Brocciu, p. 116

⑫ Product based on cheese, e.g., *fromage fort*, p. 134–136

9

The origins of cheese

*"Rest with me on green foliage: we have ripe fruit,
soft chestnuts, and plenty of fresh cheese."* VIRGIL, 42 BC

CHEESE is one of the most ancient forms of manufactured food. The first real evidence of cheese is in ancient Sumerian writings from about 3000 BC, which refer to nearly 20 soft cheeses. Remains of cheesemaking equipment discovered in Europe and Egypt also appear to date back to about 3000 BC. However, we can only guess at when the craft of cheesemaking actually started. The most likely theory is that in around 10,000 BC, when sheep and goats were domesticated, early herdspeople began to take

Cow's-milk cheeses
Since their domestication thousands of years ago, cattle have been bred selectively for the quantity and quality of milk they produce for cheesemaking.

advantage of the fact that sour milk naturally separated into curds and whey. If drained off, shaped, and dried, the curds provided them with a simple and nourishing food. Cow's-milk cheeses came two or three thousand years after the sheep and goat-milk cheeses as cattle were not domesticated until considerably later.

Cheese in ancient Greece and Rome
References to cheese and cheesemaking are dotted throughout ancient literature, including the Old Testament. Homer's *Odyssey* tells how Ulysses and his men hide in the Cyclops' cavern, while the one-eyed giant milks his ewes and goats, then curdles half the milk, drains the curds, and sets them aside in wicker baskets.

Roman cheeses

The Romans enjoyed eating cheese both raw and cooked in little cakes, called *glycinas*, made from sweet white wine and olive oil. In a treatise on farming written in AD 60–65, Roman agricultural writer Columella tells how cheeses were made from fresh milk, which was curdled by the addition of *coagulum* – rennet extracted from the fourth stomach of a lamb or kid.

The curds were pressed to expel the whey, and then sprinkled with salt and left to harden in a shady place. Columella explains that, apart from enhancing the flavor, the salt helped dry and preserve the cheese, and so the process of salting and hardening was carried on. The ripe cheeses were washed, dried, and packed for shipping, perhaps to an army depot, since cheese was included in a legionnaire's daily ration. Caesar himself is said to have eaten a blue cheese at Saint-Affrique, just to the west of Roquefort, where one of the world's most celebrated blue cheeses is still produced today.

Cheese and language

The vast network of Roman roads set up communications that influenced language. The Latin word for cheese, *caseus*, became Italian *cacio*, German *Käse* and English *cheese*, as well as Spanish *queso* and *queijo* in Portuguese. The Italian *formaggio* and French *fromage* also derive from Latin, although the root of these words is in the Greek *formos* – the Cyclops's wicker basket.

After the Romans

Soon after the collapse of the Roman Empire, Barbarian invaders overran much of Europe. Subsequent invasions by the Normans, Mongols, and Saracens, followed by successive outbreaks of the plague, devastated the continent. The ancient cheesemaking recipes and techniques, developed over thousands of years, were gradually forgotten, surviving only in the mountains and in remote monasteries. It was there that some of the oldest traditional cheesemaking methods were preserved for us to appreciate today.

The *fromager*
The makers and sellers of cheese are known in France as fromagers. *Many of these craftspeople still make and ripen cheeses in family businesses following traditional techniques passed down the generations.*

Ancient affinage
Many of the techniques for ripening cheese date back thousands of years. This process, known as affinage, *hardens the cheese so that it keeps longer.*

Cheese, wine, and bread

"Cheese is probably the best of all foods,
as wine is the best of all beverages." PATIENCE GRAY, 1957

IN FRANCE, cheese and wine have been considered natural allies for as long as people can remember. This view remains valid today, but we must not forget bread, which cements the union. Indeed, there can be few greater pleasures in life than a good, ripe *fermier* cheese, matched with a glass of quality wine and a chunk of freshly baked bread. The great advantage of this union is that cheese, wine, and bread are all foods that can be enjoyed in their "raw" state, with little or no preparation, making them an ideal choice for quick snacks or picnics. It is no coincidence, therefore, that generations of French farmworkers have relied on local cheeses, wines, and bread to fortify them while they work in the fields.

Wine with cheese
The best wine to enjoy with cheese is one that you like. By tasting a range of combinations, you can develop your own preferences.

The "Holy Trinity" of the table
Because of their close association, cheese, wine, and bread have occasionally been called the Holy Trinity of the table, an expression that may have been coined by the French humanist François Rabelais, whose writings attest to a great liking for food. Born at Chinon in around 1494, he would, of course, have tasted at least

Crusty French bread
This long crusty baguette is traditionally eaten fresh from the bakery. With a hunk of cheese and a good wine it makes a simple, hearty meal.

some of the outstanding goat-milk cheeses Touraine is still famous for today.

Rabelais was a Roman Catholic monk for much of his life and was thus familiar with the concept of the Holy Trinity – inseparable God the Father, God the Son, God the Holy Spirit – yet even he admitted that some cheeses are better served with fruit, than bread: "There is no match you could compare to Master Cheese and Mistress Pear."

The action of yeasts and bacteria
Although bread, cheese, and wine are produced from different materials – bread is made from grain, wine from grapes, and cheese from milk – they each depend on yeasts and bacteria for their development. Without the changes brought about by fermentation, bread doughs would not rise, wines would be devoid of alcohol, and cheeses would simply not taste like cheese. In addition, it is the action of the fermentation that makes all of these products keep.

Just as the flavor, body, and bouquet of a wine depend on the grape variety, production techniques, and the technique and length of aging, so the taste, texture, flavor, and aroma of cheeses depend on the milk from which they are produced – cow, goat, ewe, or mixed milks – and the methods used to make and ripen them.

Accompanying breads
The combination of foods is a matter of harmony and contrasts, be it in looks, textures, temperatures, flavors, or smells, all of which are subject to personal likes

and dislikes. A simple rule of thumb might be that the more delicate the cheese, the whiter and less salted ought to be the bread to go with it, while spiced breads, which are often made with sour milk and thus already contain a dairy flavor, are most enjoyable with a powerful blue cheese.

Which wine to choose

Although much advice is given on which wines should be selected to accompany a particular food or dish, there are no hard and fast rules. The best selections are almost always based on individual tastes because different people naturally prefer different combinations. The only way to know and develop your own preferences is to sample as many wines as possible with as wide a variety of foods as you can.

Compared with a dish composed of a number of ingredients, cheese is a unique product that may be matched relatively easily with a wine. Matches are usually made in terms of texture and taste rather than smell, and a particular wine is often selected to accompany a particular cheese on the basis of similarities, contrasts, or complementary characteristics.

A smooth, fatty cheese may go very well with a similarly smooth, slightly oily wine, while a cheese with high acidity often contrasts very well with a sweet, alcoholic wine. Very salty cheeses may be complemented by a wine with good acidity. It is worth bearing in mind that, as a general rule, the longer a cheese is left to ripen, the more it will dominate and "attack" the flavor of a wine.

Many people erroneously believe that cheese should be eaten exclusively with red wine. One of the principal reasons for this may be that cheeses are usually served at the end of a meal, when it is difficult to return to a dry white wine after a red, especially if the red is full-bodied. It is true, however, that white wines go better with many cheeses than reds, and it is well worth sampling a few combinations for the experience.

Many of the wines recommended by Robert and Isabelle Vifian in this book come from the same region as the cheese with which they are matched. Their choice is often based on the traditional combinations of wine and cheese favored by the local people.

Wine is not the only drink that goes well with cheese, however. In areas such as Normandie, where little or no wine is produced, the cheeses are often better matched with a good local beer or cider, or sometimes even coffee. With cheeses that have been cured in *eau-de-vie* it is worth trying a good *marc*.

It is important to remember that the wine suggestions in this book are no more than pointers – it is individual taste and pleasure that count most of all.

An alternative to meat
Cheese is a valuable source of protein and an appetizing alternative to meat as a main meal served with potatoes, fresh green salad, and a good wine.

French cheeses today

"How can anyone be expected to govern a country with 325 cheeses?" GENERAL CHARLES DE GAULLE

SINCE CHARLES DE GAULLE made his famous statement over 30 years ago, the number of cheeses produced in France has, according to recent estimates, increased to around 500 – a count that could be higher still if we include local, homemade cheeses that are unlikely to be found outside their region of production. We might deduce from these figures alone that French cheesemaking is prospering, an impression confirmed by official statistics as well as the wide range of cheeses offered in many shops, restaurants, and supermarkets.

Changing attitudes
A growing preference for vegetarian foods and a modern tendency for people to graze during the day rather than sit down to cooked meals, both favor cheese.

A wide variety
The increased demand for a wider variety of cheeses has led to the mass-production of cheeses such as Camembert, which is now available worldwide.

Nothing could be easier, tastier, or more nourishing than a light meal of a few good pieces of cheese, with bread, salad, and fresh fruit on the side. No doubt we shall continue to see cheeses being offered at the end of a formal lunch or dinner. However, more and more people accept that unless we plan our menus in order to leave room for cheese, only the heartiest of appetites can do them justice.

The effect of the supermarket
One of the greatest changes to the sale and production of French cheeses has been the increase in numbers of supermarkets. Even in traditionally rural areas of France, supermarkets are gradually replacing the village shops that used to sell a wide variety of household goods, food, and drink. Despite constant criticism by people who have forgotten the frustrations of not finding what they want in the village shop, supermarkets have brought down prices and offer a wider variety of fresher produce. Cheeses, however, pose a problem for supermarkets since most of them require expert care if they are to be allowed to reach maturity when their textures and flavors are at their peak. The village grocer might have had the knowledge and patience to mature some Camembert or Brie, but he also took the risk of being left with some rather smelly old cheeses that no one would buy. Supermarkets, which rely on a quick turnover and are best at selling large quantities of uniform goods, cannot afford to take this risk and prefer to stock mainly *industriel* (factory), rather than *artisanal* (artisan) or *fermier* (farmhouse) cheeses.

Gourmet cheese shops
It is at the specialty cheese shop – in a small town or a large city – where the best cheeses can be bought. Just like people with a passion for good wines, lovers of cheese have become both better informed and more demanding in their choice. What they are looking for is character and flavor, the attributes given to a cheese by the care and attention of

the artisan cheesemaker using traditional techniques rather than by the technician applying science in a factory.

The traditional cheesemaker is backed up by the careful husbandry of the farmer producing the finest milk. However, it is not only the traditional cheeses that are proving so popular. New cheeses, too, are being developed and made by hand, in limited numbers, on small farms in many areas of France.

Into the future

Over the last 50 years, French cheese-making has been subject to a number of European regulations that are too often based on the methodology of the factory and do not take account of the advantages of the farm. They tend to be drawn up by scientists and, as a result, are unsympathetic to the needs of France's many *artisanal* and *fermier* cheesemakers,

several of whom have been producing traditional cheeses for generations. Unless people discover for themselves the superiority of a good, handmade *fermier* cheese over one that has been mass-produced in a factory, they will never understand why it is so important – and worthwhile – to protect and promote small-scale cheesemaking.

Ultimately, the future of France's many traditional cheeses depends on people being aware of what is available, knowing what to select or buy in a shop or a restaurant, and asking for it if is not already on display. This book will provide you with the information you need – now it's up to you to go out and taste them.

Cheese markets

Some of the best regional fermier *and* artisanal *cheeses can be found in cheese markets, where local cheesemakers often have their own stalls.*

Map of France

THIS MAP shows the administrative regions (*régions*) of France, each of which is made up of a number of standard-sized departments (*départements*). In total there are 96 departments and 22 regions, all of which are listed below. To find out where a cheese is produced, first look up the minimap that accompanies the entry in the book and make a note of the name of the region and the number of the department. The red spot shows you roughly where to look on the map. The list below gives the names of the departments, many of which are named after rivers.

Alsace
Bas-Rhin (67),
Haut-Rhin (68)

Aquitaine
Dordogne (24),
Gironde (33) Landes (40),
Lot-et-Garonne (47),
Pyrénées-Atlantiques (64)

Auvergne
Allier (03), Cantal (15),
Haute-Loire (43),
Puy-de-Dôme (63)

Bourgogne
Côte d'Or (21),
Nièvre (58),
Sâone-et-Loire (71),
Yonne (89)

Bretagne
Côtes-du-Nord (22),
Finistère (29),
Ille-et-Vilaine (35),
Morbihan (56)

Centre
Cher (18), Eure-et-Loire
(28), Indre (36),
Indre-et-Loire (37),
Loir-et-Cher (41),
Loiret (45)

Champagne-Ardenne
Ardennes(08), Aube (10),
Marne (51),
Haute-Marne (52)

Corse
Corse-du-Sud (2A),
Haute-Corse (2B)

Franche-Comté
Doubs (25), Jura (39),
Haute-Sâone (70),
Territoire de Belfort (90)

Ile-de-France
Paris (Ville de) (75),
Seine-et-Marne (77),
Yvelines (78),
Essonne (91),
Hauts-de-Seine (92),
Seine-Saint-Denis (93),
Val-de-Marne (94),
Val-d'Oise (95)

Languedoc-Roussillon
Aude (11), Gard (30),
Hérault (34), Lozère (48),
Pyrénées-Orientales (66)

Limousin
Corrèze (19), Creuse (23),
Haute-Vienne (87)

Loire (Pays de la)
Loire-Atlantique (44),
Maine-et-Loire (49),
Mayenne (53), Sarthe (72),
Vendée (85)

Lorraine
Meurthe-et-Moselle (54),
Meuse (55), Moselle (57),
Vosges (88)

Midi-Pyrénées
Ariège (09), Aveyron (12),
Haute-Garonne (31),
Gers (32), Lot (46),
Hautes-Pyrénées (65),
Tarn (81),
Tarn-et-Garonne (82)

Nord-Pas-de-Calais
Nord (59),
Pas-de-Calais (62)

Normandie (Haute-)
Eure (27),
Seine-Maritime (76)

Normandie (Basse-)
Calvados (14),
Manche (50), Orne (61)

Picardie
Aisne (02), Oise (60),
Somme (80)

Poitou-Charentes
Charente (16),
Charente-Maritime (17),
Deux-Sèvres (79),
Vienne (86)

**Provence-Alpes-
Côte-d'Azur**
Alpes-de-Haute-Provence
(04), Hautes-Alpes (05),
Alpes-Maritimes (06),
Bouches-du-Rhône (13),
Var (83), Vaucluse (84)

Rhône-Alpes
Ain (01), Ardèche (07),
Drôme (26), Isère (38),
Loire (42), Rhône (69),
Savoie (73),
Haute-Savoie (74)

62

Nord-Pas-de-Calais

59

80

76

02

08

Picardie

60

Normandie
(Haute-)

55

57

95

27

51

Lorraine

67

78 92 75 77

54

94

Ile-de-France

91

Champagne-Ardenne

Alsace

88

28

10

52

68

72

45

89

70

90

Centre

21

Franche-Comté

41

25

37

Bourgogne

18

58

86

36

71

39

03

Charentes

01

74

16

87

23

63

42

69

Limousin

73

Auvergne

19

38

Rhône-Alpes

24

15

43

05

46

07

26

47

48

82

84

04

06

12

30

Provence-Alpes-Côte-d'Azur

32

Midi-Pyrénées

13

83

2B

31

34

Corse

Languedoc-Roussillon

11

09

2A

66

Abbaye de Cîteaux

Although the Abbey of Saint-Nicholas-des-Cîteaux dates back some 900 years, production of this *fermier* cheese began as recently as 1925. It is as soft to the eye as it is to the palate, and rather milder than the majority of washed-crust cheeses. Sixty tons are made every year from the milk of 70 Montbéliard cows. Most of the cheeses are eaten locally.

❢ Beaujolais or Bourgogne, young and fruity, chilled

Semi-hard pâte; uncooked, unpressed

Essential Facts
- ⊝ 7.1 in diameter
  1.4 in high
- ⚖ 1.5 lbs
- ▭ 45%
- ✔ All year

Smooth, washed grayish yellow rind

Bourgogne (21)

Raw

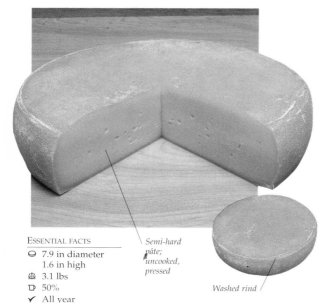

Abbaye de la Joie Nôtre-Dame

This *fermier* cheese has been produced by the nuns of the Abbaye de la Joie Nôtre-Dame since 1953. The recipe was passed on to the convent when it became independent from the Abbaye de la Coudre (p. 210). This fine and elegant cheese is one of the numerous descendants of Port-du-Salut (p. 173), the very first French monastery cheese, which it resembles both in appearance and taste. During affinage it is washed with brine for four to six weeks.

❢ Bordeaux, young and fruity

Essential Facts
- ⊝ 7.9 in diameter
  1.6 in high
- ⚖ 3.1 lbs
- ▭ 50%
- ✔ All year

Semi-hard pâte; uncooked, pressed

Washed rind

Bretagne (56)

Raw

Abbaye du Mont des Cats

The monks of the abbey, near the town of Godewaersvelde (Plain of God) in Flanders, started production of this *artisanal* cheese in 1890 using the Port-du-Salut recipe (p. 173). It is made in a small independent dairy from milk that has been bought in from neighboring farms. The cheese shown has been cured using modern methods and is not yet ripe. The small holes are characteristic of this cheese. Locally, it is often served as a breakfast cheese with coffee. Affinage takes a minimum of one month, during which time the cheese is regularly washed with brine dyed with *rocou*, a reddish extract of annatto seeds.

❦ Graves

Nord-Pas-
de-Calais (59)

Raw

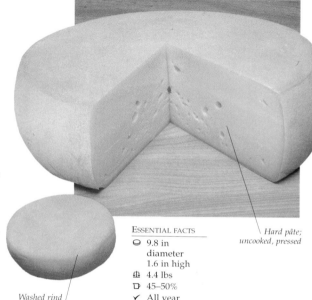

*Hard pâte;
uncooked, pressed*

Washed rind

ESSENTIAL FACTS

◯ 9.8 in
  diameter
  1.6 in high
⚖ 4.4 lbs
◷ 45–50%
✔ All year

Abbaye de la Pierre-qui-Vire

Both this cheese and the Boule des Moines (below) are *fermier* cheeses made by 12 of the 85 monks at the Abbaye de la Pierre-qui-Vire from the milk of 40 cows. Since the monks use neither chemical fertilizers nor pesticides, both cheeses are organic. During the affinage of two weeks the cheese is washed with brine. It should be eaten when young.

❦ Beaune

Boule des Moines

This soft, fresh version of the above cheese was launched to boost sales. The flavored pâte has a strong smell of garlic.

❦ Irancy, young and fruity

Bourgogne
(89)

Raw

*Soft pâte, smooth
and supple;
uncooked, unpressed*

Washed rind

**Abbaye de la
Pierre-qui-Vire**

ESSENTIAL FACTS

◯ 3.9 in
  diameter
  1 in high
⚖ 7.1 oz
◷ Not defined
✔ All year, best
  in summer
  and autumn

*Soft pâte, mixed
with garlic, chives,
and pepper*

**Boule des
Moines**

ESSENTIAL FACTS

◯ 2–2.8 in diameter
⚖ 3.5 oz
◷ Not defined
✔ All year, especially
  summer and autumn

Creamy to pale yellow pâte, supple without elasticity, with small, even holes; half-cooked at 113–122°F, pressed

Dark yellow to brown rind, with cloth traces and a blue casein label on the side

This Abondance *d'alpage fermier* has had an affinage of ten months

This Abondance *d'hiver fermier* has had an affinage of seven months

ESSENTIAL FACTS

- 14.9–16.9 in diameter
  2.8–3.7 in high
- 5.4–17.6 lbs
- 2 oz min. per 3.5 oz cheese
- 48% or 9 oz min. per 3.5 oz cheese
- Autumn for cheeses made at a *chalet d'alpage*

ABONDANCE (AOC)

This medium-sized mountain cheese from Haute Savoie in the Rhône-Alpes is produced using milk from cows of the Abondance, Montbéliard, and Tarine breeds. The animals must not be fed any silage or other fermented fodder. The *fromage d'alpage* (p. 54) shown here was made in September at an alpine *chalet*. It has a strong smell and a distinct and complex flavor, with a balance of acidity and sweetness and a long aftertaste. The crust, including the gray layer beneath, should be removed before eating.

Artisanale, coopérative, and *industriel* versions of Abondance are produced, but around 40% of the 383 tons made each year are *fermier* cheeses, and production is increasing. *Fermier* cheeses have an oval, blue *casein* label on the side, while all other versions have a square label. Affinage takes at least 90 days during which time a maximum of three samples are taken from the core of the cheese with a cheese iron.

❢ Vin de Savoie, Côtes de Nuits Villages, Morey St. Denis, Fixin

AOC REGULATIONS: ABONDANCE

1. The milk may be heated once to a maximum of 104°F, but only at the renneting. Systems or machinery that would allow the rapid heating to above 104°F before renneting may not be kept on the premises.

2. Salt is applied to the surface of the cheese either directly or with brine.

3. A *casein* label must bear the following information: France; Abondance; the ID number of the place of production: *fermier* for the farm category of cheeses.

AOC GRANTED 1990

Rhône-Alpes (74)

Raw, whole

How Abondance is Made

It takes 26.4 gallons of milk from cattle grazing in the mountain pastures to make a single Abondance of 20.9 lbs.

Renneting and coagulation
When the rennet is added, the milk is heated to 90–95°F. Coagulation (**2**) takes 35 minutes.

Cutting the curd (*le décaillage*)
The curd (*caillé*) is carefully cut into small pieces and stirred vigorously to separate out the whey. As it separates, the curd turns grainy (**3**). The whey, which is usually thrown away, contains proteins and sugars.

Scalding
The curd is heated to 86°F and on to 122°F, over 45 minutes. The whey continues to separate, while the curd turns into grains the size of wheat, with a milky color, rubbery consistency, and slightly sugary taste. Scalding dries the curd and cooks it. If the curd is heated too quickly or too much the pâte may break or swell during affinage.

Drawing off (*le soutirage*)
The curd is gathered, or "drawn off" in a linen gauze (**4**).

First pressing
The curd is pressed into a wooden hoop mold lined with gauze (**1**). A rope can be tightened to adjust the diameter of the cheese, which expands above and below the hoop (**6**). Seven or eight filled hoops are stacked (**7** and **8**) and pressed in the *pressoir* for 20 minutes. The curd grains begin to stick to each other.

Second pressing and labeling
The molds are turned immediately and *casein* labels slipped in on the side. After the fourth turning, in the evening, when the wet gauze is changed for a dry one, the molds are pressed at maximum force. The curd grains fuse, and the cheese takes its final shape. The cheese is taken out of the mold and left for a day to let the pâte cool.

Salting
The cheese is soaked in brine for 12 hours to speed up the formation of the crust, improve its appearance, and reduce the risk of mould. The cheese is allowed to dry for 24 hours.

Affinage
The affinage takes place over a minimum of 90 days in a well-ventilated cellar. On alternate days the surface of the cheese is rubbed with coarse salt and wiped with a cloth soaked in *morge*. The abrasive action of the salt limits the growth of mold and helps build up the strong crust (**9**) that conserves these large cheeses for a long time. *Morge* is made by mixing brine with the sticky, light-brown substance found on the crusts of old cheeses.

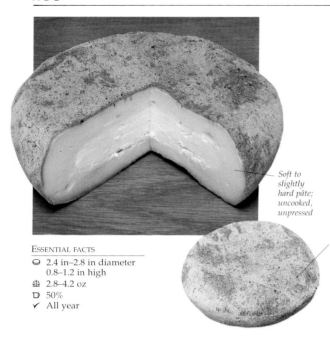

Soft to
slightly
hard pâte;
uncooked,
unpressed

ESSENTIAL FACTS

- ⊖ 2.4 in–2.8 in diameter
  0.8–1.2 in high
- ⚖ 2.8–4.2 oz
- ⊅ 50%
- ✓ All year

Aisy Cendré

This *artisanal* cheese from
Bourgogne is made by burying a
young cheese in ashes for a month.
A number of cheeses can be used
as a base for Aisy cendré but the
one shown here is a young
Epoisses de Bourgogne (p. 133),
a strong, washed cheese. It is not
yet matured and would be perfect
for people who prefer an unripe
center. The heart is white, with
the texture of plaster, and is
surrounded by a more creamy
pâte. The salty taste indicates
that it is still young.

❢ Hautes Côtes de Nuits Villages

Rind covered
with ashes

Bourgogne
(21)

Raw,
whole

Categories and conditions of production

The four main categories of production
permitted by the AOC (see page 77) are
fermier, *artisanal*, *coopérative*, and *industriel*.

The category of *fermier* is not a guarantee of
quality, however, it suggests that a cheese
is made according to traditional methods.

CATEGORY	CONDITIONS OF PRODUCTION	QUANTITIES PRODUCED	WHERE THE CHEESES ARE SOLD
Fermier (made in a farmhouse, *chalet d'alpage*, *buron*, or other mountain hut)	An individual producer uses the milk of animals (cows, goats, sheep) raised on his or her farm to make cheese following traditional methods. Milk from neighboring farms is not allowed. Only raw milk may be used.	Small	Regional markets and a few *fromageries* in large towns. Some are exported to other countries.
Artisanal	An individual producer uses the milk of animals raised on his or her farm, or brings in milk to make cheese. (The producer is the owner of the dairy but all the milk may be bought elsewhere.)	Small to medium	Regional markets, and *fromageries* in towns and suburbs.
Coopératives (also *fruitières*)	The cheese is made in a single dairy with milk provided by members of the cooperative.	Medium to large	All of France.
Industriel	The milk is bought from a number of producers, sometimes from distant regions. Production is industrial.	Large	All of France; sometimes exported to other countries.

ARÔMES AU GÈNE DE MARC

This is a seasonal *artisanal* cheese that is ready to eat at the end of autumn. It is produced following a traditional method of curing cheeses in the wine-growing region of Lyon. Ripe cheeses such as Rigotte (p. 176), Saint-Marcellin (p. 182), Pélardon (p. 167), and Picodon (p. 170) are placed in a barrel of *marc* for a minimum of one month. The *marc,* which consists of the damp skins, seeds, and stalks left after the grapes have been pressed, permeates the cheese and flavors it. This cheese needs to be eaten with wine.

🍷 *Marc* de Côtes du Rhône;
🍷 Muscat de Beaumes de Venise

Soft to hard pâte

Rhône-Alpes (69)

Not defined

Natural rind, covered with marc de raisins

ESSENTIAL FACTS

- 2.4–2.8 in diameter 0.8–1.2 in high
- 2.8 oz
- Not defined
- ✓ End of autumn, winter

ARÔMES AU VIN BLANC

This cheese is made by filling the bottom of a large jar with white wine and put a goat cheese such as Saint-Marcellin (p. 182) on a wire rack just above the wine. The jar is then sealed tightly and left for two to three weeks. As the wine evaporates, the cheese absorbs its aroma, while the pâte grows soft and moist. This is a refined and sought-after cheese, worthy of Lyon, the city of gourmets. It should not be eaten on its own.

🍷 Bourgogne, St. Romain

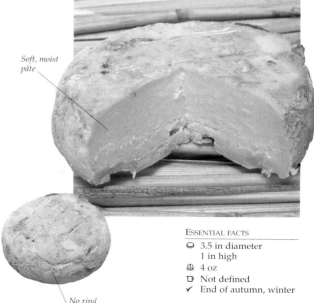

Soft, moist pâte

Rhône-Alpes (69)

Not defined

No rind

ESSENTIAL FACTS

- 3.5 in diameter 1 in high
- 4 oz
- Not defined
- ✓ End of autumn, winter

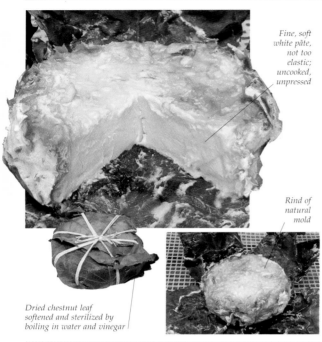

Fine, soft
white pâte,
not too
elastic;
uncooked,
unpressed

Rind of
natural
mold

Dried chestnut leaf
softened and sterilized by
boiling in water and vinegar

BANON À LA FEUILLE

This small mountain cheese was made by a couple from the village of Puimichel near the town of Banon in Provence. *Fermier, artisanal*, and *industriel* versions are produced. After an affinage of two weeks, the cheese is dipped in *eau-de-vie* and wrapped in a chestnut leaf. The *eau-de-vie* protects the cheese against bad mold. The Banon shown has been made with goat's milk only. The pâte has a milky smell when young. As it ripens, the surface takes on the color and aroma of the leaf.

Marc of the region,
♀ Vin de Cassis

ESSENTIAL FACTS
- ⊖ 2.4–2.8 in diameter
  1.2 in high
- ⚖ 3.2–4.2 oz
- ♉ 45%
- ✔ All year (cow); spring to autumn (goat)

Rind
covered
in dried
savory

Soft pâte;
uncooked,
unpressed

ESSENTIAL FACTS
- ⊖ 2.4 in diameter
  1.2 in high
- ⚖ 4.2 oz
- ♉ 45%
- ✔ All year (cow); spring to autumn (goat)

POIVRE D'ÂNE /
PÈVRE D'AÏ

Pèvre d'aï is the old Provençal name given to *Satureia hortensis* or summer savory, a southern European herb with a peppery bite, similar to thyme and mint. The cheese used is the same as for Banon à la Feuille and may be made solely with either goat's or cow's milk, or a mixture of the two. Affinage, in dried savory, takes one month. *Fermier, artisanal*, and *industriel* versions are produced.

♀ Coteaux d'Aix *rosé*

Provence-
Alpes-Côte-
d'Azur (04)

Raw

BARGKASS

Le Thillot, where this *fermier* cheese is produced, is a little village in the Vosges mountains of northeast France, famous for its cheeses, the best-known being Munster (p. 158). In the local dialect, *barg* means mountain, *kass* cheese. Bargkass has a soft but firm pâte, which is slightly elastic, with a few small holes. It has a light, soft smell and a rounded, relaxed taste with a slightly acid aftertaste. The cheese is best eaten with black sourdough bread. Affinage takes between six and eight weeks, during which time the cheese is brushed and turned once a week.

♥ Pinot Noir

Light brown or brown rind marked by the cloth during pressing

Slightly elastic pâte; uncooked, pressed

Lorraine (88)

Raw

ESSENTIAL FACTS
- 11.8 in diameter 2.4 in high
- 15.4–17.6 lbs
- Not defined
- May to October

BEAUMONT

This *industriel* cheese was first made in 1881 at Beaumont, near Geneva, using the same method as for Tamie (p. 187). It is one of the first mass-produced cheeses to use raw milk. Affinage takes four to six weeks, during which time the cheese is washed.

♥ Vin de Savoie, Hautes Côtes de Beaune

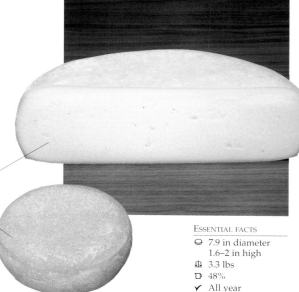

Semi-hard pâte, elastic to touch; uncooked, pressed

Pinkish-yellow, washed rind

Rhône-Alpes (74)

Raw

ESSENTIAL FACTS
- 7.9 in diameter 1.6–2 in high
- 3.3 lbs
- 48%
- All year

Slightly concave circumference

ESSENTIAL FACTS

- ⊖ 13.8–29.5 in diameter
  4.3–6.3 in high
- ⚖ 44–154 lbs
- ♣ 2.2 oz min. per
  3.5 oz cheese
- ▷ 48%
- ✓ All year; autumn if
  made in a *chalet d'alpage*

*Hard, yellowish
rind forms during
affinage*

Affinage of five to six months

BEAUFORT (AOC)

Beaufort is a large, round mountain cheese produced in the province of Savoie in the French Alps. Large cheeses with cooked and pressed pâtes are commonly called *gruyères* in France (not to be confused with Swiss Gruyère). The average weight of a Beaufort is 99 lbs, or all the milk produced by a herd of 45 cows in one day. Around 3.2 gallons of milk make 2.2 lbs of Beaufort. A good cheese should have a moist, sticky crust and a slightly concave surface due to the *cercle de Beaufort* used to shape it (p. 20).

Types of Beaufort

Three versions of Beaufort are produced: Beaufort, Beaufort *d'été* (summer Beaufort) and Beaufort

Rhône-Alpes
(73, 74)

Raw,
whole

d'alpage, which is made in *chalets* in the mountains. The pâte of a winter cheese is white, that of a summer cheese, pale yellow. It is said that the chlorophyll from the grass and carotene from the alpine flowers give the summer cheeses both color and flavor.

Production and affinage

Fermier, chalet d'alpage, coopérative, and *industriel* versions of Beaufort are made. Affinage takes at least four months from the date of production, within areas specified by the AOC at below 59°F with at least 92% humidity, during which time the cheese is constantly wiped and rubbed with brine.

In November, five- or six-month-old Beauforts (shown top right) appear on the Parisian markets and are the first of the *fromages d'alpage*. They have a soft, clear scent of milk, butter, flowers, and honey. The supple pâte has a flowery aroma, as well as a hidden acidity and saltiness. The taste lingers on the palate. Beaufort goes well with white wine.

After an affinage of one year in a dark, cool cellar at 46.4–48.2°F and 98% humidity, the cheese is washed with brine and turned twice a week. At this time, the crust is moist to the touch. Under the crust there is a thin, gray layer which gradually melts into the pâte. The cheese has a complex flavor with a strong aroma, and the taste of salt has grown subtler.

The Beaufort cows

Mahogany-colored Beaufort cows, the Tarines or Tarentaises, are indispensable in the making of Beaufort cheese. This ancient mountain breed, originally from the Indo-Asian continent, crossed Central Europe before reaching France. The cows were named Tarines in 1863 and were entered in the *Herd Book* in 1888. During the winter they are kept in sheds to protect them from the heavy winter snow and according to AOC regulations, they are not allowed to be fed any silage or other

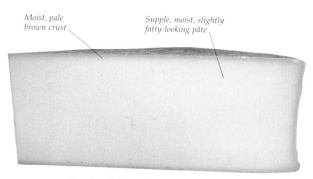
Moist, pale brown crust — *Supple, moist, slightly fatty-looking pâte*

Beaufort *d'alpage* after an affinage of five to six months

After an affinage of approximately one year

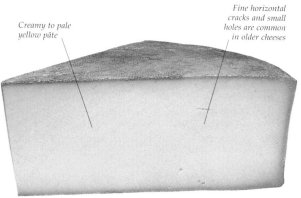
Creamy to pale yellow pâte — *Fine horizontal cracks and small holes are common in older cheeses*

Affinage of approximately one-and-a-half years

fermented fodder. In spring, they are taken high into the mountains to graze on the lush grass and flowers of the alpine meadows. In autumn they descend to the lower meadows, returning to the villages before the winter snows settle. They are a strong, hardy breed that adapt well to changes in temperature, and move easily over rocky terrain. Their milk is of excellent quality, with a fat content of 36.3% and protein content of 31.8%. They calve once a year and in the ten years of its working life, each cow produces an average of 4.8 tons of milk, which is also used to make several other great mountain cheeses such as Tomme de Savoie (p. 182) and Emmental (p. 132).

♍ Seyssel, Chablis

AOC REGULATIONS: BEAUFORT

1. The milk must be taken into the dairy immediately after milking. Only where refrigeration tanks are in use on the farm may it be transported once a day only. If the milk is refrigerated, the rennet must be added within 24 hours of milking, or 36 hours in winter.

2. No system or machinery that would allow the milk to be heated above 104°F before renneting is allowed on the premises.

3. The name of the cheese must be shown in blue *casein* letters that must always remain legible.

4. The terms *été* and *alpage* may be used only as follows: *été* for dairy products from June to October, including those made at a *chalet d'alpage*; *alpage* for summer products made twice a day at an alpine *chalet* with the milk from a single herd (no other milk may be mixed with it).

5. The salt must be applied to the surface of the cheese either directly or with brine.

6. If the cheese is sold cut and prepacked, the pieces must present a portion of the crust characteristic of the Beaufort appellation.

AOC GRANTED 1976

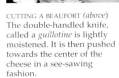

CUTTING A BEAUFORT (*above*)
The double-handled knife, called a *guillotine* is lightly moistened. It is then pushed towards the center of the cheese in a see-sawing fashion.

THE CHEESE IRON (*top*)
This is used for taking samples from the inside of a cheese. The pâte of a young Beaufort yields easily to the iron.

CHAMBÉRY CELLAR (*above*)
In M. Provent's cellar in Chambéry, 1,000 cheeses may be stored in the month of November.

Bleu

Bleu d'Auvergne (AOC)

There are two different sizes of Bleu d'Auvergne. The larger size has a diameter of 7.9 in, with a height of 3.2–3.9 in and weight of 4.4–6.6 lbs. The smaller size is 3.9 in diameter, varies in height, and weighs any from 12.6 oz to 2.2 lbs. Although these cheeses are traditionally round, a rectangular version is produced for export and prepack sale. This is 11.4 in long, 3.6 in wide, 4.3 in high, and weighs 5.5 lbs. The cheeses shown here are part of the 134 tons that were made with raw milk, out of a total 9,125 tons produced in 1991. The pâte is sticky, moist, and crumbly, with an even spread of veins, and its taste is tart and gluey. The spice of the mold blends perfectly with the well-integrated salt. This cheese is delicious in salad dressings, with chicory, nuts, or raw mushrooms. It also makes an excellent seasoning for hot, fresh pasta.

Both *coopérative* and *industriel* versions are made within the areas specified by the AOC. Affinage takes a minimum of four weeks from the date of production for cheeses weighing over 2.2 lbs, and two weeks for those weighing less.

The AOC was granted in 1975.

Ɏ Sauternes, Maury (VDN)

Natural rind

Pâte evenly veined with blue mold; uncooked, unpressed

Auvergne (63, 15, 43); Midi-Pyrénées (12, 46); Limousin (19); Languedoc-Roussillon (48)

Raw, pasteurized

Essential facts

- ⊖ 7.9 in diameter (large); 3.9 in diameter (small) 3.2–3.9 in high (large); variable (small)
- ⚖ 4.4–6.6 lbs (large); 2.2 lbs (small)
- ⦙ 1.8 oz min. per 3.5 oz
- ⭗ 50%
- ✔ All year

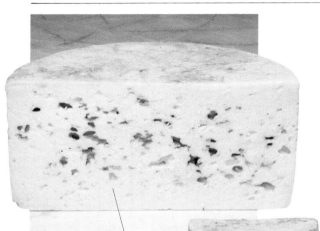

ESSENTIAL FACTS

⊖ 7.9 in diameter
3.2–3.9 in high
⊕ 5–6.6 lbs
∴ 1.9 oz min.
per 3.5 oz cheese
⊅ 45%
✔ All year

Yellowish or white pâte with veins of blue mold; uncooked, unpressed

Natural rind

BLEU DES CAUSSES (AOC)

This commercially produced *coopérative* or *industriel* cheese is a mild cow's-milk version of Roquefort (p. 178). The solid flavor is a result of the affinage which lasts at least 70 days, (usually three to six months) and takes place in natural caves called *fleurines* (p. 178) in the limestone plateaus of the Causses. The pâte of the summer cheeses is moist and ivory-yellow; winter cheeses are white and have a strong taste. They are best when matched with a naturally sweet white wine of good acidity, especially at the end of a meal.

The AOC was granted in 1975.

♀ Barsac *moelleux*,
Banyuls Grand Cru (VDN)

Midi-Pyrénées
(12, 46);
Languedoc-
Roussillon (48,
30, 34)

Raw

BLEU DE COSTAROS

This traditional *fermier* cheese from the village of Costaros in the Auvergne is known locally as *fromage à vers*, meaning cheese eaten by worms – a reference to the cheese mite (*le ciron*) that lives in it. The slightly hard, elastic pâte is irregularly punctured by small holes and is sticky, with a faint smell and flavor of mold. A local cheesemaker says that she eats the crust – "Oh, yes, all of it, even the worms."

♀ Loupiac, Rivesaltes (VDN)

Uncooked, unpressed pâte

Hard natural rind forms during affinage

ESSENTIAL FACTS

⊖ 3.9 in diameter
2.8–3.2 in high
⊕ 1.2–1.3 lbs
⊅ Not defined
✔ All year

Veins of natural concentrated mold

Auvergne
(43)

Raw

BLEU DU HAUT JURA (AOC)

This mild blue cheese is also known as Bleu de Gex or Bleu de Septmoncel, but its official name is Bleu du Haut Jura. The rind is covered with a layer of white, powderlike mold that should be gently wiped off before eating. The pâte's aroma evokes the milk of rich pastures. Locally, it is often eaten with boiled potatoes.

The cows that are milked to make this cheese graze in the mountains of the Jura. It is said that the mold of the mountain grass and flowers passes into their milk where it flourishes. Today, spores of the blue mold *Penicillium glaucum* are introduced into the milk. During affinage, air is inserted with a syringe into the pâte to allow the mold to grow internally.

During the affinage of around one month within AOC specified areas, the cheeses are dried and ripened naturally in the cellars of a *coopérative* at a humidity of 80%.

The AOC was granted in 1977.

♉ Sainte Croix du Mont (VDN), ❢ Port

Soft, ivory pâte, evenly marbled with pale green mold; uncooked, unpressed

Rind forms naturally; thin yellowish with a dry powdery mold, may show red spots

Gex is stamped on the surface

Holes where air is inserted with a syringe

BLEU FONDU À LA POÊLE
To make this tasty recipe, simply cut the cheese into slices and melt them slowly in a frying pan. They make an excellent topping for chicken breasts, or are equally delicious spread on slices of country bread and accompanied by a glass of Vin jaune d'Arbois.

Rhône-Alpes (01); Franche-Comté (39)

Raw

ESSENTIAL FACTS
- ◯ 14.2 in diameter Height not specified
- ⚖ 16.5 lbs
- ❖ 1.8 oz min. per 3.5 oz
- ▷ 50%
- ✔ All year, best from summer

BLEU DE LANGEAC

Locally, this *fermier* cheese from the town of Langeac in the Auvergne goes by the simple name of *fromage de la région*, meaning cheese of the region. It has a completely dry crust and a slight aroma. The pâte is firm and has a definite taste of mold. This is a salty and solid cheese, made from good, strong milk. Affinage takes two months.

♀ Cérons *moelleux*, Sauternes *meilleur marché*, Banyuls (VDN)

Yellowish pâte, veined with natural mold; uncooked, unpressed

ESSENTIAL FACTS
- ◯ 3.9–4.7 in diameter 1.6 in high
- ⚖ 1–1.1 lbs
- ⬜ Not defined
- ✓ All year

Rough, dry rind forms naturally during affinage

Auvergne (43)

Raw

BLEU DE LAQUEUILLE

Antoine Roussel from the village of Laqueuille first made this cheese in 1850 with mold grown on rye bread. His statue can be seen in the village. The pâte has a slight smell of the cellar and tastes of blue mold. Bleu de Laqueuille belongs to the same family as Fourme d'Ambert (p. 138). Today, production is limited to an *industriel* version. Affinage takes three months.

♀ Monbazillac *moelleux*, Rivesaltes (VDN)

Rind forms naturally during affinage

ESSENTIAL FACTS
- ◯ 19.3 in diameter 3.7 in high
- ⚖ 5.5 lbs
- ⬜ 45%
- ✓ Summer, autumn

Soft pâte with blue mold; uncooked, unpressed

Auvergne (63)

Pasteurized

BLEU DE LOUDES

The pâte of this *fermier* cheese from the town of Loudes in the Auvergne is firm and elastic, sticky, and slightly sour, with no particular smell. The presence of the mold is not immediately obvious. The cheese shown has been cut and exposed to the air for 24 hours. Affinage takes six weeks.

♀ Sainte Croix du Mont *moelleux*, Rivesaltes (VDN)

Firm pâte peppered with natural blue mold and a few holes, firm; uncooked, unpressed

Hard, dry rind forms naturally during affinage

Auvergne (43)

Raw

BLEU DU QUERCY

A mild, commercially produced *bleu industriel* from the Quercy region suitable for the uninitiated who have yet to acquire a taste for blue cheeses. Affinage takes three months.

♀ Cérons *moelleux*, Maury (VDN)

Pâte regularly veined, with natural green mold; uncooked, unpressed

Rind appears naturally during affinage

Midi-Pyrénées (46)

Pasteurized

ESSENTIAL FACTS
⊖ 7.1 in diameter
   3.5–3.9 in high
⚖ 5.5 lbs
↻ 45%
✓ All year

BLEU DE SASSENAGE

This traditional mountain cheese, a sweet *bleu*, was first made by monks, and the recipe spread to the surrounding villages. In a charter of 1338, Baron Albert of Sassenage allowed the free sale of the cheese made by people on his land. Today production is principally *industriel*. The summer version has a simple flavor of the milk produced by cows grazing in the mountains and is characterized by a comforting roundness and the faint perfume of the mold. Affinage takes two to three months.

♀ Barsac *moelleux*, Banyuls

ESSENTIAL FACTS

Soft pâte; uncooked, unpressed

⊖ 11.8 in diameter
    3.2 in high
⧄ 11–13.2 lbs
♌ 45%
✓ Summer, autumn

Natural white and reddish rind

Rhône-Alpes
(38)

Pasteurized

BRESSE BLEU

This commercially produced *industriel* cheese was first made after World War II in the province of Bresse in southern France. The soft pâte is peppered with small patches of blue mold. Three different sizes are produced. The large size is around 3.9 in diameter, 2.6 in high, and weighs 1.1 lbs. The medium size is 3.2 in diameter, 1.8 in high, and weighs 8 oz. The small size is just 2.4 in diameter, 1.8 in high, and weighs 4.4 oz. Affinage takes two to four weeks.

♀ Monbazillac *moelleux*, Rivesaltes (VDN)

ESSENTIAL FACTS

Soft, supple pâte; uncooked, unpressed

⊖ 3.9 in diameter
    2.5 in high
⧄ 1.1 lbs
♌ 55%
✓ All year

Rind of white mold

Rhône-Alpes
(01)

Pasteurized

Bleu de Termignon

Termignon is the name of the village in which this cheese is produced, at an altitude of 4,265 ft in the French Alps. This is an outstanding cheese of great quality, a little fatty, natural and down-to-earth, made by just one woman in very limited quantities, in a *chalet d'alpage*. She keeps her nine cows high up in the National Park of Vanoise, where the animals feed on grass and flowers. It is here that the source of the mold may be found. The mold passes into the milk to create a refined flavor that spreads throughout the cheese. Its crust is white, brown, hard, and looks like a rock, and the pâte is crumbly. The blue mold is natural and is not artificially induced as in most other blue cheeses. It develops and expands much more slowly and less evenly. During affinage, the cheeses are regularly turned and wiped for four to five months.

♀ Tokay Selection de Grains Nobles *moelleux*, Rivesaltes Grand Cru (VDN)

Dry cheese

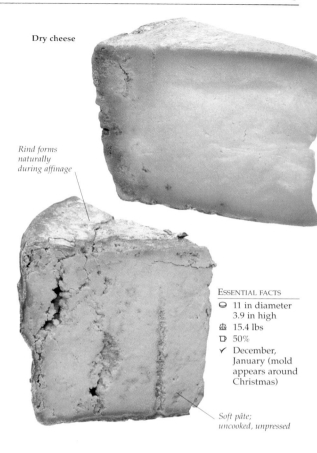

Rind forms naturally during affinage

Soft pâte; uncooked, unpressed

Essential facts
- ◯ 11 in diameter 3.9 in high
- ⚖ 15.4 lbs
- ⌗ 50%
- ✔ December, January (mold appears around Christmas)

 Rhône-Alpes (73)

 Raw

Le Petit Bayard

This *artisanal* cheese from the Laiterie Col Bayard in the Dauphiné region has an affinage of about one month.

♀ Côtes de Provence

Essential facts
- ◯ 4.7–5.1 in 2 in
- ⚖ 1 lb
- ⌗ 45%
- ✔ All year

Rind of natural mold

Pâte is uncooked, unpressed

Provence-Alpes-Côte d'Azur (05) Raw

BOULE DE LILLE / MIMOLETTE FRANÇAISE

The name Boule de Lille allegedly derives from the *cave d'affinage*, or ripening cellar, in the city of Lille where affinage originally took place. The name Mimolette derives from *mi-mou* or half-soft. Some say this cheese originated in Holland, while others maintain that it has always existed in France. The true story behind its origins is probably that during the 17th century, the French minister Colbert forbade the import of foreign goods, including cheese, and the French began making Mimolette themselves. The method of production is the same as for the Dutch cheese Edam.

This is a northern *coopérative* or *industriel* cheese, about the size of a baby's head, flattened at top and bottom, with no distinct aroma. The pâte is semi-soft at the beginning, then slowly hardens and dries as the cheese ripens and finally cracks. Results of ripening vary, depending on the level of humidity in the cellar. The minimum affinage takes about six weeks; three months for a young Mimolette; six months for a *demi-étuvée* or *demi-vieille* (half-old); twelve months for a *vieille en étuvée* (old); and two years for a *très vieille* (very old) cheese. The color of the pâte changes from carrot to orange brown, and with it the taste. The dry cheese can be grated and used for cooking.

♈ Banyuls (VDN)

Hard, dry, yellowish-orange to light brown rind

Semi-hard to hard pâte; half-cooked, pressed

Affinage of 18 months

Affinage of 24 months

Pâte varies in color from yellowish-orange to red, with a few small holes

ESSENTIAL FACTS

○ 7.9 in diameter
  5.9 in high
⚖ 4.4–8.8 lbs
• 1.9 oz per 3.5 oz cheese
▢ 40%
✓ All year

Nord Pas-de-Calais (62)

Pasteurized

Brebis de Pays

BREBIS DE PAYS DE GRASSE

This *fermier* cheese is made in the area around the town of Grasse. The ewes, whose milk is used to make the cheese, feed on the grass and lavender of the arid mountain plateaus, exposed to the pure air of the Alps and the Mediterranean breezes. The taste is light, and slightly acid for a sheep's cheese made with quality milk. Brebis de Pays de Grasse is a perfect accompaniment to a baguette hot out of the oven. Affinage takes about six weeks.

♀ Cassis

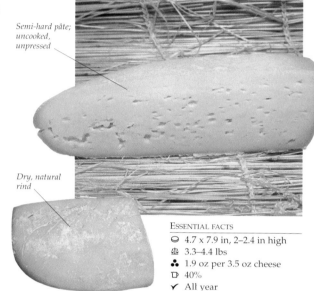

Semi-hard pâte; uncooked, unpressed

Dry, natural rind

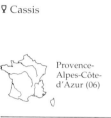

Provence-Alpes-Côte-d'Azur (06)

Raw

ESSENTIAL FACTS
- ⊖ 4.7 x 7.9 in, 2–2.4 in high
- ⚖ 3.3–4.4 lbs
- ❖ 1.9 oz per 3.5 oz cheese
- ◻ 40%
- ✔ All year

BERGER PLAT

This *fermier* cheese is produced on a farm called Le Berger des Dombes in the province of Lyons. It was first made as a result of the introduction of Lacaune sheep into the region, the same breed as the ewes of Roquefort (p. 178). The rind is white or beige with a pale blue mold. Berger Plat is a cheese of gentle scent and taste. During affinage, the cheeses are left to rest on a bed of straw for 15–21 days.

♟ Coteaux de Lyonnais, Beaujolais

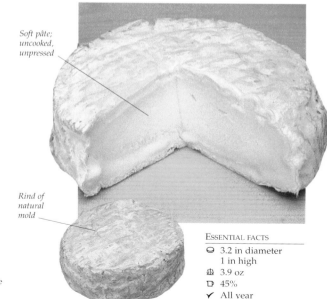

Soft pâte; uncooked, unpressed

Rind of natural mold

Rhône-Alpes (01)

Raw, whole

ESSENTIAL FACTS
- ⊖ 3.2 in diameter 1 in high
- ⚖ 3.9 oz
- ◻ 45%
- ✔ All year

37

Brebis du Bersend

This *fermier* cheese from the village of Bersend is one of the few sheep's cheeses produced in the province of Savoie. Until the 19th century, ewes were reared in this mountainous area, close to the Swiss and Italian borders. Their numbers fell but at last appear to be on the rise again. Affinage takes a minimum of two months in a natural cellar.

℣ Roussette de Savoie

Rind of natural white, brown, or gray mold

⊖ 4.7 in diameter
    2 in high
🝭 1.3 lbs
🗇 45%
✔ Best in summer

Semi-hard pâte, slightly elastic under pressure; uncooked, unpressed

Rhône-Alpes (73)

Raw

Brebis du Lochois (pur)

This *fermier* cheese is a recently introduced sheep's cheese in an area dominated by goat cheeses. There are only two producers in the whole of the Touraine. The cheese shown here was made in the village of Perrusson near the town of Loches. Affinage takes at least two weeks.

℣ Menetou Salon

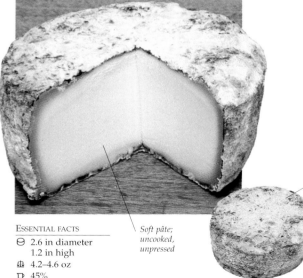

Rind of natural mold

⊖ 2.6 in diameter
    1.2 in high
🝭 4.2–4.6 oz
🗇 45%
✔ Best end of winter
    to summer

Soft pâte; uncooked, unpressed

Centre (37)

Raw

LE CAUSSEDOU

This mild, gentle *fermier* cheese is produced by La Ferme Poux-del-Mas in the Quercy region. In French a *causse* is a limestone plateaus, for which the Quercy is famous, and *doux* means soft, describing the nature of the Caussedou. A natural blue mold appears on the rind after a few days. Affinage takes a minimum of 15 days at 55.4°F.

❚ Cahors

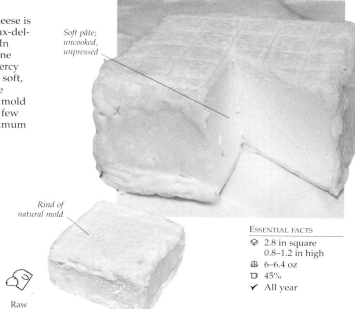

Soft pâte; uncooked, unpressed

Rind of natural mold

Midi-Pyrénées (46)

Raw

ESSENTIAL FACTS
◈ 2.8 in square
   0.8–1.2 in high
▦ 6–6.4 oz
▷ 45%
✔ All year

FROMAGE DE BREBIS

This is a rich *fermier* cheese produced by GAEC Saint-Pierre in the village of Meyrueis. It is a thick cheese, with a robust flavor. In a cheese weighing 3.4 oz, 0.9 oz are fat, which accounts for a lot of calories! Affinage takes five to ten days.

❚ Minervois

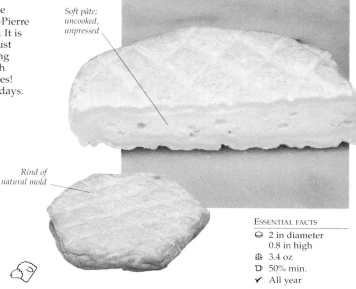

Soft pâte; uncooked, unpressed

Rind of natural mold

Languedoc-Roussillon (48)

Raw

ESSENTIAL FACTS
◡ 2 in diameter
   0.8 in high
▦ 3.4 oz
▷ 50% min.
✔ All year

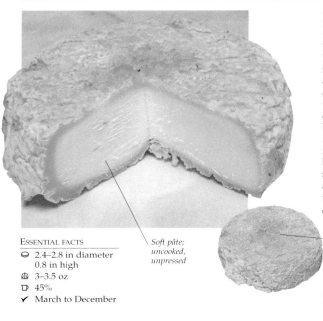

FROMAGE FERMIER PUR BREBIS

This *fermier* cheese is produced by the GAEC La Bourgeade near Saint-Hilaire Foissac on the western edge of the Massif Central. The cheese shown here looks soft at the center and harder at the edges since it was bought at the beginning of its affinage from the farm where it was made. The flavor is slightly sour, with a well-balanced saltiness and a subtle sweetness that leaves a pleasant aftertaste. Affinage takes one to four weeks.

❡ St. Pourçain

Rind of natural mold

Soft pâte; uncooked, unpressed

ESSENTIAL FACTS
- ◡ 2.4–2.8 in diameter 0.8 in high
- ⚖ 3–3.5 oz
- ▯ 45%
- ✔ March to December

Limousin (19)

Raw

FROMAGEON FERMIER AU LAIT CRU DE BREBIS

Although it is made from the same ewe's milk as Roquefort, the Fromageon is a very different cheese, with a mild flavor. It is produced according to traditional *fermier* methods on a farm belonging to J. Massebiau at La Cavalerie in Rouergue. Affinage takes a minimum of 10 days.

❡ Côtes du Roussillon

Rind of natural mold

Soft pâte; uncooked, unpressed

ESSENTIAL FACTS
- ◡ 2.4–2.8 in diameter 0.8 in high
- ⚖ 3 oz
- ▯ Not defined
- ✔ End of winter to summer

Midi-Pyrénées (12)

Raw

Le Lacandou

In the northern part of the Aveyron, where the mountains stretch as far as the eye can see, M. Lacan makes the Lacandou following traditional *artisanal* methods. The farmer who produces the milk does not feed any silage to his ewes; they graze on the mountainside. Affinage takes three weeks.

❢ Côtes du Roussillon, Crozes Hermitage

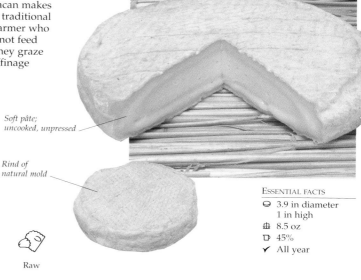

Soft pâte;
uncooked, unpressed

Rind of
natural mold

Midi-
Pyrénées
(12)

Raw

ESSENTIAL FACTS
- 3.9 in diameter
  1 in high
- 8.5 oz
- 45%
- All year

Moularen

Two women make this *fermier* cheese in the village of Montlaux, at an altitude of 1,969 ft, where it snows occasionally. The ewes stay outdoors for eight months of the year and lamb in both October and March, enabling them to produce milk all year round. As with many washed-rind cheeses, the surface of Moularen cheese is pale orange. The pâte is creamy and thick and pleasant in the mouth. Affinage takes three weeks.

❢ Bandol or Bandol *rosé*

Soft pâte;
uncooked,
unpressed

Orange rind
washed with brine

Provence-
Alpes-Côte-
d'Azur (04)

Raw

ESSENTIAL FACTS
- 3.8 in diameter
  1 in high
- 8 oz
- 50%
- Best from end of
  winter to summer

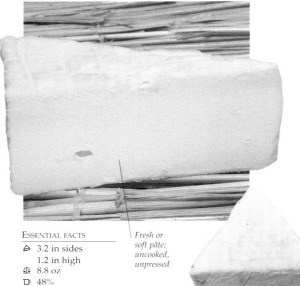

PÉRAIL

This *fermier* or *artisanal* cheese is made according to traditional methods on the limestone plateaux of the Causse du Larzac in the province of Rouergue. It has a smell of ewe's milk and a smooth texture like very thick cream. The flavor is soft and velvety. Affinage takes at least one week.

❦ St. Chinian

Soft pâte; uncooked, unpressed

Rind of natural mold

ESSENTIAL FACTS
- ⊖ 3.2–3.9 in diameter
  0.6–0.8 in high
- ⚖ 2.8–4.2 oz
- ☐ 45–50%
- ✔ Winter to summer

Midi-Pyrénées (12)

Raw

TRICORNE DE MARANS

The Tricorne was extinct for many years, but in 1984 production was started up again at the coastal town of Marans. The cheese shown was produced by two women using milk produced by their 150 ewes. The flavor is rich and slightly sweet and sour. The quality of the milk results in a high fat content. Cow and goat's milk may be used if the ewe's milk is in short supply. For a goat cheese, 1.6 quarts of milk are needed but for a sheep's cheese of the same size just 1.7 quarts of ewe's milk is sufficient. This *fermier* cheese is usually eaten fresh, although it may be ripened for anywhere from two or three weeks to three months.

❦ Haut Poitou

Fresh or soft pâte; uncooked, unpressed

ESSENTIAL FACTS
- ⊿ 3.2 in sides
  1.2 in high
- ⚖ 8.8 oz
- ☐ 48%
- ✔ All year; end of winter for ewe's-milk cheese

Rind: none when fresh; depends on the ripening

Poitou-Charentes (17)

Raw

Brebis des Pyrénées

The cheeses shown here are from the rugged Béarn and Basque regions in the western Pyrénées, where there is a long tradition of making sheep's cheeses. Most are *fermier* cheeses made from whole raw milk, with an undefined proportion of fat. A long affinage makes them hard.

The AOC Ossau-Iraty-Brebis Pyrénées was granted in 1980. These white *fermier* cheeses are usually simply called "mountain cheeses" or "sheep's cheeses." Due to the limited amounts of ewe's milk and short period of production, almost all of these cheeses are eaten locally. It is a good idea to cut this cheese a while before eating to allow it to breathe. Brebis des Pyrénées goes well with white wines such as Jurançon *sec*, Irouléguy, Pacherenc du Vic-Bilh, and Bordeaux *sec*.

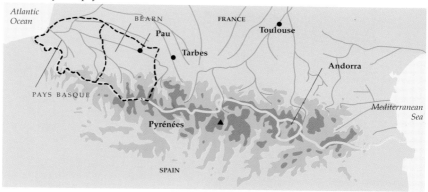

Ossau-Iraty-Brebis Pyrénées (AOC)

These cheeses are made with the milk of Manech ewes, and *fermier* (sometimes produced in *cayolars*, mountain huts), *artisanal*, *cooperative*, and *industriel* versions are produced. There are three main versions: small (Petit-Ossau-Iraty-Brebis Pyrénées); intermediate (non-*fermier*); large (*fermier*). Affinage takes at least 90 days; 60 days for the small version. The cellar must be below 54°F.

♀ Irouléguy, Graves *sec*

ESSENTIAL FACTS

⊖ 7.1–11 in diameter, 2.8–5.9 in high (sizes vary according to format)
⚖ 4.4–15.4 lbs (depending on size)
♌ 50% min.
✔ All year, depending on affinage; from autumn for mountain cheeses

AOC Regulations: Ossau-Iraty-Brebis Pyrénées

1. No ewe's milk may be made into cheese until 20 days after lambing.

2. Renneting must take place within 48 hours.

3. Coagulation is obtained by renneting. Any other enzyme is forbidden.

4. The term *montagne* may be used only for cheeses made from ewes grazing on summer pastures between May 10 and September 15.

5. Any cheese not conforming to the regulations must be sold as *fromage de brebis*, sheep's cheese.

AOC GRANTED 1980

Aquitaine (64); Midi-Pyrénées (65)

Whole

STAMP OF QUALITY
The producer imprints his initials into the rind of the cheese using special metal stamps.

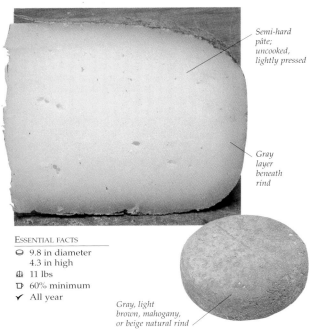

Semi-hard
pâte;
uncooked,
lightly pressed

Gray
layer
beneath
rind

ESSENTIAL FACTS

◯ 9.8 in diameter
4.3 in high
⚖ 11 lbs
🗘 60% minimum
✓ All year

Gray, light
brown, mahogany,
or beige natural rind

ABBAYE DE BELLOC

This *fermier* cheese is made from the milk of red-nosed Manech ewes. The milk is bought in from neighboring farms and taken to the Abbaye de Nôtre-Dame de Belloc in the Pays Basque where it is made into cheese. The cheese shown has a fine, dense pâte that is rich in fat. The strong lingering flavor, like caramelized brown sugar, is the result of a long affinage of six months, similar to aging a fine wine. It is hard to believe that the only additive is salt. Bread and wine go well with this cheese, which is one of the few Pyrénéan sheep's cheeses to be found in Paris.

𝖸 Pacherenc du Vic-Bilh, Bordeaux *sec*

Aquitaine
(64)

Raw,
whole

ARDI-GASNA (1)

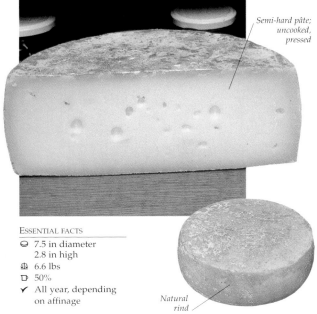

Semi-hard pâte;
uncooked,
pressed

In the Basque language, *ardi* means ewe and *gasna* is cheese. When asked who produces Ardi-Gasna, the owner of the cheese shop where it was bought in Saint-Jean-Pied-de-Port said, "My shepherd made it." The shepherd tends 200 to 250 sheep and in May he moves up to the mountains, where he milks the ewes and makes the cheese. The end product is the result of a long-standing agreement between the shepherd and the shop owner, who ripens each cheese with great care. The rind is yellow, orange, beige, and slightly moist. The pâte under the rind is grayish, the taste refined. This is a *fermier* cheese with an affinage of at least three months.

❦ Margaux, Madiran

ESSENTIAL FACTS

◯ 7.5 in diameter
2.8 in high
⚖ 6.6 lbs
🗘 50%
✓ All year, depending
on affinage

Natural
rind

Aquitaine
(64)

Raw,
whole

ARDI-GASNA (2)

This *fermier* cheese is made at the farm of Aire-Ona high in the Pyrénées, where 250 ewes and 60 cows are reared. In the Basque language *aire* means air and *ona* means pure or good. In spring the animals are taken up to graze on the lush alpine pastures over the summer. The spring cheese, made from ewe's milk, is highly recommended. In November the animals come down from the mountains, and the calves and lambs are born. During winter they are fed on corn and hay. Affinage may last up to two years but the young cheese, ripened for two to three months, has a pleasant aroma.

Semi-hard pâte; uncooked, lightly pressed

Natural rind

❢ Irouléguy,
Côtes de Bordeaux (young)

Aquitaine
(64)

Raw, whole

ESSENTIAL FACTS
- ⊖ 10.6 in diameter
  3.2–3.5 in high
- ⚖ 8.8 lbs
- ↻ Not defined
- ✔ Best in spring

FROMAGE DE VACHE BRÛLÉ

These two *fermier* cheeses are made on the Ferme Aire Ona from cow's milk. The Fromage de Vache Brûlé is scented with charred oak wood. The pâte is fine and a little sour.

❢ Bergerac, light and fruity

CAILLÉ DE LAIT DE VACHE

This fresh cheese is produced from November 1 on. The cheese is mixed with sugar or honey and eaten with coffee, or mixed with sugar and Armagnac for dessert.

☕ Coffee

Pâte is semi-hard; uncooked, slightly pressed

Rind of charred oak

Raw, whole

Aquitaine
(64)

ESSENTIAL FACTS
- ⊖ 5.1–5.9 in diameter
  2–2.4 in high
- ⚖ 2.2–2.9 lbs
- ↻ Not defined
- ✔ Best in spring

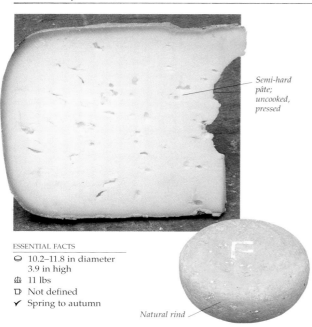

Semi-hard *pâte*; uncooked, pressed

ESSENTIAL FACTS

- 10.2–11.8 in diameter
  3.9 in high
- 11 lbs
- Not defined
- Spring to autumn

Natural rind

AUBISQUE PYRÉNÉES

The letter "F" stamped on this young, *fermier* cheese is the initial of one of three shepherds who, according to local people, are the only producers of this cheese in the Vallée d'Ossau in the province of Béarn. It is made from a mixture of ewe and cow's milk, the proportion of which varies according to season and availability; the flavor is mild and smooth. Generally, the higher the percentage of cow's milk, the softer the flavor. The mixture of the two milks requires a shorter affinage of two months than that required by a pure ewe's-milk cheese.

❦ Madiran (young), Côte de Blaye

Aquitaine (64)

Raw

ESSENTIAL FACTS

- 7.5 in diameter
  3 in high
- 5.5 lbs
- Not defined
- Best at end of summer

Semi-hard *pâte*; uncooked, pressed

Rind is hard, natural

BREBIS PAYS BASQUE LE CAYOLAR

A young *fromager* goes to market in the morning in a van. On arrival, he opens one side of the van, disclosing a mobile cheese shop. His *fermier* cheese has a brown rind, a viscous gray and shiny *pâte*, and holes due to the pressure applied in the manufacturing process and during the affinage of seven months. The proportion of fat is probably very high. The name could not be more straightforward: Brebis, Pays Basque, le Cayolar, in other words a ewe's cheese made in a *cayolar*, or mountain hut, in the Basque Country. This one was bought in Saint-Jean-Pied-de-Port.

❦ Pacherenc du Vic-Bilh

Aquitaine (64)

Raw, whole

BREBIS

This *fermier* cheese, which was bought in the little mountain village of Izeste in the Vallée d'Ossau, is made in a *cayolar*, or mountain hut. It is surprisingly strong given the smooth, mild flavor of the milk. The letters "C" and "D" stamped in the rind are the initials of the shepherd and owner – M. Daniel Casau. Affinage takes three months.

♀ Irouléguy, Graves *sec*

Semi-hard pâte; uncooked, slightly pressed

Natural rind

 Aquitaine (64)

 Raw, whole

ESSENTIAL FACTS
- ◉ 10.2 in diameter 3.2 in high
- ⚖ 8.9 lbs
- ⅁ Not defined
- ✔ Best at end of summer

MIXTE

A stream, the Gave d'Ossau, passes through the village of Izeste from its source on the Pic du Midi d'Ossau, which reaches a height of 9,472 ft. In the village, there is a little house at the entrance of which a small sign reads: "cow, goat, ewe." The locals come here with their churns to buy milk. Just inside the door two or three cheeses are displayed, which the owner of the house cuts on a wooden board. The flavor of these cheeses is compact, with an aroma that fills the mouth. The strength of this cheese is surprising considering that the milk is so mild and smooth. Affinage takes three months.

♀ Irouléguy, Graves *sec*

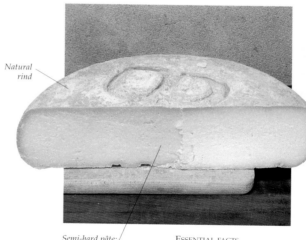

Natural rind

Semi-hard pâte; uncooked, slightly pressed

 Aquitaine (64)

 Raw, whole 50% of each

ESSENTIAL FACTS
- ◉ 10.6–12.2 in diameter 3.2 in high
- ⚖ 11.2 lbs
- ⅁ Not defined
- ✔ Best at the end of summer

BREBIS PYRÉNÉES

At the market in the town of Saint-Jean-de-Luz a *fromager* and his daughter, who is also his apprentice, sell large, hard *fermier* cheeses that no one else is allowed to touch. They have been produced on a farm near Arudy, a town in the Vallée d'Ossau. They have an affinage of six to ten months.

♀ Pacherenc du Vic-Bilh

Semi-hard pâte; uncooked, pressed

ESSENTIAL FACTS
- ⊖ 10.2–11 in diameter
  3.5–3.9 in high
- ⊕ 11–13.2 lbs
- ↻ Not defined
- ↣ All year, depending on affinage

Natural rind, dry and hard

Aquitaine (64)

Raw, whole

FROMAGE DE BREBIS

The region where this *fermier* mountain cheese is produced is often snowbound in the winter, with limited means of transportation. Cheese is an important food since it can be made with the plentiful summer milk and stored for months. Fromage de Brebis is made for six to seven months of each year, and has an affinage of eight months. It is a large and heavy cheese, with a reddish brown rind. The yellow pâte is compact, and the rind, which preserves it, quite solid. This is a tasty cheese that is well worth chewing for a while to allow all the flavors to develop. Most of the production is consumed in the region.

♀ Pacherenc du Vic-Bilh, Côtes de Blaye

Semi-hard pâte; uncooked, pressed

ESSENTIAL FACTS
- ⊖ 9.8 in diameter
  3.5 in high
- ⊕ 11 lbs
- ↻ Not defined
- ↣ Best in autumn

Natural rind

Aquitaine (64)

Raw

FROMAGE DE BREBIS ET VACHE FERMIER

This *fermier* cheese, made from a mixture of cow's and ewe's milk. The "S" stamped on the rind is the initial of the cheesemaker, M. Sanche, who makes only 200 cheeses in a year and sells them wholesale to M. J-C. Chourre when they are still *blanc*, or fresh. M. Chourre, who has ten farms under contract to produce these cheeses, ripens and sells them. There are always some 1,500 cheeses ripening in his cellar, which has been in his family for generations. The quality of the cheeses depends on the milk – the ewes that give the best milk are two to three years old. Affinage takes around three months.

❢ Irouléguy

Hard pâte with small holes; uncooked, slightly pressed

Natural, reddish-yellow rind

Aquitaine (64)

Raw

ESSENTIAL FACTS

◒ 9.5–10.2 in diameter
  3.2 in high
⚖ 7.7 lbs
◻ Not defined
✔ All year, best in
  summer

FROMAGE DE BREBIS VALLÉE D'OSSAU (AOC)

A superb *fromagerie*, or cheese shop, can be found at Saint-Jean-de-Luz, a port near the French-Spanish border and a base for tuna fishing boats. Here you can buy sheep's cheeses from the two main cheese-producing regions of the Pyrénées: the Béarn and the Pays Basque. The owner, M. C. Dupin, is a *maître affineur*, a master cheese ripener. His cheeses are refined and elegant, a perfect union of mountains and soil, ewe, shepherd, and *affineur*, with all the balanced flavors this imparts to the palate. Affinage lasts five months. Match this cheese with an Irouléguy, the red wine of the Pays Basque.

❡ Irouléguy, Entre Deux Mers *sec*

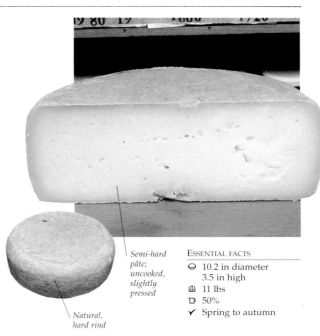

Semi-hard pâte; uncooked, slightly pressed

Natural, hard rind

Aquitaine (64)

Raw, whole

ESSENTIAL FACTS

◒ 10.2 in diameter
  3.5 in high
⚖ 11 lbs
◻ 50%
✔ Spring to autumn

Semi-hard pâte; uncooked, pressed

Natural rind

ESSENTIAL FACTS

- ◯ 3.5–10.2 in diameter
  2–4.3 in high
- ⚖ 1.1–13.2 lbs
- 🌡 Not defined
- ✓ Summer to winter

FROMAGE FERMIER AU LAIT DE BREBIS

This sweet, salty *fermier* cheese from the province of Béarn in the Pyrénées, is produced at the Ferme Penen in three different sizes: large, medium, and small. The owner of the farm milks the ewes, makes the cheese, and sells it at the town market. Of her cheeses she says, "People now prefer young cheeses, not too salty. I make them to be eaten immediately. It is better to sell them quickly, especially the heavy cheeses. But a minimum of salt is necessary. It's really best to leave them a while, but then they get smaller and more expensive." At the start of affinage the cheese are wiped, then brushed over a period of four months.

🍷 Jurançon *sec*

Aquitaine (64)

Raw, whole

FROMAGE FERMIER AU LAIT DE VACHE

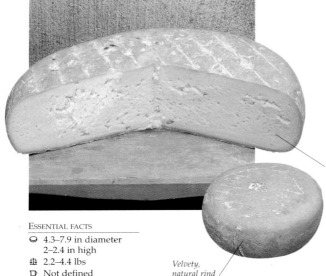

Semi-hard pâte; uncooked, pressed

Velvety, natural rind

This cow's-milk cheese, like the ewe's-milk cheese shown above, is another *fermier* cheese produced by the Ferme Penen in the province of Béarn. It comes in three different sizes: large, medium, and small. During affinage it is wiped and brushed, sometimes with salt, and then left for at least two months.

🍷 Madiran

ESSENTIAL FACTS

- ◯ 4.3–7.9 in diameter
  2–2.4 in high
- ⚖ 2.2–4.4 lbs
- 🌡 Not defined
- ✓ All year, best in spring

Aquitaine (64)

Raw

FROMAGE D'OSSAU, LARUNS

This *fermier* cheese is made in the Hameau de Bagès, in the department of Laruns, one of the cheesemaking centers of the Ossau Valley. It has a robust flavor and is traditionally eaten at the end of a meal consisting of a nourishing local soup called *garbure* (made from leeks, cabbage, celery, white beans, bacon, goose confit, and goose fat simmered together for three to four hours) followed by roast lamb. Affinage takes five months.

♀ Jurançon *sec*

Semi-hard pâte; uncooked, pressed

Hard, natural rind

 Aquitaine (64)

 Raw, whole

ESSENTIAL FACTS
- 7.9–9.8 in diameter 4.7 in high (not level)
- 11–13.2 lbs
- Not defined
- Best at the end of summer

FROMAGE DE VACHE

This is a *fermier* cheese made in Hameau de Bagès, in the department of Laruns in the Ossau Valley. Surrounded by mountains and just 18 miles from the Spanish border, the town perches high in the Pyrénées at an altitude of 1,742 ft, where the air is pure and cold. The cheese has a rich, complex flavor. Affinage takes at least two months.

❢ Madiran

Pâte is semi-hard; uncooked, pressed

Natural rind

 Aquitaine (64)

 Raw

ESSENTIAL FACTS
- 8.3–9.5 in diameter 2.4 in high
- 6.6–7.7 lbs
- Not defined
- Best in spring

FROMAGE DE PAYS, MIXTE

A sign in the shop in the area of the Col d'Aubisque where this cheese was bought says simply Fromage de Pays, regional cheese. Most of the farms in the area raise cows and ewes. When there is not enough ewe's milk for making cheese, cow's milk is added. The pâte is sweeter, closer to butter, yellower, and less dry when the two milks are mixed. The usual affinage of this fermier cheese is eight months.

♀ Jurançon *sec*

Semi-hard pâte, yellowish; uncooked, pressed

Natural rind

ESSENTIAL FACTS
- ⊖ 9.8 in diameter
  3.5 in high
- ⚖ 10.1 lbs
- ⟁ Not defined
- ✓ All year, depending on affinage

Aquitaine (64)

Raw

Semi-hard pâte; uncooked, pressed

LARUNS

The rind of this *fermier* cheese is dry, while the pâte is gray, very crumbly, with the color of a ripe ewe's cheese. The affinage of six months has given the cheese a balanced blend of acidity, salt, and fat. The strong animal smell of sheep adds flavor to the cheese. A total lack of softness is one of the characteristics of the cheeses from Ossau. Every year, a cheese fair is held at Laruns, where shepherds from all over the region come to show and sell their products, and price levels are fixed for the next 12 months. Because ewe's milk is more concentrated than cow's milk, only 5.8 quarts are used to make 2.2 lbs of cheese, compared with 10.6 quarts of cow's milk.

♀ Jurançon *sec*

ESSENTIAL FACTS
- ⊖ 11 in diameter
  3.5 in high
- ⚖ 11 lbs
- ⟁ Not defined
- ✓ All year

Natural rind, hard and dry

Aquitaine (64)

Raw

MATOCQ (AOC)

Few cheeses of the Pyrénées have a label and an AOC. This *artisanal* cheese made by M. C. Matocq is salty, solid, and well structured, with an affinage of four months.

♀ Jurançon *sec*

Pâte is semi-hard; uncooked, pressed

Natural rind

Aquitaine (64)

Raw, whole

ESSENTIAL FACTS

⊖ 10.2 in diameter
3.7 in high
⚖ 9.3 lbs
🗋 50%
✓ All year, best at end of spring to autumn

MATOCQ

This is a cow's-milk Matocq. It is as rich as the sheep's version. Annual production of sheep's cheeses amounts to 200 tons, mixed cheeses (half ewe's milk, half cow's milk) to 110 tons, and cow's cheeses to 220 tons. Their affinage takes some six to eight months in cellars, although some are left to mature for a whole year. M. Matocq's cheeses are exported to Germany, Belgium, and the United States in increasing numbers each year.

♀ Jurançon *sec*

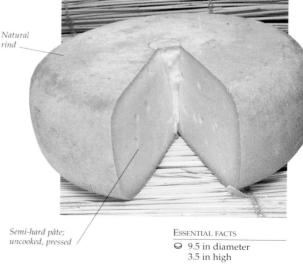

Natural rind

Semi-hard pâte; uncooked, pressed

Aquitaine (64)

Whole

ESSENTIAL FACTS

⊖ 9.5 in diameter
3.5 in high
⚖ 9.3 lbs
🗋 50%
✓ All year

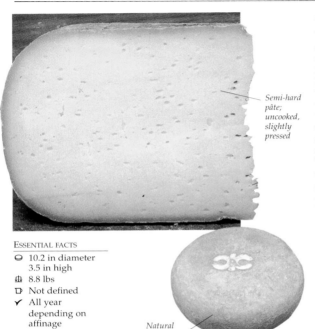

Semi-hard
pâte;
uncooked,
slightly
pressed

OSSAU FERMIER

This *fermier* cheese has an affinage of four and a half months. Cheeses from the Pyrénées are never ripened in a hurry. The one shown here is a little young but perfect, with small holes spread evenly throughout the pâte. This cheese tastes dry and salted. It has a good scent of well-integrated fat. As it is chewed, all the flavor of sweet and sour and the aroma are released. This is a strong cheese with nothing soft or flamboyant about it.

🍷 Madiran (type Château Montus), Pauillac

ESSENTIAL FACTS
- ◯ 10.2 in diameter
  3.5 in high
- ⊕ 8.8 lbs
- ↧ Not defined
- ✔ All year
  depending on
  affinage

Natural
rind

Aquitaine
(64)

Raw,
whole

Making cheese in the mountains

Summer arrives late in the French Alps, but each year, as soon as the last of the winter snow has disappeared from the summits, the *alpage*, or summer migration of herds, begins. In mid to late June, herds of cattle, often owned by more than one farmer, are entrusted to herdsmen or women, known as *alpagistes*, who accompany them to the upper slopes. The animals move along at their own pace, grazing and browsing on flowers. The *alpagistes* stay in *chalets*, where they milk the cows twice a day and make cheese. The *chalets* are scattered all over the mountains and provide a kind of cheesemaking relay since the animals do not stop at a single place but keep on climbing. When all the grass in one area is eaten, the herd moves on up the mountain in search of new pastures. By the middle of August, the herd will have reached almost 9,843 ft, just below the snowline. The first snows give the signal for the descent; stage by stage,

MOUNTAIN MILK
The rich and creamy milk produced by cattle grazing on the upper alpine slopes is used by the *alpagiste* to make cheese in *chalets* on the way up the mountain.

the *alpagiste* takes the animals back down the same slopes, which are rich and grassy again. On Saint Michael's Day, September 29, the herd returns to the village. The cows go back to their sheds to calve, and the production of winter cheeses begins.

In the Pyrénées a similar summer migration, known as *transhumance*, takes place, but here, the animals are sheep and goats tended by shepherds.

TOURMALET

Despite the imposing size of most Pyrénéan cheeses, there are some of a size that is easier to sell and buy. The Tourmalet, named after a mountain in the region where it is produced, is an *artisanal* cheese made with ewe's milk. It has a solid, pleasantly rustic flavor and aroma and easily holds its own against the bigger cheeses. Affinage takes one month.

Ÿ Jurançon *sec*

Semi-hard pâte; uncooked, pressed

Natural, hard rind

Aquitaine (64)

Raw

ESSENTIAL FACTS
⊖ 3.9 in diameter
2.8 in high
⚖ 1.3 lbs
Ɖ 50%
✓ All year

LE PETIT PARDOU

This cheese is a cow's-milk version of the Tourmalet shown above. Both cow's and ewe's versions are *artisanal* cheeses made in the town of Laruns.

❢ Madiran, Fronsac

Semi-hard pâte; uncooked, pressed

Natural, hard rind

Aquitaine (64)

Not defined

ESSENTIAL FACTS
⊖ 3.9 in diameter
2.8 in high
⚖ 1.3 lbs
Ɖ 50%
✓ All year

Brie

Rind of thin, white
mold, with red
patches and lines

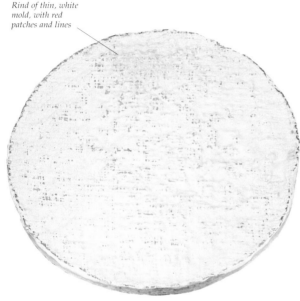

Soft, even-textured,
cream pâte;
unpressed, uncooked

ESSENTIAL FACTS

- ⊖ 14.2–14.6 in diameter
  1.2–1.4 in high
- ⚖ 5.5–6.6 lbs
- ♣ 1.6 oz min. per
  3.5 oz cheese
- ⏸ 45%
- ✓ All year

**AOC REGULATIONS:
BRIE DE MEAUX**

1. The milk may be heated to a
maximum of 98.6°F once and only
at the renneting.

2. The cheese is cast manually into
its mold with a special *pelle à Brie*
(Brie shovel).

3. The cheese is salted with dry salt
exclusively.

AOC GRANTED 1990

BRIE DE MEAUX (AOC)

Situated some 131 miles east of
Paris, the green region of Brie has
a long history of cheesemaking.
One reason for the rise in
importance of the cheese was
the proximity of the region to
Paris, which was a great center of
cheese consumption. The
geographical separation between
the places of production and
affinage is a Brie tradition.

When a Brie de Meaux is sold,
at least half the thickness of the
cheese should be ripe. This is a
refined cheese with a balanced
appearance and smell, and the
sweetness one would expect from
a first-class dairy product. The
cheese shown here is well ripened,
with a slight smell of mold. Its rind
looks like white velvet and when
the cheese is very ripe, the top and
sides will redden. The pâte is
compact, even-textured, and the
color of straw. It has a a slight scent
of mold, and is full of sweet as well
as smoky aromas, with a rich,
condensed flavor.

Brie de Meaux is an *artisanal*
or *industriel* cheese, and it must
be cured within the AOC regions
shown beside the map at the foot
of this page, as well as in parts
of Hautes-de-Seine (92), Seine-
Saint-Denis (93), Val-de-Marne (94),
and Paris (75).

During production of the cheese
the curd is barely cut. Drainage is
spontaneous and liquid evaporates
from the large surface. If drainage
is too quick, the cheese may split.
Affinage normally takes eight weeks.

🍷 St. Julien,
Vosne Romanée, Hermitage

Île-de-France (77);
Champagne-
Ardennes (10, 51,
52); Centre (45);
Lorraine (55);
🍇Bourgogne (89)

Raw

BRIE FERMIER

The workshop in the Laiterie Ganot, the dairy where this *fermier* Brie is made, stands next to a cow shed. The hot, ammonia-laden air that flows from the shed is said to encourage the development of mold. Using traditional methods, Mme. Clein makes the cheese, and Mme. Ganot cures it and then sells it at the markets of Meaux and Melun. She says: "It's good with green apples and walnuts and perhaps a glass of champagne." Since it is not the right size, it cannot be called a Brie de Meaux AOC. The color of the rind, with red marks from lying on straw, is that of a ripe Brie full of flavor and aroma. Affinage takes at least two months.

❦ St. Julien, Vosne Romanée, Hermitage

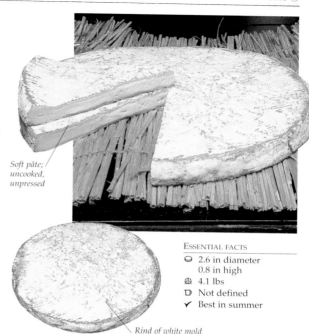

Soft pâte; uncooked, unpressed

Île-de-France (77)

Raw

Rind of white mold

ESSENTIAL FACTS

- ⊖ 2.6 in diameter
  0.8 in high
- ⚖ 4.1 lbs
- ▯ Not defined
- ✔ Best in summer

BRIE NOIR

The aged Brie shown on the right has had an affinage of about a year. It is thick and velvety. The locals soak it in their *café au lait* for breakfast.

❦ Château Chalon *jaune*, Arbois *jaune*

Rind is crumbly

Dry pâte needs to be chewed

Île-de -France (77)

Raw

ESSENTIAL FACTS

- ⊖ 11.8 in diameter
  8 in high
- ⚖ 3.2 lbs
- ▯ Not defined
- ✔ All year

Rind of thin, white mold, with brown or red stains and lines

Soft, even-textured pâte of uniform cream color; uncooked, unpressed

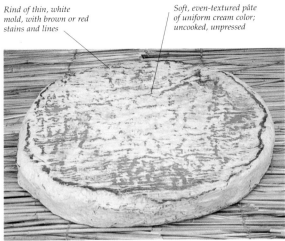

Affinage of ten weeks

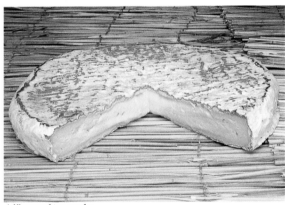

Affinage of ten weeks

Fresh cheese

BRIE DE MELUN (AOC)

Brie de Melun and Brie de Meaux are both from the same region, but whereas the Meaux is refined and relaxed, Melun is strong, robust, and salty. This difference derives from the varying methods of production. Coagulation for Meaux takes less than 30 minutes thanks to renneting, while Melun depends on lactic fermentation, which takes at least 18 hours. The affinage also takes longer and cheeses are left to mature for a minimum of four weeks, but usually seven to ten.

The *artisanal* cheese shown has a musty smell, and the pâte is creamy, sweet, and slightly salty.

Most Brie de Melun is eaten in the region and sold fresh or ripe at local markets. The fresh cheese is sour due to the lactic fermentation, and sweet, like good thick milk.

The AOC was granted in 1990.

❦ Bourgogne

ESSENTIAL FACTS

- ⊖ 10.6–11 in diameter
  1.4–1.6 in high
- ⚖ 3.3–4 lbs after 4 weeks of affinage
- ❖ 1.4 oz for 3.5 oz cheese
- ⛉ 45%
- ✔ All year

AOC REGULATIONS: BRIE DE MELUN

1. The milk must be heated once to a maximum of 86°F at the renneting.

2. Coagulation must be caused mainly by lactic fermentation but also by renneting.

3. Coagulation must take at least 18 hours.

4. Drainage must be slow.

5. The curd must be cast manually.

6. The cheese must be salted exclusively with dry salt.

AOC GRANTED 1990

Ile-de-France (77); Champagne–Ardenne (10); Bourgogne (89)

Raw

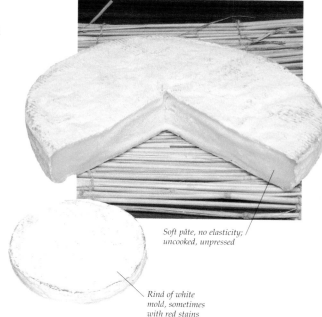

BRIE DE COULOMMIERS

It is said that Coulommiers is the ancestor of all Brie cheeses. Until 1984, this *fermier* version of the Brie de Coulommiers was produced by Mme. Storme, who used to raise 50 cows. The cheeses were then taken to be ripened for four weeks by a family firm in the region, the Société Fromagère de la Brie.

The local people prefer it when it is firm, not runny. Its sweet aroma and smell of mold spread in the mouth. Today, the *fermier* version is no longer made, and only an *artisanal* version is produced.

♥ Bourgogne, Bordeaux, Côtes du Rhône

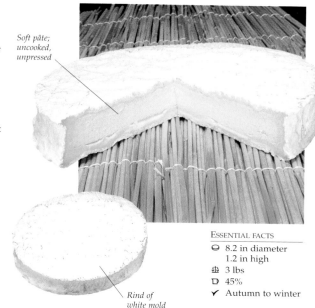

Soft pâte; uncooked, unpressed

Rind of white mold

Ile-de-France (77)

Raw

ESSENTIAL FACTS
- ⊖ 8.2 in diameter
  1.2 in high
- ⚖ 3 lbs
- Ð 45%
- ✔ Autumn to winter

BRIE DE MONTEREAU

This *artisanal* cheese is close to Brie de Meaux in taste. Its aftertaste and smell are strong for a Brie. The cheese photographed is still quite young. Affinage usually takes five to six weeks.

♥ Bourgogne, Bordeaux, Côtes du Rhône

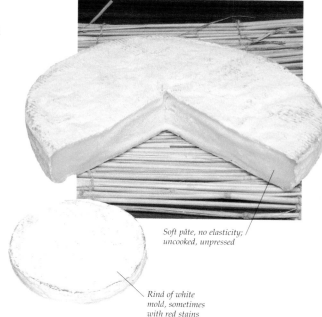

Soft pâte, no elasticity; uncooked, unpressed

Rind of white mold, sometimes with red stains

Ile-de-France (77)

Raw

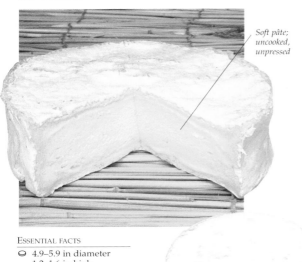

Soft pâte;
uncooked,
unpressed

COULOMMIERS

Brie cheeses come in three sizes: large, medium, and small. The Coulommiers is small but quite thick. The one shown here is at the point of affinage, which is how the local people prefer it. It has a small heart with the sourness of a fresh cheese, set in a pâte of pale yellow that has a sweet and melting taste. In this one single cheese, it is possible to see the different stages of affinage.Production may be *fermier*, *artisanal*, or *industriel*, with an affinage of eight weeks for the raw milk version and at least four weeks for the pasteurized milk.

❢ Bourgogne, Bordeaux, Côtes du Rhône

Rind of white mold,
with some red stains

ESSENTIAL FACTS

- ◯ 4.9–5.9 in diameter
  1.2–1.6 in high
- ⚖ 14.1–17.6 oz
- ⁙ 4.9 oz min. per cheese
- ◖ 40% min.
- ✔ End of summer
  (*fermier*); all year
  (pasteurized)

Ile-de-France
(77)

Raw or
pasteurized

LE FOUGERUS

This *artisanal* cheese belonging to the Brie group is slightly larger than a Coulommiers. Originally, it was made on a farm for family consumption, with the fern leaf serving as decoration and flavoring. It was commercially produced for the first time at the beginning of the 20th century. The scent of the fern blends with the smell of the mold. The pâte is supple and sweet and has a salty taste. Affinage takes four weeks.

Rind of
white mold

❢ Bourgogne, Bordeaux, Côtes du Rhône

ESSENTIAL FACTS

Soft pâte;
uncooked,
unpressed

- ◯ 6.3 in diameter
  1.6 in high
- ⚖ 1.4 lbs
- ◖ 45–50%
- ✔ Spring to autumn

Ile-de-France
(77)

Raw

BRIE DE NANGIS

This *artisanal* cheese was ousted by the Brie de Melun (p. 58) and disappeared from the market for some time. It was revived by a single maker but is no longer made in the town of Nangis. The heart of the cheese shown here is barely ripe and would suit those who prefer their Brie young. Affinage takes four to five weeks.

❢ Bourgogne, Bordeaux, Côtes du Rhône

Soft pâte; uncooked, unpressed

Rind of white mold

Ile-de-France (77)

Raw

ESSENTIAL FACTS
- ◯ 7.9–9 in diameter
  1.6 in high
- ⚖ 2.2–2.7 lbs
- ◻ 45%
- ✓ Summer to winter

BRIE LE PROVINS

After a total, but happily short, disappearance, the Provins has made a modest reentry; although production is limited to just one cheesemaker. The heart of this medium-sized Brie is on the point of turning into a creamy pâte. It no longer rasps on the tongue nor the bottom of the mouth. Some people like young Brie, but it is best when ripened (right) because the bouquet of the milk, a lingering aroma, and a clear and refined smell of mold are fully developed. It is an *artisanal* cheese with an affinage of four to five weeks.

❢ Bourgogne, Bordeaux, Côtes du Rhône

Soft pâte; uncooked, unpressed

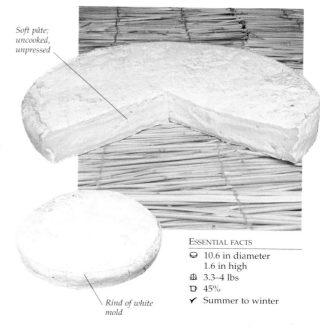

Rind of white mold

Ile-de-France (77)

Raw

ESSENTIAL FACTS
- ◯ 10.6 in diameter
  1.6 in high
- ⚖ 3.3–4 lbs
- ◻ 45%
- ✓ Summer to winter

Cabécou / Rocamadour (AOC)

Made with raw goat's milk from the plains, this tiny, but highly pleasing cheese matures well, acquiring body and presence. Each year some 490 tons are produced in the triangle between Rocamadour, Gramat, and Carlucet. In the *langue d'Oc*, the old language of the south, a *cabécou* is a small goat. The fresh, young spring cheeses, smelling of grass and milk, are well worth trying. Under the name of Rocamadour this cheese was granted AOC status on March 16, 1996.

Cabécou de Gramat

Soft pâte;
uncooked,
unpressed

❶

Rind of
natural
mold

Rind of
natural
mould

❷

Cabécou

Soft pâte;
uncooked,
unpressed

❸

Picadou

CABÉCOU DE GRAMAT

This *fermier* cheese has an affinage of a minimum of ten days

♀ Jurançon *sec*, Vouvray sec, Tursan

ESSENTIAL FACTS
- ⊖ 1.6–2 in diameter
  0.4–0.6 in high
- ⚖ 1.1–1.4 oz
- ⧠ 45%
- ✓ Spring to autumn

CABÉCOU

A *fermier* Cabécou from the region of Quercy.

♀ Jurançon *sec*, Vouvray sec, Tursan

PICADOU

This cheese is produced by wrapping a ripe Cabécou in walnut or plane leaves. It is then sprayed with *marc* of plums and preserved in an air-tight container. The crushed pepper adds spice to an already piquant cheese.

⧠ *Marc, Eau de vie* of plums

Midi-
Pyrénées
(46)

Raw

Cabécou de Rocamadour (AOC)

These small *fermier* and *artisanal* cheeses are small and mature rapidly. They have a thin rind, and a tender, creamy pâte with a subtle scent reminiscent of milk and mold. The aftertaste is equally light, of sugar and hazelnuts. Affinage takes anything up to four weeks. The cheeses shown here have all had different periods of affinage.

❦ Gaillac, ♀ Bergerac *sec*

Midi-Pyrénées (46)

Raw

Essential facts
- 1.6–2 in diameter
  0.4–0.6 in high
- 1.1–1.4 oz
- 45%
- Spring to autumn

Soft to hard pâte; uncooked, unpressed

Rind of thin, natural mold depending on affinage

Affinage of about one week **6**

Affinage of about six weeks **4**

Affinage of about two weeks **7**

Affinage of about two weeks **5**

Affinage of about four weeks **8**

How Camembert is Made

Normandie is a mild region in northern France where it tends to rain a lot. The gentle sun and humidity produce lush green grass on which the typical black-and-white Normande cows can feed. Their milk is of excellent quality, and has made Normandie famous for its butter and cream, as well as its noble cheeses such as Pont l'Evêque, Livarot, and Camembert.

Since 1981, François Durand, who was born in Paris in 1961, has produced Camembert *fermier* just outside the village of Camembert in Normandie. He makes at least 650 cheeses a week. Total production of the cheeses takes two days. Although it is of an excellent quality, his cheese has not been granted an AOC, which recognizes Camembert de Normandie only.

CAMEMBERT *FERMIER*
This colorful sign advertising farmhouse Camembert, marks the entrance to the farm where François Durand has made cheeses since 1981.

MILK FROM NORMANDE COWS
The cows are milked twice a day, once in the morning and once in the evening.

THE STARTER
The day before production, the starter is added.

WARMING THE MILK
The warm milk is poured into buckets. The air is near 100% humidity.

MILKINGS
The milk is transported from the milking place in refrigeration tanks.

SKIMMING
Fat (20%) is skimmed off. The milk is heated.

RENNETING
Liquid rennet from the fourth stomach of a calf is mixed in.

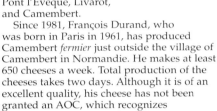

COAGULATION
Coagulation occurs over a period of 90 minutes to 2 hours.

PREPARING THE SURFACE
A grooved, stainless-steel table is covered by a mat of boiled poplar wood.

PLASTIC MOLDS
The molds in which the cheese is made are perforated.

CLEANING THE CURD
A brush is used to remove any impurities that gather on the surface of the curd.

CUTTING THE CURD
The curd is cut four times vertically and horizontally with a large knife.

LADLING OUT THE CURD
The curd is emptied out of the bucket and into the molds.

FILLING THE MOLDS
The ladle used has the same diameter as the molds themselves.

FOUR LAYERS OF CURD
Each mold is given one ladle full of curds, four times around.

THE FIFTH LAYER OF CURD
One hour later a fifth ladle of curds is added to the molds.

DRAINING OFF THE WHEY
The whey drains naturally with the weight of the curd. It is fed to pigs.

TURNING
Seven hours later, each mold is carefully turned by hand.

METAL PLATE
A metal plate is laid on the white cheese which is left to rest for the night.

REMOVING THE MOLD
The next day, the molds are removed. The metal plate helps the cheeses to drain.

REMOVING THE PLATES
The metal plates are removed from each cheese.

ADDING THE MOLD
Three sorts of *Penicillium candidum* diluted in water are sprayed on the cheeses.

SALTING THE TOP AND SIDES
After five days, fine dry salt is applied directly to the tops and sides.

SALTING THE UNDERSIDE
The cheeses are lined up, flipped over and the underside lightly salted.

ADDING MOLD TO THE TOP
The new top of each cheese is sprayed with diluted mold.

DRYING
The cheeses are left to rest for a night before going to the drying room.

DRYING ROOM
This room is set at 55°F, 85% humidity. The cheeses stay here for two weeks.

FIFTH DAY
After five days the cheeses are still quite deep and developing a crust.

EIGHTH DAY
After eight days, the cheeses have shrunk. They are turned during drying.

TWO WEEKS
After two weeks the white mold characteristic of Camembert has developed.

WRAPPING
The cheeses are then wrapped in wax paper ready for packing.

PACKING
The cheeses are put in wooden boxes and sent to the *fromager* or cheese shop.

READY TO EAT
After 2 weeks ripening at a *fromager* the Camemberts are ready to eat.

CAMEMBERT DE NORMANDIE (AOC)

To many people, the name of Camembert is synonymous with French cheese. Even before Camembert was granted its AOC in 1983, it was the most copied cheese in the world. You should always choose a Camembert by eye: the shape should be intact, and the rind covered in white mold, with reddish stripes and stains. The pâte should be creamy yellow, supple and give slightly to finger pressure. There should be a light smell of mold and the taste may be too salty at times. The locals prefer Camembert *moitié affiné* – half and half – when the *filet* or heart is still white and not yet creamy.

Coopérative and *industriel* versions of Camembert are produced, with an affinage of a minimum of 21 days from the date of manufacture within the AOC areas listed. Today, it is hard to find good Camembert: a young cheesemaker has taken up the production of Camembert *fermier* (p. 64) but his cheese has yet to be granted an AOC.

❡ St. Emilion, St. Estèphe

Rind of white mold pierced by red stains

AOC REGULATIONS: CAMEMBERT DE NORMANDIE

1. Concentrated or powdered milk, lactic proteins, or coloring may not be added to the milk.

2. The milk must not be heated above 98.6°F.

3. The uncut curd must be sliced vertically.

4. The curd must be cast with a ladle whose diameter corresponds to that of the mold: the operation is undertaken in stages, with a minimum of four successive fillings (pp. 64–65).

5. Salting is carried out with dry salt exclusively

6. After salting the cheeses are taken to the drying room, where the temperature is between 50°F and 57°F: they are left in wooden boxes. Before this, they may be placed on boards, in cellars at 46 or 48°F.

7. The words *Fabrication traditionnelle au lait cru avec moulage à la louche* may appear on the label of a cheese benefiting from the AOC. *Fabriqué en Normandie* indicates the place of production on the labels of cheeses not benefiting from the AOC.

AOC GRANTED 1983

ESSENTIAL FACTS

⊖ 4.1–4.3 in diameter
  1.2 in high
⚖ 8.8 oz min.
⁂ 4.1 oz per cheese
🏷 45% min.
✓ All year

Normandie
(14, 50, 61, 27, 76)

Raw

CAMEMBERT AFFINÉ AU CIDRE DE LA MAISON

This cheese is a specialty of the cheesemaker who makes it by soaking a young Camembert with its white rind on in cider for about 15 days. The cheese absorbs the taste of the cider and the aroma of the apple. Its smell stings the nose a little.

❢ Beaujolais, 🍶 Cider

Marks from cloth
used during affinage

CŒUR DE CAMEMBERT AU CALVADOS

This is a peeled Camembert, soaked in Calvados, which is a spirit distilled from cider; both the Calvados and the cheese are Norman specialties.

🍶 Cidre-Jasnières, Calvados,

Decorated with
a walnut

CANCOILLOTTE / METTON

A cheese called Metton, of which both *artisanal* and *industriel* versions are produced, is used to make Cancoillotte. The Metton is made from skimmed milk, which is coagulated, thinly cut, and heated to a maximum of 140°F, pressed, pounded, and then ripened for a few days. Cancoillotte is made by melting the Metton in a little water or milk over a low heat and adding salt and butter. Hot or cold the Cancoillotte is spread on bread and eaten for breakfast or as a snack, sometimes with vegetables or meat. It is sold in containers, plain, with butter, garlic, or white wine. The taste is simple. La Cancoillotte is a popular food in the Franche Comté.

❢ Côtes du Jura
Bourgogne Passetoutgrains

Metton has a
granular
consistency

Metton

Pale yellow, lightly
salted, and creamy,
with the consistency
of liquid honey

Cancoillotte

Franche-
Comté (25)

Skimmed

Cantal, Salers, Laguiole, and Aligot

Affinage of six months

Ivory semi-hard, compact pâte; uncooked, pressed twice

CANTAL / FOURME DE CANTAL (AOC)

Fermier, coopérative, and *industriel* versions of Cantal are produced. A piece of Cantal feels heavy and moist, and the pâte will melt in the hand when kneaded. The salt that is added to it brings out the full flavor of this cheese. A well-ripened Cantal has a strong taste, while a young cheese has the sweetness of raw milk.

AOC granted 1980

❢ Côtes d'Auvergne, Chatêaugay; Moulin à Vent Calvados

ESSENTIAL FACTS

- ⊖ 13.8–16.5 in diameter (average); 14.2–15.8 in high
- ⚖ 77.2–99.2 lbs
- ❣ 2 oz min. per 3 oz matured cheese; 1.9 oz min. for *fromage blanc* just after pressing
- ⏦ 45%
- ✔ All year

Auvergne (15, 43, 63,); Midi-Pyrénées (12); Limousin (19)

Raw, pasteurized

Dark yellow natural rind with red and orange stains

Aluminium ID tag: CA indicates Cantal; 15 is the department of production; EE is the maker's code

After only eight days of affinage

How Cantal is Made

Cantal is made in accordance with strict AOC regulations.

Renneting
The milk is heated to 89.6°F. The curd forms approximately one hour after renneting.

Cutting the curd
The curd is cut into cubes, then brewed: the whey is removed.

First pressing
The curd is gathered in a compact mass and quantities of 76.4–220 lbs at a time are wrapped in a cloth and passed through the press (**1**). This results in a thick slice called a *tome* (**2**), which is cut and pressed several times to expel the whey.

1. The curd is wrapped in a cloth and passed through the *press-tomme.*

Maturing of the shape
After pressing, the *tome* is allowed to rest for eight hours at 53.6–59°F. This encourages the natural development of lactic acids that protect and modify the structure of the *tome*, necessary for its affinage. The matured *tome* is broken in small pieces with the help of a grinding machine. Although this process is commonly used in other countries, in France it is unique to the production of Cantal.

2. The *tome* is cut before being pressed again to expel the whey.

Curing with salt
The *tome*, reduced to nut-sized pieces, is salted, with a minimum of 0.9 oz salt per 2.2 lbs of volume in summer, 0.7 oz in winter, and then brewed. The salt dissolves and mixes evenly with the *tome*. The next day, when the *tome* has gathered, it is rapidly crumbled; a handful is squeezed tightly and then thrown. If the pieces come away from the hand easily, curing is complete.

3. The ground *tome* is placed in a cloth-lined metal mold.

Casting and pressing
A cloth-lined mold is filled with ground *tome* (**3**), closed with metal lid, and then passed through the press (**4**). After 48 hours, the cheese is removed from the press, the cloth changed, and the cheese is passed through the press three or four times.

Affinage
Once the cheese has assumed the definitive shape of the Fourme de Cantal, it is removed from the mold and transferred to the *cave d'affinage*, a cool (50°F), damp (90% humidity), dark, and lightly ventilated room. For at least 30 days from the date of production, the cheese is rubbed and turned twice a week. There are three stages in the affinage: 30 days gives a young, white, sweet cheese; two to six months gives a golden, medium cheese (*entre-deux* or *doré*) cheese; six months gives a dark yellow, old (*vieux* or *charactère*) cheese.

4. Each cheese is pressed three or four times over 48 hours.

Firm, yellow, semi-hard pâte; uncooked, pressed twice

Affinage of ten months

Dry, natural rind

Dry Matter per 3.5 oz Cheese				
Cantal	**Salers**	**Laguiole**	**Beaufort**	**Brie**
2 oz min.	2 oz min.	2 oz min.	2.2 oz min.	1.6 oz min.

Fat Content per 3.5 oz Cheese				
Cantal	**Salers**	**Laguiole**	**Beaufort**	**Brie**
0.9 oz min.	0.9 oz min.	0.9 oz min.	1 oz min.	0.7 oz min.

Salers (AOC)

For 2,000 years, Salers and Cantal have been produced in the mountains of the Auvergne following traditional methods that have remained fundamentally the same. Salers is the *fermier* version of Cantal, and the AOC regulations stipulate that it must be made with the milk of cows that grazed on mountain pastures in summer; Cantal is made from the milk of the other seasons. Of the 32 AOC cheeses currently registered in France, Salers is the only entirely *fermier* cheese: its red aluminum tag states this. Affinage in the areas defined by the AOC is for a minimum of three months from the date of production. The cheese is ripened and preserved at a temperature below or equal to 53.6°F.

How dry matter affects the flavor

Salers and Cantal are not cooked-pâte cheeses, but they are pressed twice and the *tome* is ground between pressings, which is why they contain more than 2 oz dry matter; a cooked and pressed cheese such as Beaufort (p. 26) contains even more. Usually, half of a cheese is composed of water, and it is rare that the percentage of dry matter should exceed 1.8 oz per 3.5 oz cheese. The high percentage of dry matter in Salers shows that it is a compact cheese with a firm pâte. As a result, it has volume, complexity, and an unequaled quality of flavor.

Period of production

The mountains of Cantal are snowbound for half the year. In April or May, the cows and herders leave for the mountains. Huts of stone called *burons* serve as living quarters, as well as dairies and ripening cellars. In the Savoie region of the Alps, these are called *chalets*. In 1948, there were 1,000 *burons* in the region and the cheeses made there were called Salers *haute montagne*. Now there are only 20 *burons* left. In 1961, a law decreed that Salers *haute montagne* must be made between May 20 and September 30 but this period was extended to May 1 to October 30.

Production

Salers is produced by 92 farms. Each farm raises 35 to 50 cows. Every herd produces one Salers of approximately 88 lbs per day, the equivalent of 92.5–105 gallons of milk. The number of Salers made by all of the farms during the six months of the permitted season in 1991 amounted to some 18,000 cheeses, or 799 tons (compared with 17, 760 tons of Cantal).

Cows

Salers cows calve about once a year and give between 7.3 and 8.6 quarts of milk per day or 3.3 tons milk per year. It is of high quality and has a 34% protein content and 38% fat content. Equally appreciated for its meat, this breed of cow originates from the Massif Central. It is robust, and even-tempered, with a reddish-brown coat and lyre-shaped horns.

Affinage of ten months

The cheese shown opposite has had an affinage of ten months. The letters and numerals SA 15 HK on the red tag refer to the department and the maker. The crust is brown

and resembles the surface of a dry rock. It is created by being repeatedly rubbed and left in a cool cellar at a temperature of 53°F. Its thickness protects the pâte, which is the color of egg yolk and gives off a strong, meaty smell. The pâte is firm yet surprisingly soft, and leaves a moist, fatty feeling on the tongue. In the mouth, the flavor opens up and has a full, sweet, nutty aroma of arnica, anemones, dandelions, gentians, and other mountain flowers that blossom in summer, as well as the tang and sourness of old salt. Salers is a strong cheese.

Affinage of 18 months

The rind of the cheese shown below is fissured and a bloom has formed after 18 months. This is caused by cheese mites that eat the rind and invade the pâte. Some people wait for this stage of the affinage: they scrape the powder from the rind and eat the cheese.

▼ St. Pourçain, Touraine

ESSENTIAL FACTS
- ⊖ 15–19 in diameter (before affinage) 11.8–15.8 in high
- ⊕ 77–110 lbs
- ⁂ 2 oz min. per 3.5 oz ripened cheese
- ♉ 45% min. 3.5 oz min. per 100 g cheese
- ✓ All year depending on affinage; a Salers made in May can be eaten in autumn

Affinage of 18 months

Midi-Pyrénées, Limousin (15, 43, 63)
Raw, whole summer milk

Firm, yellow, semi-hard pâte; uncooked, pressed twice

Natural, dry, light, orange and white rind, darkens with affinage

⊖ 15.8 in diameter
  11.8–15.8 high
⚖ 66–110 lbs
∴ 2 oz min. per 3.5 oz cheese
⛿ 45% min., 0.9 oz min.
  per 3.5 oz cheese
✓ All year depending
  on affinage

LAGUIOLE (AOC)

Laguiole derives its name from the village on the plateau of Aubrac. The name is pronounced *laïyole* – without the g. It has a firm, golden pâte and a thick rind. Cantal (p. 68), Salers (p. 70), and Laguiole share the same method of production, their size and shape are almost identical, and they all contain a high percentage of dry matter.

Affinage takes at least four months from the date of production in the listed areas. The temperature of affinage and conservation must be below 57°F.

The AOC was granted in 1976.

The history of Laguiole

According to local history, Laguiole was first made at a monastery in the mountains of Aubrac during the 19th century. The monks taught their method of production to the *buronniers,* who still make cheese in their *burons* or mountain huts.

Production reached its peak at the beginning of the 20th century. At that time, the summer migration of herds and herders lasted just 142 days, from May 25 to October 13. A cow then produced only 110 lbs cheese – not only did the cows of the Aubrac breed give no more than a maximum of 3–4 quarts of milk per day, but cheese production too was limited to the period of migration. Despite this, 1,200 *buronniers* produced 770 tons of high-quality Laguiole each summer.

An association is established

Towards the end of the 19th century, an association was formed to boost sales and the village of Laguiole became the center of production for this cheese.

In 1939, the association changed its role to protection of the cheese. Despite this, a sharp decrease in the work force reduced the number of *burons* to 55. During the 1960s, annual production decreased to 33 tons. To put an end to this, the Coopérative Fromagère Jeune Montagne was created in 1960. In 1976, production was finally allowed throughout the year.

Cows

Sadly, there has been a marked decline in the quality of Laguiole cheeses since 1981, due to the introduction of Holstein cows. These cows, originally from Holland, produce a lot of milk but the protein content is inferior to that of the Aubrac breed. The Holsteins did not adapt well to its new environment, so studies were carried out to find a better breed that could adapt to the climate and soil of Aubrac. A Swiss breed, the Pie-Rouge-de-l'Est, was selected: these cows give 1,268 gallons of milk in 300 days, with a protein content of 32.5%. Further studies are still underway to reach a goal of 1,321 gallons per year of a milk, with a minimum of 32% protein.

Production

Laguiole is made in three different departments. With 47 villages producing 649 tons (1991), there is no comparison with the Salers (770 tons) nor the Cantal (17,760 tons).

Although most of the production is *coopérative*, there are currently three *burons* that make Laguiole from raw milk produced on the plateau of Aubrac, but this cheese is sold to tourists without being ripened for the minimum of four months stipulated by the AOC.

❡ Côtes du Frontonnais

HOW A LARGE, ROUND CHEESE IS CUT

When cutting a large, round cheese, some of which, like Laguiole, can weigh as much as 110 lbs, great care must be taken to make straight, clean cuts through the pâte.

1. The first step is to stand the cheese firmly on one end ready to make the first vertical cut.

2. Using a strong cheese wire, the cheese is first cut from top to bottom in two equal halves.

3. Each half is then cut horizontally into two halves.

4. Each piece is then cut into triangles of various sizes.

KNIVES OF LAGUIOLE
In the past, the people of Laguiole worked in Spain over the winter. While there, they came across jackknives. When they returned to France, they began to make similar knives. These were so successful that they became known as knives of Laguiole.

Midi-Pyrénées (12); Auvergne (15); Languedoc-Roussillon (48)

Raw, whole

ALIGOT / TOMME FRAÎCHE

There are two possible origins for the name of this cheese. One theory says that *aligot* is a corruption in the local language of the Latin *aliquid*, meaning "something," which was the word used by pilgrims begging for money in the medieval monasteries. Monks gave them soup with bread and fresh *tomme*, meaning a lump of cheese. The second possible origin comes from the ancient French verb *alicoter*, which meant "to cut." In due course this was shortened to *aligot*.

Fermier, coopérative, and *industriel* versions of Aligot are produced. This cheese is used in many dishes and is often eaten with potatoes. A specialty of the region is Aligot with mashed potatoes. Pieces of Aligot are mixed quickly and melted in hot mashed potatoes, then seasoned with garlic, the juice of grilled sausages, salt, and pepper. Another local dish is Aligot with *tripoux* or chestnut purée, accompanied by the favorite local red wine, St. Pourçain.

🍷 St. Pourçain

Fresh, white, spongy, elastic, nonsalted pâte

ESSENTIAL FACTS

⊕ 44 lbs, also vacuum packs of 4.4–11 lbs

🧀 45%

✓ All year, especially spring to summer

COOKING CHEESE
Melted Aligot can stretch six to ten feet when pulled with a spatula and must be eaten piping hot.

Auvergne; (15), Midi-Pyrénées, (12)

Raw or pasteurized

CARRÉ DE L'EST

This cheese has a moist rind that sticks to the fingers and feels elastic. The pâte is evenly perforated and is soft, sticky, salty, and melts in the mouth. The cheese is easiest to eat when covered with mold. *Coopérative* and *industriel* versions are produced, with an affinage of three to four weeks.

❢ Coteaux Champenois, Pinot Noir d'Alsace, Sancerre

Alsace,
Champagne-
Ardenne,
Lorraine

 Pasteurized

ESSENTIAL FACTS

◈ 3.4 in square 1–1.2 in high
⚖ 8.8–10.6 oz
▱ 45%
✔ All year

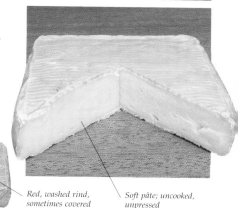

Red, washed rind, sometimes covered with white mold

Soft pâte; uncooked, unpressed

....

SAINT-RÉMY

This mild-flavored cheese belongs to the same family as Carré de l'Est (above). It tastes similar to Camembert and is neither weak nor strong. Saint-Rémy is ideal if you like just a small piece of washed-rind cheese. Production is *industriel*, with an affinage of two to three weeks.

❢ Pinot Noir d'Alsace, Sancerre

Lorraine
(55)

 Pasteurized

ESSENTIAL FACTS

◈ 3.5 in square 1.2 in high
⚖ 8.8 oz
▱ 45–50%
✔ All year

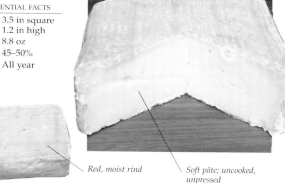

Red, moist rind

Soft pâte; uncooked, unpressed

....

LE SAULXUROIS

This *artisanal* cheese, which comes from from Saulxures in the region of Bassigny in Champagne, also belongs to the same family as the Carré de l'Est (above). It tastes salty. Affinage takes at least three weeks, during which time the cheese is washed with brine.

❢ Coteaux Champenois, Pinot Noir d'Alsace, Sancerre

Champagne-
Ardenne (52)

 Raw

ESSENTIAL FACTS

◈ 3.5 in square 1.2 in high
⚖ 8.8 oz
▱ 45%
✔ All year

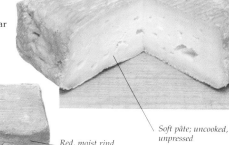

Red, moist rind

Soft pâte; uncooked, unpressed

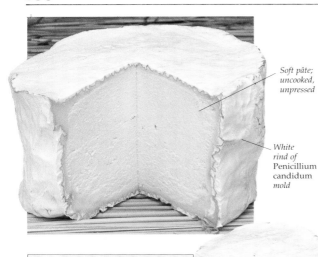

Soft pâte; uncooked, unpressed

White rind of Penicillium candidum mold

CHAOURCE (AOC)

Not all cheeses need to mature. The cheese shown is very young and melts in the mouth like light snow. Production is *artisanal* and *industriel* within specified areas of Bourgogne and Champagne. Affinage takes a minimum of two weeks and usually at least one month.

◊ Champagne *rosé*,
♥ Coteaux Champenois, Irancy, Sancerre

ESSENTIAL FACTS

⊖ 5.4–3.5 in diameter, 2.4–2.8 in high, small; 4–4.3 in diameter, 2–2.4 in high, large
⚖ 8.8 oz min. small; 1 lb min., large
◻ 50% min.
✓ All year, best summer to autumn

Champagne-Ardenne (10); Bourgogne (89)

Not defined

AOC REGULATIONS: CHAOURCE

1. Coagulation must be mainly lactic and last for at least 12 hours.

2. Drainage must be spontaneous.

AOC GRANTED 1977

CHAUMES

This *industriel* cheese is produced in Jurançon by the Fromageries des Chaumes, one of the biggest cheesemaking companies in France producing cheeses from cow and ewe's milk, low-fat cheeses, and blue cheeses. It is easy to eat, with practically no smell at first; some people may find it a little bland. Affinage takes four weeks.

♥ Madiran, Côtes de Bourg

Semi-hard pâte; uncooked, unpressed

ESSENTIAL FACTS

⊖ 7.9–9 in diameter 1.6 in high
⚖ 4.4 lbs
◻ 50%
✓ All year

Washed rind

Aquitaine (64)

Pasteurized

The Appellation d'Origine Contrôlée

The Appellation d'Origine Contrôlée, or AOC, applies to wines, *eaux-de-vie*, dairy, and farmhouse products. It guarantees that a product of quality has been produced within a specified region by the correct method. The AOC is regulated by laws, the first of which was the Law for the Protection of the Place of Origin on May 6, 1919. This law specifically defines the place of origin of a product, including province, region, and commune. Since then, there have been numerous revisions until the present day, when the Institut National Appellation d'Origine (INAO) was put in control. This branch of the Ministry of Agriculture represents the triumvirate of manufacturers, consumers, and the government.

The INAO has established precise definitions for the cheeses themselves, such as their milk, regions, methods of production, and the length of affinage. Any violation is liable to prosecution, and penalties consist of imprisonment of three months to one year, and a fine. Some of the most important points of current AOC regulations are given in this book.

There are 34 AOC cheeses. AOC status for two other cheeses has been applied for: Tomme de Savoie (p. 184) and Valençay (p. 84).

Production of AOC cheeses is increasing, with 148,350 tons in 1985; 148,350 tons in 1986; 149,431 tons in 1987; 153,379 tons in 1988; in 1989; 164,320 tons in 1990; and 166,299 tons in 1991. In 1991, the production of Abondance (p. 20) increased by 52.6%; that of Mont d'Or (p. 228), by 46.4%.

Prices of cheese vary depending on the shop and the degree of affinage. Large hard cheeses are sold by weight; smaller soft cheeses are often sold by the piece.

In the table (right) the left column gives the year when the AOC was granted; the column on the far right tells you where to find details of the cheese in this book.

Obligatory mark for all AOC cheeses

YEAR	CHEESE	PAGE
1975	Bleu d'Auvergne	29
1975	Livarot	152
1976	Beaufort	26
1976	Comté	112
1976	Fourme d'Ambert	134
1976	Laguiole	72
1976	Maroilles	154
1976	Pont-l'Evêque	172
1976	Reblochon	175
1979	Saint-Nectaire	184
1977	Bleu du Haut Jura	31
1977	Chaource	76
1977	Neufchâtel	162
1978	Munster	158
1979	Bleu des Causses	30
1979	Salers	70
1980	Brie de Meaux	56
1980	Brie de Melun	58
1980	Cantal	68
1981	Mont d'Or	228
1983	Camembert de Normandie	66
1990	Abondance	20
1991	Epoisses de Bourgogne	133
1991	Langres	151

YEAR	CHEESE	PAGE
1975	Selles-sur-Cher	83
1976	Crottin de Chavignol	80
1976	Pouligny-Saint-Pierre	81
1983	Picodon	170
1988	Cabécou/de Rocamadour	63
1990	Chabichou du Poitou	79
1990	Sainte-Maure de Touraine	82

YEAR	CHEESE	PAGE
1979	Roquefort	178
1980	Ossau-Iraty-Brebis Pyrénées	43

YEAR	CHEESE	PAGE
1988	Brocciu	116

Chèvre de la Loire (AOC)

The Loire River rises in the Massif Central from where it flows into the Atlantic Ocean. At some 629 miles long, it is the longest river in France. It flows first to the north, then west. Soft plains spread around this giant curve in a region justly called the Garden of France. The countryside is sprinkled with Renaissance castles and there is an abundance of wines and cheeses.

In the 8th century, the Saracens were repelled at Poitiers. These people were originally Arabs, who for centuries had been settled in the south of Spain and gradually moved north into France. When they were expelled from France, they left behind not only goats, but also the recipes for making cheese from their milk.

Villages on either side of the river produce goat cheese of different sizes. They have delicately varied tastes and include five AOCs: in the eastern part of the area, there is Crottin de Chavignol (p. 80), shaped like a drum; to the west, Sainte-Maure de Touraine (p. 82), a thick stick covered with powdered charcoal; to the north of the central region, Selles-sur-Cher (p. 83), also covered with charcoal ash; and to the south, a small black pyramid, Valençay (p. 84), which is a candidate for an AOC of its own; to the west is Pouligny-Saint-Pierre (p. 81), a slightly more slender pyramid; and southwest, Chabichou du Poitou (opposite).

How goat-milk cheeses are made

According to French tradition, goat's cheese should be on the table from Easter to All Saints' Day in November. Coagulation of goat's milk is usually caused by lactic fermentation. The ferment (also called starter) is mixed into the milk. The milk rests for a night and turns sour. It is then heated to 64–68°F. A very small amount of rennet is introduced and the milk rests for another 24 hours. The curd is neither cut nor heated, mixed nor pressed: drainage is instant as the curd is ladled into the molds, and the whey runs off through the fine holes in the sides and base. The cheese is cured dry – *affiné à sec* – in a cool and well-ventilated room at 52°F and 80% humidity, which is relatively dry compared with cellars at 90 to 100%. The drying process of both rind and pâte must be balanced, otherwise the rind will wrinkle and the whey left in the pâte will stick to it from the inside. Although blue mold will appear naturally on the rind, a covering of oak ash and charcoal powder helps to create an environment that encourages its development.

PERFORATED MOLDS
The holes in the molds used to make Valençay (left), and Selles-Sur Cher (right) allow the whey to drain off quickly.

ADDING ASH
Covering the rind of the cheese with ash, encourages the blue mold to appear.

CHABICHOU DU POITOU (AOC)

Poitou is the most important goat-breeding region in France and consequently produces many goat's-milk cheeses. This cheese, has a delicate and slightly sweet flavor with little salt and a faint acidity. Production can be *fermier*, *coopérative*, or *industriel*.

The AOC was granted in 1990.

♥ Sancerre, Pouilly Fumé

ESSENTIAL FACTS

- ⊖ 2.4 in diameter base, 2 in top 2.4 in high
- ⚖ 3.5 oz–5.3 oz
- ∴ 1 oz min. per cheese
- ⊅ 45% min.
- ✓ All year; spring to autumn (*fermier*)

Poitou-Charentes (16, 79, 86)

Whole

Thin rind of white, yellow, or blue mold

Soft, even-textured pâte becomes hard and brittle when mature; uncooked, unpressed

CHABICHOU / CHABIS

This *fermier, artisanal,* or *industriel* produced cheese has an affinage of 10 to 20 days. The cheeses shown here are all versions of Chabichou that were bought and photographed before the AOC was granted in 1990. The variety of sizes and shapes is interesting.

♥ Sancerre, Menetou Salon

ESSENTIAL FACTS

- ⊖ 2.6 in diameter base, 2 in top 2.8 in high
- ⚖ 4.2 oz
- ∴ 1.4 oz min. per cheese
- ⊅ 45%,
- ✓ All year; spring to autumn (*fermier*)

Poitou-Charentes (16)

Raw, whole

Chabis   Chabichou

Chabichou *fermier*   Chabichou

Soft white or ivory-colored
pâte; uncooked, unpressed

Thin rind of blue
or white mold;
sometimes no
mold

Affinage of two weeks

Affinage of four months

Affinage of five months

ESSENTIAL FACTS

⊖ 1.6–2 in diameter
2.1–3.9 oz high

⚖ 60–110 g

🗖 45% min.

⁛ 1.3 oz min. per cheese

✔ All year; spring to
autumn (*fermier*)

CROTTIN DE CHAVIGNOL (AOC)

This cheese is also known as Chavignol and should be hard, black, and knobby on the surface.

A fresh white Crottin weighs about 4.9 oz and does not yet look like a true Crottin de Chavignol. After two weeks, it weighs only about 3.9 oz. The rind begins to take on a bluish hue and the pâte becomes glossy. It is a little salty and the balance of sourness, sweetness, and the smell of milk enhance the taste. At this point, the cheese is ready to eat. After five weeks, the cheese is dry and has shrunk. The smell is strong and the pâte has a meaty texture, with a robust flavor. This is a ripe Crottin. After four months, it weighs only 1.4 oz. The rind is rough and hard and should be removed by grating.

Annual production amounts to some 16 million cheeses, which may be *fermier*, *artisanal*, or *industriel*. Affinage must take place within AOC specified areas. It must lasts at least ten days from the date of production, but usually two to four weeks is allowed. The temperatures must be kept low and the room well ventilated.

Hot Crottin on salad with wine vinegar makes a good appetizer.

♀ Sancerre de Chavignol

AOC REGULATIONS:
CROTTIN DE CHAVIGNOL

1. Coagulation is mainly lactic with a small amount of rennet.

2. The curd may be drained in advance.

3. The words *fabrication fermière* or *fromage fermier* are forbidden for cheese made with frozen curd.

AOC GRANTED 1976

Bourgogne
(58); Centre
(45, 18)

Whole;
frozen curd
may be used

POULIGNY-SAINT-PIERRE (AOC)

This cheese is nicknamed the Pyramid or the Eiffel Tower because of its cone shape. The cheese shown was ripened for four weeks until it was ready to be eaten. The rind is dry with a good, natural blue mold. The pâte shows an amazing whiteness and is fine-textured, moist, soft, and crumbly. It smells of goat's milk and straw. An exquisite sourness spreads in the mouth, followed by a salty taste, and then sweetness. A softer sourness dissolves at the end, although it leaves an aftertaste. After another six or seven days the rind is even more beautiful and complex: the colors are richer in tone, it becomes knobby, and the mold spreads.

Production may be *fermier* or *industriel*, and affinage takes two weeks from the date of production, usually four or five weeks. There are two labels: green for the Pouligny *fermier*; red for the *industriel* Pouligny *laitier* (dairy).

♀ Reuilly, Sancerre

ESSENTIAL FACTS

◈ 2.6 in square base
3.2–3.5 in high

⚖ 8.8 oz

⁂ 3.2 oz min. per cheese

⛁ 45% min. per cheese

✔ All year; spring to autumn (*fermier*)

AOC REGULATIONS: POULIGNY

1. Coagulation is mainly lactic, with a small amount of rennet.

2. The words *fabrication fermière* or *fromage fermier* are forbidden for cheeses made with frozen curd.

AOC GRANTED 1976

Centre (36)

Whole

Rind of natural mold

Soft pâte; uncooked, unpressed

White or ivory, fine-textured pâte; uncooked, unpressed

Dried for 24 hours

Affinage of three weeks

Rind of natural mold, sometimes covered with ashes

Affinage of six weeks

Long, truncated log

SAINTE-MAURE DE TOURAINE (AOC)

The method of production for this cheese is faithful to tradition (p. 78). The milk is heated to 164°F, then coagulated for 24 hours, cast in a long mold, and drained spontaneously. The cheese is then taken out of its mold and a long straw is inserted, the purpose of which is to hold the fragile cheese together and ventilate its interior. The cheese is then covered with salted charcoal ashes and laid on a board to complete drainage.

Production of this cheese may be *fermier, coopérative,* or *artisanal.* Affinage takes a minimum of ten days (usually, two to four weeks) after renneting, within AOC specified areas. The cheese is turned every day in a well-ventilated, cool cellar at 59°F with 90% humidity. On the tenth day, the rind is pale yellow, and has no mold. The pâte is still soft and has a sour smell. During the third week, a blue mold forms on the rind, which now appears dry. The pâte too changes from being moist to a dry, smooth, robust texture. After the fifth or sixth week, the surface of the cheese is dry and has shrunk. The mold is blue-gray and the pâte is fine-textured, firm, and smooth. This cheese is fully mature, balanced, round, with salt, sourness, and an aroma of walnut.

❢ Chinon, ♀ Vouvray

ESSENTIAL FACTS

◇ 1.2 in diameter at one end
1.6 in diameter at other
5.5 in long
⊞ 8.8 oz
♣ 3.5 oz min. per cheese
♉ 45% min., 1.6 oz min. per cheese
✔ All year; spring to autumn (*fermier*)

Centre (37, 41, 36); Poitou-Charentes (86)

Frozen curd forbidden

AOC REGULATIONS: SAINTE-MAURE DE TOURAINE

1. Coagulation is mainly lactic.

2. The fresh undrained curd (p. 78) is cast with a ladle or curd distributor.

3. Drainage must be natural and spontaneous.

AOC GRANTED 1990

Selles-sur-Cher (AOC)

A good goat's cheese is defined by its lingering scent and aftertaste. The local people eat the rind: they are the ones who cultivated its mold and they consider that it contains the true taste of the cheese. The cheese shown here was made by the Moreau family, who run l'Elevage Caprin de Bellevue.

After an affinage of four weeks, the surface of the cheese is very knobby and the rind is dry It is covered completely with a blue-gray mold, under which is a layer of powdered charcoal. The pâte is characteristic of a true goat cheese. It is slightly hard at first, then moist, heavy, and claylike as it blends and melts in the mouth. The taste is slightly sour and salty, with some sweetness. The aroma created by the goat's milk and the mold of a dark cellar remains.

Production of this cheese may be *fermier*, *coopérative*, or *industriel*. Affinage takes place within AOC stated areas over a period of at least ten days, usually three weeks.

🍷 Sancerre, Pouilly Fumé

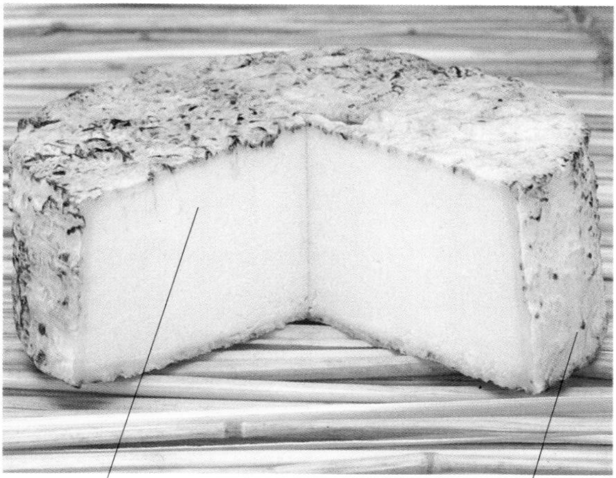

Soft pâte; uncooked, unpressed

Rind of natural mold, covered with salted charcoal ash

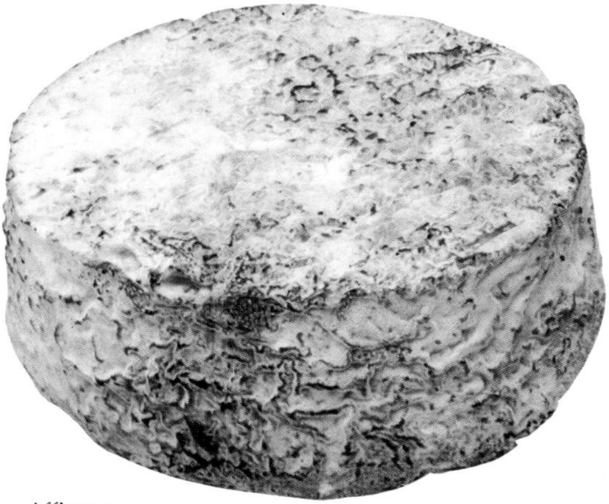

Affinage of 4 weeks

AOC Regulations: Selles-sur-Cher
1. Coagulation is mainly lactic with a small amount of rennet.
2. The curd is cast with a ladle.
AOC granted 1975

Essential facts

- 3.2 in diameter base
  2.8 in diameter top
  0.8 –1.2 in high
- 7 oz min. when fresh, otherwise 5.3 oz
- 2 oz min. per cheese
- 45% min.
- All year; spring to autumn (*fermier*)

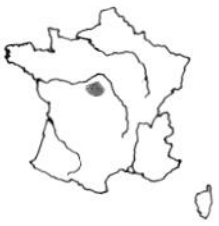

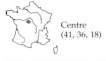

Centre
(41, 36, 18)

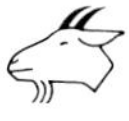

Whole

Soft, firm, moist pâte; uncooked, unpressed

VALENÇAY

The province of Berry has long been the source of famous cheeses. These include Crottin de Chavignol (p. 80); Selles-sur-Cher (p. 83); and Pouligny-Saint-Pierre (p. 81).

Valençay was originally shaped like a perfect pyramid. On his return from the disastrous campaign in Egypt, Napoléon stopped at the castle of Valençay and seeing the cheese that reminded him of the Egyptian pyramids, he drew his sword and chopped off the top.

When making a Valençay, the drained curd is cast in a mold, then it is removed, covered with salted charcoal ashes, and ripened in a well-ventilated room at 80% humidity. Production may be *fermier*, *artisanal*, or *industriel*. Affinage takes three weeks, after which a natural mold covers the surface.

ESSENTIAL FACTS

◈ 2.4 in square base, 1.4 in square top, 2.4 in high
⚖ 7.1–8.8 oz
⏲ 45% min. per cheese
♣ 3.2 oz min. per cheese
✔ Spring to autumn

❡ Quincy, Reuilly, Sancerre

Centre (36)

Raw or pasteurized

Rind of natural mold, covered with ashes

Chèvre de Coin

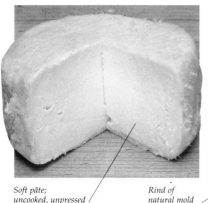

Soft pâte; uncooked, unpressed

Rind of natural mold

ESSENTIAL FACTS

⊖ 2.4 in diameter 1.2 in high
⚖ 4.6 oz
⏲ Not defined
✔ April to November

AMBERT / CROTTIN D'AMBERT

Goat cheese is rare in the Auvergne. The village of Saint-Just, in the suburbs of Ambert where this cheese is made, lies at an altitude of 2,756 ft above sea-level. This is a *fermier* cheese with an affinage of ten days.

❢ Côte du Forez, Beaujolais *primeur*

Auvergne (63)

Raw

Anneau du Vic-Bilh

This *fermier* cheese looks hand made and its flavor has the right balance of sourness and saltiness. The cheesemaker says, "We southern people like it young." Affinage takes at least ten days.

Ⓥ Pacherenc du Vic-Bilh

ESSENTIAL FACTS
- ☺ 3.9 in diameter
  1.2 in hole
  0.8 in high
- ⚖ 7.1–8.8 oz
- 🜏 45%
- ✓ Spring to autumn

Midi-Pyrénées (65)

Raw

Rind of natural mold powdered with charcoal

Soft, perfectly white pâte; uncooked, unpressed

Apérobic

The word *bic* derives from *bicot*, a small goat. This tiny *fermier* cheese is made with goat's milk in spring and summer, a mixture of goat and cow's milk in autumn, and cow's milk only in winter. It has a mild flavor, with a pleasant tang of the mold. Although Apérobic may be the smallest cheese in the world, it is ripened with care for 15 days.

Ⓥ Bourgogne Aligoté

ESSENTIAL FACTS
- ◈ 0.6 in diameter base, 0.8 in high
- ⚖ 0.1 oz
- 🜏 Not defined
- ✓ All year; spring to autumn for goat's-milk cheeses

Bourgogne (71)

Raw, whole

Rind of natural mold

Soft pâte; uncooked, unpressed

Autun

This *fermier* cheese has a fine texture. The flavor is rich, refined, and rounded, with a hint of acidity. Affinage takes at least three weeks.

Ⓥ Mercurey, Rully

ESSENTIAL FACTS
- ☺ 2 in diameter, 3.2 in high
- ⚖ 9.5–10.6 oz
- 🜏 Not defined
- ✓ Spring to autumn

Bourgogne (71)

Raw

Rind of natural mold

Soft, white pâte, even-textured and compact; uncooked, unpressed

BEAUJOLAIS PUR CHÈVRE (PETIT)

This *artisanal* cheese comes from the village of Saint-Georges-de-Reneins, in the Beaujolais region. Affinage usually takes four to five weeks until the pâte hardens. The cheese shown was ripened for six weeks by a *fromager* in the city of Lyon and is completely mature. It has a slightly sour taste.

❦ Beaujolais, young and fruity

ESSENTIAL FACTS
- ⬭ 2 in diameter 0.8 in high
- ⊕ 1.6 oz
- ▯ 45%
- ✓ April to October

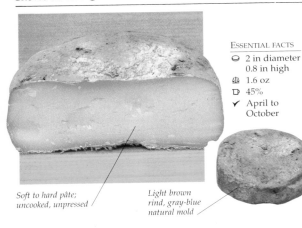

Soft to hard pâte; uncooked, unpressed

Light brown rind, gray-blue natural mold

Rhône-Alpes (69)

Not defined

BESACE DE PUR CHÈVRE

This *fermier* cheese is made by a woman on her small farm at the foot of Mont Tournier, in Savoie, at an altitude of 2,874 ft. She shapes the cheeses by hand, squeezing each one in a cloth. It is at its best after two weeks of affinage.

❦ Crépy, Seyssel

ESSENTIAL FACTS
- ⬭ 3.2 in diameter 1.6 in high
- ⊕ 6 oz; 9.2 oz fresh
- ▯ 45%
- ✓ Spring to autumn

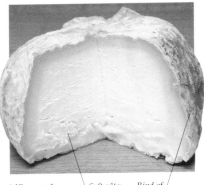

Affinage of two weeks

Soft pâte; uncooked, unpressed

Rind of natural mold

Fresh cheese

Rhône-Alpes (73)

Raw

BIGOTON

This is a light and simple *fermier* cheese produced by a farm in the Orléanais region called La Chèvrerie d'Authon. Affinage takes at least 15 days.

❦ Coteaux du Vendômois, young and fruity

ESSENTIAL FACTS
- ⬭ 2–2.4 in wide 4–5 in long 1.6 in high
- ⊕ 4.6–5.3 oz
- ▯ 45%
- ✓ Spring to autumn

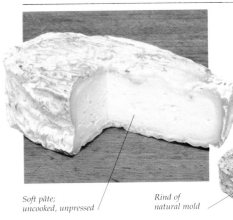

Soft pâte; uncooked, unpressed

Rind of natural mold

Centre (41)

Raw

BILOU DU JURA (LE PETIT)

This goat cheese comes from the Franche-Comté region, where goat cheese is generally quite scarce. It is made with high-quality milk, and is as good as the goat cheese of the Loire. Affinage takes at least ten days.

♀ Côtes du Jura

ESSENTIAL FACTS
- ⊖ 2.4–2.8 in diameter
  1.2 in high
- ⬤ 3.5–5.3 oz
- ◻ 45%
- ✓ Spring to autumn

Franche-Comté (39)

Raw

*Rind of
natural mold*

*Soft pâte;
uncooked, unpressed*

BONDE DE GÂTINE

This high-quality *fermier* cheese produced by the GAEC de la Fragnée comes from the marshy Gâtine area of Poitou. Affinage usually takes from four to ten weeks, but the cheese is almost ready after just six weeks. The pâte has a pronounced acidity and saltiness and melts in the mouth, leaving a light but rich aroma.

♀ Haut Poitou

ESSENTIAL FACTS
- ⊖ 2–2.4 in diameter
  2–2.4 in high
- ⬤ 4.9–5.6 oz
- ◻ 45%
- ✓ Spring to autumn

Poitou-Charentes (79)

Raw

*Rind of
natural mold*

*Soft white pâte;
uncooked, unpressed*

LE BOUCA

This *fermier* goat cheese has a strong, milky aroma and a perfect balance of acidity and saltiness. The cut pâte of the cheese shown here looks good and shows the right degree of firmness. Affinage takes at least ten days.

❢ Touraine

ESSENTIAL FACTS
- ⊖ 2.8 in diameter
  1.6 in high
- ⬤ 7.1 oz
- ◻ 40–45%
- ✓ All year, especially spring to autumn

Centre (37)

Raw

*Rind of natural mold,
covered with charcoal
powder*

*Soft pâte;
uncooked,
unpressed*

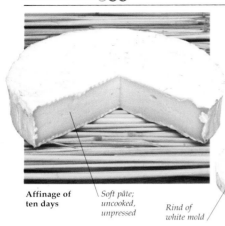

Affinage of ten days | *Soft pâte; uncooked, unpressed* | *Rind of white mold*

ESSENTIAL FACTS

⊖ 3.9 in diameter 1 in high

⚖ 2.8 oz

🍶 50%

✔ All year

BOUGON

This cheese is made by a *coopérative* from raw milk. It looks like a Camembert and is packaged in a box made of thin wood. The label says to store at below 46°F and leave at room temperature for one hour before serving. The pâte is firm and both rind and pâte taste the same. Affinage takes two to three weeks.

🍷 Haut Poitou

 Poitou-Charentes (79)

 Raw; pasteurized for export

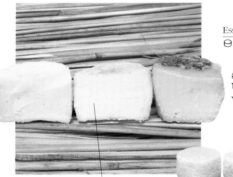

Affinage of two weeks | *Soft to hard pâte; uncooked, unpressed* | *Rind of natural mold*

ESSENTIAL FACTS

⊖ 1.2 in diameter, 1.2 in high

⚖ 0.7–1.4 oz

🍶 45%

✔ All year, depending on affinage

BOUTON DE CULOTTE

These little cheeses are eaten by the locals as they pick grapes in autumn. They may be made using goat or cow's milk, or a mixture of both. Production is either *fermier* or *artisanal*. A blue mold appears on the rind after two weeks of affinage. After a month, the pâte turns yellow and tingles on the tongue.

🍷 Bourgogne Aligoté

 Bourgogne (71)

Raw

Affinage of one month | *Soft pâte; uncooked, unpressed* | *Pear-shaped, pierced by a straw*

Rind of natural mold

ESSENTIAL FACTS

◊ 1.3 in diameter base; 1 0.5 in diameter top, 1.6 in high

⚖ 0,5 oz

🍶 45%

✔ Spring to autumn

BOUTON D'OC

These unusual, pear-shaped, *fermier* cheeses are sold by the dozen and make a good accompaniment to an apéritif. The pâte has a very fine texture and a pleasant flavor. Because of their small size, they ripen quickly. Affinage takes at least 10 days.

🍷 Gaillac *perlé* or *mousseux*

 Midi-Pyrénées (81)

 Raw

BRESSAN

Although this *fermier* cheese is made with goat's milk, cow's milk may be added depending on the season and maker. After a week of affinage, the cheese shown here has a good, balanced flavor, both sweet and sour, that strengthens with age. In the province of Bresse it is eaten for breakfast with jam. Affinage takes at least one week.

♀ Bugey, Seyssel, Roussette de Savoie

ESSENTIAL FACTS
⊖ 2 in diameter base, 1.6 in diameter top, 1.6 in high
🝆 3.5 oz
🗗 45%
✓ Spring to autumn

Affinage of one week   *Soft to hard pâte; uncooked, unpressed*

Rhône-Alpes (01); Bourgogne (71)   Raw

Rind of natural mold

BRIQUE ARDÉCHOISE

This cheese is the product of a combination of the talent of the cheesemaker, the high quality of milk used in production, and the careful affinage. The result is an elegant cheese. This is a *fermier* cheese with an affinage of three to four weeks. It is slightly pungent and goes well with a robust wine.

♀ Hermitage, St. Joseph, St. Péray

ESSENTIAL FACTS
⊘ 1.6–2 in wide 4.3 in long 1.2 in high
🝆 5.3 oz
🗗 Not defined
✓ Spring to autumn

Affinage of four weeks   *Soft pâte; uncooked, unpressed*

Rhône-Alpes (07)   Raw

Rind of natural mold

BRIQUE DU FOREZ

The cheese shown here was made from a mixture of goat and cow's milk. Since there is neither the smell nor flavor of goat's milk, it probably contains a higher percentage of cow's milk. Production may be *fermier* or *artisanal*, with an affinage of two to three weeks.

❣ Beaujolais, Côtes Roannaises

ESSENTIAL FACTS
⊘ 2–2.4 in wide 5.1 in long 1.4 in high
🝆 12.6–14 oz
🗗 40–45%
✓ All year; spring to autumn for pure goat--milk cheeses

Affinage of three weeks   *Soft pâte; uncooked, unpressed*

Auvergne (63); Rhône-Alpes (42)   Raw, whole

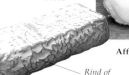

Rind of natural white mold

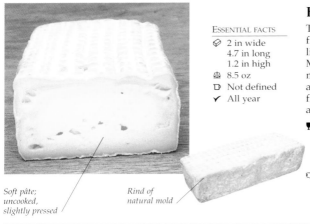

BRIQUETTE DE COUBON

ESSENTIAL FACTS

⬦ 2 in wide
4.7 in long
1.2 in high
⚖ 8.5 oz
⧖ Not defined
✔ All year

This *fermier* cheese, which comes from Velay in the Auvergne, looks like a small brick, or *briquette*. Many *briquettes* made from various milks are currently being produced all over France; this one is made from cow's milk. Affinage takes at least eight days.

❦ St. Pourçain

Soft pâte; uncooked, slightly pressed

Rind of natural mold

Auvergne
(43)

Raw

BÛCHETTE D'ANJOU

ESSENTIAL FACTS

⬦ 1.6 in diameter
4.7 in long
⚖ 3–3.5 oz
⧖ 45%
✔ Spring to autumn

This *artisanal* cheese from Anjou was modeled on Sainte-Maure (p. 82). It is a young, almost fresh cheese, with a faint smell of milk and slightly acidic taste. The rind, which is covered in charcoal powder, may be eaten but the cheese tastes better without it. Affinage takes two weeks.

❦ Saumur, Anjou Villages

Rind of natural mold

Soft pâte, uncooked and unpressed

Pays de la
Loire (49)

Raw

BÛCHETTE DE BANON

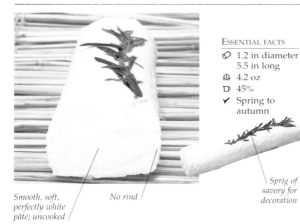

ESSENTIAL FACTS

⬦ 1.2 in diameter
5.5 in long
⚖ 4.2 oz
⧖ 45%
✔ Spring to autumn

The light sourness of this fresh *fermier* cheese blends with the aroma of the savory, giving it the typical taste and smell of Provence. This is a cheese to eat under a shady tree on a warm summer's day, preferably at the beginning rather than the end of a meal. Bûchette de Banon can be eaten fresh or allowed to ripen for a maximum of a week.

❦ Coteaux d'Aix *rosé*

Smooth, soft, perfectly white pâte; uncooked

No rind

Sprig of savory for decoration

Provence-
Alpes-Côte-
d'Azur (04)

Raw

CAPRI LEZÉEN

Each of these *fermier* cheeses produced by the GAEC du Capri Lezéen is wrapped in a chestnut leaf and packaged in a thin wooden box. The sticky, pale gold rind has a very light blue mold. The distinctive flavor comes from the creamy, slightly runny pâte. Affinage takes eight to 15 days at 100% humidity, which is high for a goat cheese.

♀ Haut Poitou

ESSENTIAL FACTS
- ⊖ 3.2 in diameter 0.6 in high
- ⚖ 4.2 oz
- ⅅ 50%
- ✓ All year

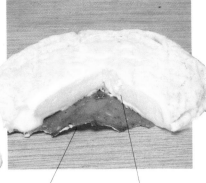

Poitou-Charentes (79)

Raw

Natural rind

Chestnut-leaf wrapper

Very soft pâte; uncooked, unpressed

CAPRICORNE DE JARJAT

This *fermier* cheese, made by R. Gribaldi, belongs to the same family as Picodon (p. 170). It has a good mold and tingles in the mouth, which makes it a good accompaniment to a glass of wine. Affinage generally takes up to three or four months, at 90% humidity, but it can be eaten fresh.

♀ St. Péray, Crozes Hermitage

ESSENTIAL FACTS
- ⊖ 4 in diameter 1.4 in high
- ⚖ 8.8 oz
- ⅅ 45%
- ✓ All year

Rhône-Alpes (07)

Raw

Affinage of one month

Rind of natural white and blue mold

Soft pâte; uncooked, unpressed

LE CATHELAIN

The word *cathelain* means goat in the old dialect of Savoie. The cheese shown is very young and has a smooth, slightly sour pâte that melts in the mouth. Affinage of this *fermier* cheese takes 15 days.

♀ Crépy

ESSENTIAL FACTS
- ⊖ 2.8 in diameter 1.6 in high
- ⚖ 6 oz
- ⅅ 45%
- ✓ Spring to December

Rhône-Alpes (73)

Raw

Natural rind

Soft pâte; uncooked, unpressed

ESSENTIAL FACTS

- ⊖ 2–2.4 in diameter
  2.8–3.2 in high
- ⚖ 7.1 oz
- 🗋 45%
- ✔ Spring to autumn

*Soft, refined pâte;
uncooked, unpressed*

*Rind of blue or white
natural mold*

CHAROLAIS / CHAROLLES

This *fermier* or *artisanal* cheese, comes from the granite plains of the Charolais region of Bourgogne. It enhances all the best flavors of the milk, and the saltiness, acidity, and sweetness of its aroma open up in the mouth. The colors and texture of the mold are pleasing, with a lingering aftertaste. Affinage lasts two to six weeks.

♀ Mercurey, Rully, Montagny

Bourgogne
(71)

Raw

ESSENTIAL FACTS

- ◈ 2.8–3.2 in square
  base, 1.6 in square
  top, 2.8 in high
- ⚖ 8.8 oz
- 🗋 45%
- ✔ Spring to autumn

*Soft pâte;
uncooked, unpressed*

*Rind of
natural mold*

CHEF-BOUTONNE

This cheese should suit modern tastes for young rather than ripe cheeses. Young cheeses are light and simple, without strong flavors. In addition to this flat-topped pyramid, there are round and square versions of the Chef-Boutonne. This is a *fermier* or *coopérative* cheese with an affinage of two weeks.

♀ Haut Poitou

Poitou-
Charentes (79)

Raw

ESSENTIAL FACTS

- ⊖ 2.4 in diameter
  1.2–1.6 in high
- ⚖ 3.5 oz
- 🗋 45%
- ✔ Spring to the
  end of autumn

*Soft pâte;
uncooked, unpressed*

*Rind of
natural mold*

CHÈVRE FERMIER

This *fermier* goat cheese is produced by the Ferme Marchal near the town of Le Thillot in Lorraine. The cheese shown here is still slightly moist, with blue and brown mold, and the beginnings of a dry rind. It has a good balanced flavor of salt and acidity. Affinage takes two to four weeks.

♀ Vin gris des Côtes de Toul (*rosé*)

Lorraine
(88)

Raw

CHÈVRE FERMIER ALPILLES

This young, *fermier* cheese is produced by a farm at the foot of the Alpilles, a range of small mountains in Provence. It has a robust flavor, which improves with age. Affinage usually takes a minimum of ten days.

♀ Bellet, Côtes de Provence

ESSENTIAL FACTS

⊖ 2.4 in diameter
   0.8 in high
⚖ 2.1 oz
🌡 45%
✔ All summer

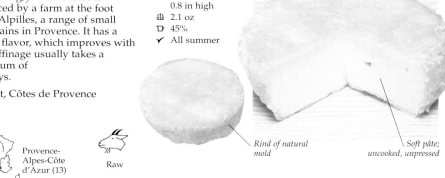

Provence-Alpes-Côte d'Azur (13)

Raw

Rind of natural mold

Soft pâte; uncooked, unpressed

CHÈVRE FERMIER DU CHÂTEAU-VERT

This *fermier* cheese comes from the slopes of Mont Ventoux in Provence. Its rind is covered in charcoal powder with a coating of white-gray mold. The pâte is smooth, slightly sour, and sweet. Affinage takes at least two weeks.

♀ Côtes du Ventoux *blanc* and *rosé*

ESSENTIAL FACTS

⊖ 2.4 in diameter
   0.8 in high
⚖ 2.5 oz
🌡 45%
✔ Spring to autumn

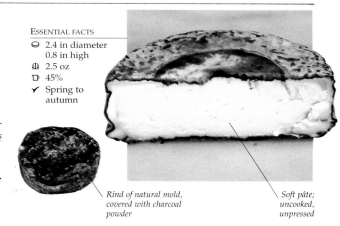

Provence-Alpes-Côte d'Azur (84)

Raw

Rind of natural mold, covered with charcoal powder

Soft pâte; uncooked, unpressed

CIVRAY

This soft goat cheese from the plains around the town of Civray in the department of Vienne, comes from the same family as Chabichou (p. 79). The natural mold gives it a pleasant flavor and it has a fine pâte, with pronounced acidity and little sugar. This is a *fermier* cheese with an affinage of a minimum of two weeks.

♀ Haut Poitou

ESSENTIAL FACTS

⊖ 2–2.4 in diameter
   base, 2 in top
   2 in high
⚖ 3.9–5.3 oz
🌡 45%
✔ Spring to autumn

Poitou-Charentes (86)

Raw

Rind of natural mold

Soft pâte; uncooked, unpressed

ESSENTIAL FACTS

⊖ 2 in diameter
2.8–3.2 in high
⚖ 5.3 oz
◻ 45%
✔ Spring to autumn

CLACBITOU

Like the Charolais (p. 92), which it resembles, this recently created *fermier* cheese comes from the Charolais region of Bourgogne. It tastes best when it is still quite young. Affinage takes two to three weeks.

♀ Bourgogne Aligoté de Bouzeron

Bourgogne (71)

Raw

Soft pâte; uncooked, unpressed

Rind of natural mold

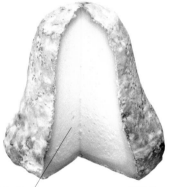

ESSENTIAL FACTS

◈ 3.5 in diameter base, 3.5 in high
⚖ 8.8 oz
◻ 45%
✔ Spring to autumn

CLOCHETTE

This *fermier* cheese is made by the GAEC Jousseaume in the village of Saint-Estèphe. Its pleasant aroma is a combination of both the mold and the cellar in which the cheese was ripened. Affinage takes at least two weeks.

♀ Haut Poitou

Poitou-Charentes (16)

Raw

Soft pâte; uncooked, unpressed

Rind of natural mold

CŒUR DE BERRY

ESSENTIAL FACTS

⊖ 3.5 in wide
3.9 in long
1.2 in high
⚖ 5.3 oz
◻ 45%
✔ Spring to autumn

This *artisanal* cheese belongs to the same family as Selles-sur-Cher (p. 83) but it is heart-shaped. Affinage takes at least two weeks and the rind is covered with charcoal powder.

♀ Quincy, Reuilly

Centre (36)

Raw

Soft pâte; uncooked, unpressed

Rind of natural mold

LE CORNILLY

These three *artisanal* cheeses from the province of Berry show different stages in the affinage, which usually takes from three to four weeks – although sometimes there is none at all. They have very little smell and a nutty flavor.

Ÿ Quincy, Reuilly

ESSENTIAL FACTS
⊖ 2–3.2 in diameter base, 2 in diameter top 2.8 in high
⚖ 5.3–8.8 oz
⏪ 45%
✓ All year

Rather soft to hard pâte; uncooked, unpressed

Centre (36)

Raw

Rind of natural mold

Fresh cheese | Ripe cheese | Dry cheese

COUHÉ-VÉRAC

This *fermier* or *artisanal* cheese blends the flavors of the leaf in which it is wrapped, with those of its mold. Affinage takes three to four weeks.

Ÿ Haut Poitou

ESSENTIAL FACTS
⊗ 3.5 in square, 1.2 in high
⚖ 1.8 oz
⏪ 45%
✓ Spring to autumn

Poitou-Charentes (86)

Raw

Plane or chestnut leaf

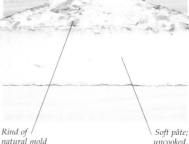

Rind of natural mold

Soft pâte; uncooked, unpressed

CROTTIN DE PAYS

This sweet, soft *fermier* cheese from the Albigeois region of Languedoc is made with mountain goat's milk. It is completely organic, and no chemical fertilizers are used on the pastures. Affinage takes around two weeks.

Ÿ Gaillac

ESSENTIAL FACTS
⊖ 2 in diameter 1.2 in high
⚖ 1.8 oz
⏪ 45%
✓ All year except in January, best from spring to autumn

Midi-Pyrénées (81)

Raw

Rind of natural mold

Soft pâte; uncooked, unpressed

⬧ 2.8 in diameter base, 2 in high

⚖ 7 oz

⊓ 45%

✓ All year

Soft pâte; uncooked, unpressed

Rind of natural mold

FIGUE

During its affinage, which lasts for at least two weeks, this *artisanal* cheese is squeezed, and molded in a cloth. It is about the size of an adult fist and crumbles easily. Occasionally it is covered with charcoal powder. It is made in a similar way to Besace de Pur Chèvre (p. 86).

♀ Bergerac *sec*

Aquitaine (24)

Raw

Soft pâte; uncooked, unpressed

Rind of natural blue and brown mold

Affinage of one month

FOURME DE CHÈVRE ARDÈCHE

This slightly sour *fermier* cheese needs an affinage of six weeks.

♀ St. Péray

ESSENTIAL FACTS

⊖ 3.5 in diameter, 5.9 in high

⚖ 2.2 lbs

⊓ 45%

✓ Spring to autumn

Rhône-Alpes (71)

Raw

ESSENTIAL FACTS

⊖ 3.9 in diameter 1.2 in high

⚖ 8 oz

⊓ 40%

✓ Spring to autumn

FROMAGE DE CHÈVRE ARIÈGE

Acidity and sweetness are pronounced in this *fermier* cheese, which is made at a farm on a mountainside close to the town of Foix in the Central Pyrénées. Affinage takes at least ten days.

♀ Limoux, Vouvray *sec*

Soft pâte; uncooked, unpressed

Rind of white mold

Midi-Pyrénées (09)

Raw

FROMAGE DE CHÈVRE DE COIN

The people of the village of Glénat used to make *fermier* goat cheeses like the one shown here mainly for their own consumption. Gradually, the cheeses started to be sold in the market, named after their village, and commercialized, although they retain their homemade appearance. Affinage takes at least ten days.

♀ St. Pourçain

Auvergne (15)

Raw

ESSENTIAL FACTS
- ⊖ 2.4 in diameter
  0.8 in high
- ⚖ 1.8 oz
- ⅁ 45%
- ✔ Spring to autumn

Rind of / natural mold

Soft pâte; uncooked, unpressed

FROMAGE DE CHÈVRE FERMIER (1)

The *fermier* cheese shown here was made on a farm at Cierp-Gaud in the Pyrénées, at the end of a narrow mountain trail called Cap del Mail, meaning top of the rock. It is small but well made, and smells slightly of goat. It can be eaten after the fourth day of affinage.

♀ Limoux, Vouvray *sec*

Midi-Pyrénées (31)

Raw

ESSENTIAL FACTS
- ⊖ 2 in diameter
  1.2 in high
- ⚖ 3.5 oz; 7 oz (fresh)
- ⅁ 45%
- ✔ February to November

Affinage of one month

Rind of / natural mold

Soft pâte; uncooked, unpressed

FROMAGE DE CHÈVRE FERMIER (2)

This is a barely ripened, pleasantly sour *fermier* cheese that reflects the high quality of the milk from which it is made. In the town of Marciac in Gascogne, where it is produced, it is often eaten for breakfast, seasoned with ground pepper. Although it can be eaten fresh, affinage may take up to two weeks.

♀ Gaillac

Midi-Pyrénées (32)

Raw

ESSENTIAL FACTS
- ⊖ 2.4 in diameter
  1.2 in high
- ⚖ 4.2 oz
- ⅁ 45%
- ✔ Spring to autumn

Affinage of ten days

Rind of / natural mold

Soft pâte; uncooked, unpressed

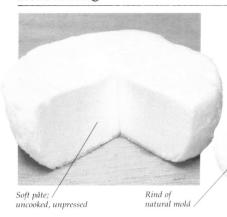

Soft pâte;
uncooked, unpressed

Rind of
natural mold

FROMAGE DE CHÈVRE LARZAC

This is a very fresh *fermier* cheese, even after a week of affinage. It has a sweet smell of good-quality milk and comes from the area known as the Causse du Larzac in the region of Roquefort, which is traditionally an area of sheep's cheeses. Affinage takes at least one week.

❢ Coteaux du Languedoc

ESSENTIAL FACTS
- ◯ 2.4 in diameter 0.8 in high
- ⚖ 2.1 oz
- ▯ 45%
- ✓ Spring to autumn

Midi-Pyrénées (12)

Raw

Soft pâte;
uncooked, unpressed

FROMAGE FERMIER

This slightly spicy *fermier* cheese is produced in the village of Granges-sur-Vologne in the mountainous region of the Vosges in Lorraine. The picture shows a cheese that has been ripened for four weeks. It is dry, hard, and covered with white, brown, and pale blue mold. Affinage takes at least ten days.

❢ Vin gris des Côtes de Toul (*rosé*)

ESSENTIAL FACTS
- ◯ 2–2.4 in diameter 1–2 in high
- ⚖ 2.5 oz
- ▯ Not defined
- ✓ Spring to end of autumn

Lorraine (88)

Raw

Soft pâte;
uncooked, unpressed

Rind of
natural mold

FROMAGE DU JAS

This *fermier* cheese is made on a farm called the Domaine Le Jas at La Roque-sur-Pernes in the Vaucluse. In old Provençal dialect a *jas* is a sheepfold. The cheese has a mildly sweet and sour flavor. Affinage takes one to three weeks.

❢ Côtes de Provence

ESSENTIAL FACTS
- ◯ 2.4 in diameter 0.8 in high
- ⚖ 2 oz
- ▯ 45%
- ✓ All year, especially spring to autumn

Provence-Alpes-Côte-d'Azur (84)

Raw

FROMAGE AU LAIT DE CHÈVRE / CHÈVRE DE PAYS

The village of Saint-Jean-de-Chapteuil, where the main industries are lace and shoemaking, has a population of just 1,700. A local farmer, J-A. Garnier, made the drum-shaped cheese shown here at the Domaine de Villeneuve. Affinage takes at least 15 days.

♥ St. Pourçain

ESSENTIAL FACTS

⊖ 2 in diameter
1.8 in high

⚖ 3.5 oz

◌ Not defined

✓ April to October

Auvergne
(43)

Raw

*Rind of
natural mold*

*Soft pâte;
uncooked, unpressed*

GALET DE BIGORRE

This *fermier* cheese is a subtle combination of flavors salt, then sourness, and finally sweetness open in the mouth. A local cheesemaker said that this cheese is best on the young side, and suggested trying it with ripe apricots. Affinage takes two weeks.

♥ Jurançon *moelleux*

ESSENTIAL FACTS

⊖ 3.5 in diameter
base, 3.2 in
diameter top
1.6 in high

⚖ 7.8 oz

◌ 45%

✓ Spring to
autumn

Midi-Pyrénées
(65)

Raw

*Rind of
natural mold*

*Soft pâte;
uncooked, unpressed*

GALET SOLOGNOT

This *fermier* cheese has a strong smell and a balanced sweet and sour flavor. One's impression of a good cheese is often influenced by the smell and flavor of its mold. An unattractive mold does little to whet the appetite and gives the cheese an unpleasant aftertaste, even if the rind is removed. Affinage takes two weeks.

♥ Reuilly

ESSENTIAL FACTS

⊖ 2.8 in diameter
base, 2.4 in
diameter top
1.2 in high

⚖ 4.2 oz

◌ 45%

✓ Spring to
autumn

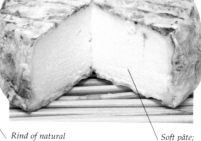

Centre
(45)

Raw

*Rind of natural
mold covered with
charcoal powder*

*Soft pâte;
uncooked,
unpressed*

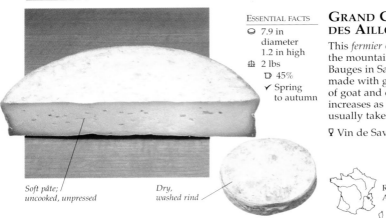

- ⊝ 7.9 in diameter
  1.2 in high
- ⚖ 2 lbs
- ⫯ 45%
- ✔ Spring to autumn

GRAND COLOMBIER DES AILLONS

This *fermier* cheese is produced in the mountains of the Massif des Bauges in Savoie. It is usually made with goat's milk or a mixture of goat and cow's milk. The flavor increases as it matures. Affinage usually takes at least four weeks.

♀ Vin de Savoie

Soft pâte;
uncooked, unpressed

Dry,
washed rind

Rhône-Alpes (73)

Raw

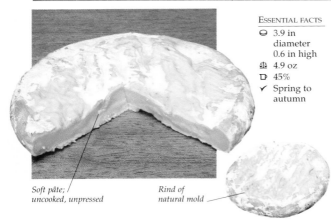

- ⊝ 3.9 in diameter
  0.6 in high
- ⚖ 4.9 oz
- ⫯ 45%
- ✔ Spring to autumn

MONT D'OR DU LYONNAIS

The characteristics of this small *fermier* or *artisanal* goat cheese from Lyon, are the blue mold and reddish rind that appear after a long and very humid affinage of two to four weeks. The cheese has a strong taste of salt, and no acidity.

♀ Beaujolais, Macon

Soft pâte;
uncooked, unpressed

Rind of
natural mold

Rhône-Alpes (69)

Raw

- ⊝ 7.9 in diameter
  0.6 in high
- ⚖ 3.5–4.9 oz
- ⫯ 45%
- ✔ All year

GALETTE DES MONTS DU LYONNAIS

This *artisanal* cheese has a soft, gentle flavor, more like milk than cheese. The consistency is so runny it is eaten with a spoon and is difficult to transport without its thin wooden container. It is made by only one cheesemaker in the Monts du Lyonnais. Affinage takes two to three weeks.

♀ Coteaux du Lyonnais

Runny pâte;
uncooked, unpressed

Rind of
natural mold

Rhône-Alpes (69)

Raw

MÂCONNAIS

This *fermier* or *artisanal* cheese, also called Chevreton de Mâcon, is made solely from goat or cow's milk, or a mixture of the two depending on the season and manufacturer. The cheese shown is hard enough to make *fromage fort* (p. 140). A faint smell of spring herbs comes from the dense pâte. Affinage takes at least two weeks.

♀ Bourgogne Aligoté

ESSENTIAL FACTS
⊖ 2 in diameter
   1.6 in high
⚖ 1.8–2.1 oz
🗇 45%
✔ All year

 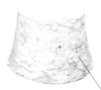

Bourgogne
(71)

Raw

Rind of natural
mold

Soft to hard pâte;
uncooked, unpressed

PAVÉ BLÉSOIS

Both square and rectangular versions of this *artisanal* cheese are produced in the Blésois region near the town of Blois on the River Loire. The rind has a dry surface covered with a blue mold. When cut, the pâte is clean, fine-textured, and tingles slightly on the tongue. Affinage takes two to four weeks.

♀ Sancerre, Pouilly Fumé

ESSENTIAL FACTS
◈ 3.2 in square, 1.2–1.6 in
   high (square);
◈ 4.3 in long
   2.4–2.8 in wide
   1.4 in high (rectangle)
⚖ 8.8 oz (square);
   10.6 oz (rectangle)
🗇 45%
✔ Spring to autumn

Rind of
natural mold

Centre
(41)

Raw

Rind of natural mold
on charcoal powder

Soft pâte;
uncooked, unpressed

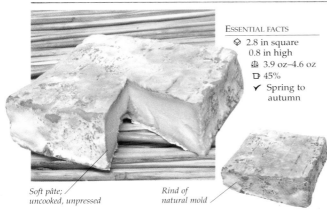

Soft pâte;
uncooked, unpressed

Rind of
natural mold

ESSENTIAL FACTS

◈ 2.8 in square
0.8 in high
⚖ 3.9 oz–4.6 oz
ᗡ 45%
✔ Spring to
autumn

LE PAVÉ

Although some people may find
this *fermier* cheese rather dry and
overripe, the pâte is firm to the bite
and slightly sticky, and the taste
has a perfect balance of acidity,
sweetness, and saltiness. The mold
is a beautiful pale blue. Affinage
takes at least four weeks.

♟ St. Péray

Rhône-Alpes
(07)

Raw

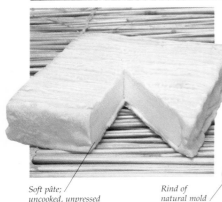

Soft pâte;
uncooked, unpressed

Rind of
natural mold

ESSENTIAL FACTS

◈ 3.2 in square
0.8 oz high
⚖ 7 oz
ᗡ 45%
✔ All year except
January; best
from spring to
autumn

PAVÉ DE LA GINESTARIÉ

This is an organic mountain goat
cheese from the Albigeois region of
Languedoc. It has an affinage of at
least two weeks, but the *fermier*
method of production is a secret.
There are traces of straw on the
rind as well as in the taste.The
straw absorbs water, and its
bacteria play a role in the ripening.

♟ Coteaux du Languedoc,
Collioure

Midi-Pyrénées
(81)

Raw

Soft pâte;
uncooked, unpressed

Rind of
natural mold

ESSENTIAL FACTS

⊖ 3 in diameter base
2.4 in diameter top
2.8 in high
⚖ 8.8 oz
ᗡ 45%
✔ Spring to autumn

POURLY

This *artisanal* cheese is produced
in the limestone plateaus of the
Auxerrois regions of Bourgogne.
It is ideal for those who like a light
goat cheese. Affinage usually takes
two to four weeks, although the
cheese may be eaten almost fresh,
after the fifth day.

♟ Sauvignon de St. Bris

Bourgogne
(89)

Raw

QUATRE-VENTS

This *fermier* cheese is made without chemical rennet since this would impair the taste. The name, which means four winds, was chosen because of the location of the farm where it is made which is on top of a hill exposed to wind from all directions. Affinage takes 12 to 15 days.

♀ St. Péray

ESSENTIAL FACTS
- ◎ 2–2.4 in diameter 1 in high
- ⚖ 2.1 oz
- ◘ 45%
- ✔ Spring to autumn

Rhône-Alpes (38)

Raw

Rind of natural mold

Soft pâte; uncooked, unpressed

PETIT QUERCY

This light *fermier* goat cheese takes its name from the province of Quercy where it is produced. The rind is attractively decorated with wild mulberry leaves. Affinage takes at least two weeks.

♀ Côtes du Roussillon

ESSENTIAL FACTS
- ◎ 3 in diameter 0.8 in high
- ⚖ 3.5 oz
- ◘ Not defined
- ✔ Spring to autumn

Mulberry leaf

Quercy

Raw

Rind of natural mold

Unripe heart

Soft pâte; uncooked, unpressed

ROGERET DE LAMASTRE

A red mold appears during the ripening of this *fermier* or *artisanal* cheese, which accounts for its other name: Fromage de Lamastre Rouge (red). The pâte is creamy and delicate. The cheese is produced in the town of Lamastre at the foot of the Monts du Vivarais. Affinage takes two to four weeks.

♀ St. Péray

ESSENTIAL FACTS
- ◎ 2.8 in diameter 0.8 in high
- ⚖ 3.5 oz
- ◘ Not defined
- ✔ All year

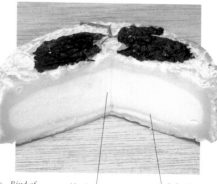

Rhône-Alpes (07)

Raw

Rind of natural mold

Soft pâte; uncooked, unpressed

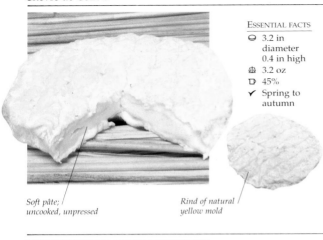

ESSENTIAL FACTS
- ⊖ 3.2 in diameter 0.4 in high
- ⚖ 3.2 oz
- ⌻ 45%
- ✔ Spring to autumn

SAINT-FÉLICIEN DE LAMASTRE

The crust, pâte, and flavor of this *fermier* cheese are soft due to the method of production, using soft curd, or *caillé doux*. Affinage takes at least two weeks.

♈ St. Péray, St. Joseph

Rhône-Alpes (07)

Raw

Soft pâte; uncooked, unpressed

Rind of natural yellow mold

ESSENTIAL FACTS
- ⊖ 4.3 in diameter 0.8 in high
- ⚖ 7.1 oz
- ⌻ 45%
- ✔ Spring to autumn

SAINT-PANCRACE

The goats on the farm where this *fermier* cheese is made graze on the slopes of Saint-Pancrace. Spots of blue mold appear on the rind as it starts to dry. The pâte is firm, smooth, and melts in the mouth, revealing a light sweetness and a mild flavor. Affinage takes two to three weeks.

♈ Condrieu, Château Grillet

Rhône-Alpes (69)

Raw

Soft pâte; uncooked, unpressed

Rind of spots of blue, natural mold

ESSENTIAL FACTS
- ⊖ 2.4 in diameter 1.2 in high
- ⚖ 5.3 oz
- ⌻ 45%
- ✔ Spring to autumn

SANTRANGES

Halfway down the River Loire in the province of Berry lies the region of Sancerrois, with three *fermier* cheeses bearing village names: Chavignol (p. 80), Crézancy, and Santranges. Chavignol is the most famous, but Santranges is also good. It is produced in small numbers and is a robust cheese to be eaten with wine. Affinage takes four weeks.

♈ Sancerre, Pouilly Fumé

Centre (18)

Raw

Soft pâte; uncooked, unpressed

Rind of natural mold

SÉCHON DE CHÈVRE DRÔMOIS

This *fermier* cheese is called a *séchon*, which means a small, dry cheese. It is named after the River Drôme in the immense Dauphiné region of southeast France where it is produced. The flavor is rather salty as well as sweet. Affinage takes at least three weeks.

♀ St. Péray

ESSENTIAL FACTS

- 2 in diameter 0.8 in high
- 1.8 oz
- 45%
- All year

Rhône-Alpes (26)

Raw

Rind of natural mold

Soft to hard pâte; uncooked, unpressed

TARENTAIS

This *fermier* cheese comes from the Tarentaise region of Savoie. After four weeks of ripening, a slight blue mold covers the rind. After another week red and blue mold develops. Affinage takes from 15 days to three months; the cheese may also be eaten fresh.

♀ Crépy

ESSENTIAL FACTS

- 2.4 in diameter 2.8 in high
- 8.8 oz
- 45%
- Spring to autumn

Rhône-Alpes (73)

Raw

Rind of natural mold

Soft pâte; uncooked, unpressed

LA TAUPINIÈRE

This new *fermier* cheese is similar in shape to Gaperon (p. 150) and is made with highly concentrated milk. It is produced with great care and attention by M. Jousseaume at his farm at St. Estèphe in the province of Angoumois. During the two-week period of affinage, the cheese absorbs natural mold in the cellar, which gives it a good flavor.

♀ Haut Poitou

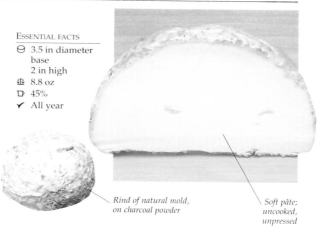

ESSENTIAL FACTS

- 3.5 in diameter base 2 in high
- 8.8 oz
- 45%
- All year

Poitou-Charentes (16)

Raw

Rind of natural mold, on charcoal powder

Soft pâte; uncooked, unpressed

Rind of
natural mold

TOUCY

ESSENTIAL FACTS

⊖ 2.4 in diameter base; 2 in diameter top, 3.2 in high
⚖ 7 oz
🌡 45%
✔ Spring to autumn

This goat cheese is made in the Auxerrois region in northern Bourgogne. It is light and easy to eat. Both *fermier* and *artisanal* versions are produced, with an affinage of at least ten days.

♈ Sauvignon de St. Bris

Bourgogne (89)

Raw

Soft pâte;
uncooked,
unpressed

Rind of natural
mold, covered with
charcoal powder

VENDÔMOIS

ESSENTIAL FACTS

⊖ 2.8 in diameter 1.2 in high
⚖ 3.5 oz
🌡 45%
✔ Spring to autumn

This *fermier* goat cheese is produced on farms in the Vendômois region north of the town of Vendôme. Although the rind of the cheese shown here would suggest that it is fully ripe, the cut pâte is somewhat young. It is fine and slightly sour. Affinage takes a minimum of ten days.

♈ Coteaux du Vendômois

Centre (41)

Raw

CROTTIN DE BERRY À L'HUILE D'OLIVE

Small goat cheeses with a mild soft pâte are soaked in olive oil flavored with pepper, thyme, rosemary, laurel, juniper berries, and garlic to make this Provençal specialty. They are usually served with bread or salad and tomatoes.

♈ Tavel *rosé*, Sancerre *rosé*

Cheese soaked
in oil and
Provençal herbs
absorbs their
flavors

Alpes-Côte-
d'Azur

Not
defined

CHÈVRE À L'HUILE D'OLIVE ET À LA SARRIETTE

Small, young Provençal goat cheeses are soaked in olive oil with berries and savory leaves to make this local specialty. Choose a cheese with no mold, which would discolor the mixture. The savory must be quite dry.

♀ Bandol *rosé*

Olive oil flavored with dried savory and berries

 Provence-Alpes-Côte-d'Azur (04)

 Not defined

Seasonal goat-milk cheeses

Jean-Pierre Moreau is the owner of the Elevage Caprin de Bellevue, where he, his wife, and two employees raise 200 goats and eight billygoats. All the goats belong to the pedigree white Saanen (top right) and brown Alpine breeds, whose quality is reflected in his cheeses. M. Moreau himself takes the cheeses to Paris twice a week.

The flavor of a goat cheese varies according to a number of factors: the breed of goat, what the animals are fed on, the way they are raised, the protein and fat content of the milk, the shape of the cheese, and the methods of coagulation and drainage. The goats first give birth at a year old, and subsequently once a year, between January and mid-March. Two or three kids are born to each goat; surplus kids are sold off immediately because their value diminishes as they grow. At the age of two, goats begin to give more milk and continue to produce it for about five years. Around 200 goats give some 3.2 quarts of milk, which is used to make 12 different cheeses.

Fresh spring milk from goats grazing outdoors on lush grass is used to make cheeses from April to May, followed by summer and autumn cheeses. Modern goat cheese is made using milk from animals kept in sheds and fed on hay. Thanks to artificial insemination and frozen curd, their cheeses can be made and sold even in winter, but they lack the flavor of the seasonal cheeses.

CHEVRETTE DES BAUGES

In the mountain region of Savoie, a cheese made from a blend of goat and cow's milk is called a *chevrette*, while a pure goat cheese is a *chevrotin*. Today, this *fermier* cheese is made only by older producers on two or three farms, and the process is in danger of dying out. The top picture shows a cheese made from three-quarters goat's milk and one-quarter cow's milk and was photographed at a cheese shop in Thonon, near Lake Geneva.

The cheese in the lower picture was made with equal proportions of the same milks; it was found in a shop in Chambéry. The owners of both cheese shops are well known for their Savoie cheeses and they also ripen them according to their own methods. Both claim that the mold that forms on a *chevrette* depends on the type of food the animals eat, their exact location on the mountainsides, and even on whether they are milked in the morning or evening.This explains why each of these cheeses has such an individual taste. Affinage takes one to three months.

♈ Seyssel

Rind of natural mold

Semi-hard pâte; uncooked, pressed

Cheese made with three-quarters goat's milk, and one-quarter cow's milk

ESSENTIAL FACTS

- ◠ 3.9 in diameter
  2 in high
- ⚖ 2.2 lbs
- ⅅ Not defined
- ✔ Early spring to early winter

Cheese made with equal proportions of goat and cow's milk

Rhône-Alpes (73, 74)

Raw

CHEVROTIN D'ALPAGE, VALLÉE DE MORZINE

The *fermier* goat cheese shown was made in a chalet in the Vallée de Morzine in Savoie. Its moist surface still shows traces of the cloth used to wrap it during affinage, which can take up to four months. The milk used to make this cheese comes from goats grazing in meadows of wild flowers in the Alps, which gives the pale yellow pâte a sugary smell and a taste of honey. Throughout the pâte there are small holes, which are characteristic of a pressed cheese. Chevrotin *d'alpage* was inspired by another great cheese, Reblochon (p. 175).

❢ Vin de Savoie

Semi-hard pâte sinks under finger pressure; uncooked, pressed

Affinage of 14 weeks

Moist rind of natural white and reddish-brown mold

Rhône-Alpes (74)

Raw

ESSENTIAL FACTS

- ◯ 6.7–7.9 in diameter 1.6 in high
- ⚖ 8.8 oz
- 🝱 Not defined
- ✔ Autumn to winter

CHEVROTIN DES ARAVIS

This *fermier* goat's cheese is sometimes made in a chalet in the Chaîne des Aravis in Savoie. Its appearance and flavor are quite different from the goat cheeses of the Loire. It has a moist, yellowish-orange rind stained with white mold. The pâte is rounded, mild, fine-textured, and melting at the edges – rather like Reblochon (p. 175) which is made using very similar methods of production. Affinage requires 95% humidity and takes three to six weeks, during which time the cheese is washed in brine, turned, and lightly pressed by hand.

❢ Vin de Savoie

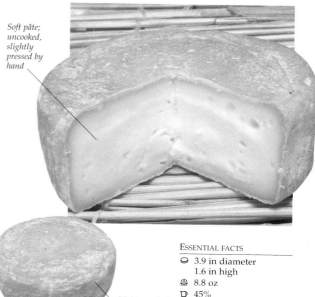

Soft pâte; uncooked, slightly pressed by hand

Rhône-Alpes (73, 74)

Raw

Moist, washed, yellowish-orange rind with powdery natural mold

ESSENTIAL FACTS

- ◯ 3.9 in diameter 1.6 in high
- ⚖ 8.8 oz
- 🝱 45%
- ✔ Summer to autumn

Rind of
natural mold

ESSENTIAL FACTS

⊖ 3.9–4.3 in diameter
2.4 in high
⚖ 1.3 lbs
🗓 45%
➵ June to December

*Semi-hard
pâte;
uncooked,
pressed*

**Affinage
of one month**

CHEVROTIN DE MACÔT

One of the prime requirements
of a good *fromagerie* is the *cave
d'affinage*, since this is where the
cheese is "finished."

When it leaves the farm where
it is made in the Tarentaise region
of Savoie, this *fermier* cheese is
white. It is taken to be ripened by
a *fromager* in his cellar, which is an
adapted bomb shelter from World
War II. This space of around
3,230 square feet cut into the
mountainside offers the ideal cool,
dark, damp conditions for affinage,
which takes between one and three
months. The cheese is initially left
to rest for a month during which
time the yellow and pink mold
opens up on the surface. The
pâte ripens slowly.

♀ Vin de Savoie

Rhône-Alpes
(73)

Raw

CHEVROTIN DU
MONT CENIS

This *fermier* goat cheese comes from
the area around Mont Cenis in
Savoie. Because of its relatively
large size, it requires a long
affinage of up to six months. The
rind, which is washed in brine,
is regularly rubbed with a cloth
soaked in liquid *morge* (p. 20). As
the rind develops, it protects the
cheese against bad mold but allows
contact between the inside of the
cheese and the natural environment
in the cellar. The cheese shown
has been ripened for a full six
months; the rind is still smooth.
The elastic pâte is beginning to
turn sticky.

♀ Crépy

*Semi-hard
pâte;
uncooked,
pressed*

ESSENTIAL FACTS

⊖ 18 in diameter
3.2 in high
⚖ 17.6 lbs
🗓 45%
➵ Best in autumn

Washed rind

Rhône-Alpes
(73)

Raw

CHEVROTIN DE MONTVALEZAN

This *fermier* cheese was discovered by a *fromager* who then helped the cheesemaker to produce it in the the Tarentaise region of Savoie. Its appearance reflects the enthusiasm and quality of their work together. It has a compact, fine, ivory pâte, which is sticky and smells of mold. Affinage takes from our to five weeks.

♀ Roussette de Savoie

Semi-hard pâte; uncooked, pressed

Rind of natural mold

Rhône-Alpes (73)

Raw

ESSENTIAL FACTS
- ⊖ 3.9 in diameter 2.4 in high
- ⚖ 1.3 lbs
- ☷ 45%
- ✔ Spring to autumn

CHEVROTIN DE PEISEY-NANCROIX

At an altitude of 4,265 ft, the tiny villages of Peisey and Nancroix in Savoie have a total of only 481 inhabitants between the two of them. Their local goat cheese is *fermier* produced with an affinage of up to six months, which is a long time considering its small size. The change in the crust is impressive; the pâte is rather sticky. This is a goat cheese of quality, with a mature taste, despite the cracks in the pâte.

♀ Roussette de Savoie

Semi-hard pâte; uncooked, pressed

Rhône-Alpes (73)

Raw

Rind of natural mold

ESSENTIAL FACTS
- ⊖ 3.9 in diameter 2.8 in high
- ⚖ 1.3 lbs
- ☷ Not defined
- ✔ Spring to autumn

Natural, stippled,
golden-yellow to
brown rind

Firm, slightly elastic, ivory
to pale-yellow pâte;
cooked below 127°F, pressed

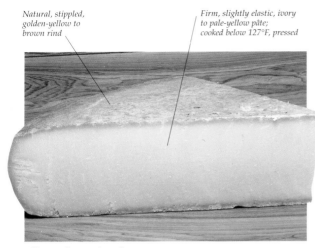

**Affinage of approximately
one year**

COMTÉ (AOC)

With Beaufort, this cheese, also called Gruyère du Comté, is the richest and most popular cheese in France. It is traditionally produced in the mountains of the Jura, where local farmers bring their milk down to the *fruitières*, which are local cooperatives managed by a group of villages. It takes as many as 140 gallons of milk, equivalent to the daily production of 30 cows, to make one Comté cheese.

Appearance and flavor
The surface of the cheese shown here is broad and flat with a moist, cool, gray, yellow, and ocher rind. When it is cut, it reveals a firm and supple pâte that melts in the mouth, leaving a sweet taste. The salt is strong but balanced and the flavor has a nutty tang. Comté is a nourishing and versatile cheese: it is a good accompaniment to an apéritif or may be eaten in a salad, with fruit, in a sandwich, or cooked in a croque-monsieur or a fondue.

Production and affinage
Consumed by 40% of the French population, Comté has the highest production figures of all French cheeses – some 38,000 tons per year. The AOC restricts production to the Franche-Comté, eastern Bourgogne, and parts of Lorraine, Champagne, and the Rhône-Alpes (see map below for specific departments). Quality is strictly controlled, and each year 5% of cheeses fail to pass the AOC tests. Affinage must take place within the AOC specified areas and needs 90 days from the date of production at below 66°F with a minimum humidity level of 92%. The cheeses are regularly wiped with brine. The rind must be treated with *morge* and stippled.

℣ Côtes du Jura (*jaune*),
Vin de Paille *doux*

ESSENTIAL FACTS

- ⊖ 15.8 in diameter
  3.5 in high
- ⚖ 121 lbs
- ♌ 45% or 1 oz min.
  per 3.5 oz cheese
- ✓ All year

Eye

THE "EYES"
The "eyes" in the pâte of the Comté are the result of careful affinage. They vary from the size of a pea to that of a small cherry. If the affinage is prolonged at low temperatures, no eye forms.

(39, 70, 90,
01, 21, 71,
52, 88,)

Raw

How to cut a Comté

To cut a whole Comté in two or four pieces, use a cutting wire. Then these pieces may be cut with a kitchen knife.

1. The cheese is first cut in half.

2. Each half is then halved.

3. A right-angle is cut off each quarter.

4. A wedge is then cut off the side of each quarter.

5. A slice is cut off the end of the quarter.

6. A second slice is cut parallel to the last.

7. The remaining quarter is cut into wedges.

8. Each quarter is cut to the same pattern.

AOC Regulations: Comté

1. The milk must be transported immediately after milking to the place of production. If the milk is refrigerated and kept at 57°F, renneting must be carried out within 14 hours. If the milk is kept at 39°F, renneting must occur within 24 hours, 36 hours in winter.

2. The milk may be heated once to a maximum of 104°F, but only at the renneting. Systems or machinery that would allow the rapid heating to above 104°F before renneting may not be kept on the premises.

3. The salt or brine is applied to the cheese.

4. The green *casein* label must be applied to the side of the cheese, bearing the month of production on the right, and the day of production on the left.

5. Grated cheese may not be sold as Comté.

AOC GRANTED 1976

Scale of Marks for AOC Assessment of Comté

Comté is graded on a scale of 1 to 20. The minimum score for an acceptable cheese is an average above 12. Cheeses with marks of 15 to 20 have green *casein* labels; those with 12 to 15 show brick-red *casein* labels.

The minimum score for taste is 3 out of 9. A score of 0 in the following areas leads to elimination from the test: shape, rind, holes, and pâte. Cheeses thus eliminated are sold as Gruyère.

Aspect	Marks	Ideal conditions for reference
Overall appearance	1/20	Rounded sides; clear-cut form: no joint between sides, top, and bottom; well-proportioned; no bulging, no stretching
Quality of rind on top, bottom, and sides	1.5/20	Treated with *morge*; stippled (with cloth marks); solid (not crumbly); clean (dry, smooth, not stained or coated); even (light orange to ocher); no defects, no cracks
Appearance of the cut and eyes	3.5/20	Holes should be present: 10 to 20 eyes on a half cheese; round, clear, cherry sized, well spread, no grooves or other defects
Quality of pâte	5/20	Even color (creamy to light orange-yellow); supple (slightly elastic); smooth (not too moist or oily); medium resistance to deformation; fine pâte (no little particles when the cheese is reduced in the mouth); should not stick to the palate
Quality of taste	9/20	Simple (no defects); nutty (walnut); fruity (apricot, dried fruits); "lactic" (milk, butter); lightly roasted (caramel); grassy (hay); balanced (sour, salty, sweet, bitter); no tingling, lingering taste.

Corse

The island of Corsica, called Corse in French, lies in the Mediterranean 106 miles south of France's Côte d'Azur and 52 miles west of Piombino on the Italian coast. The highest point is Monte Cinto, which is covered in snow for much of the year. Indeed, French writer Guy de Maupassant called Corsica "the mountain in the sea."

Corsicans see themselves as independent and some even refer to France as "the Continent." The language is closer to Italian than French and the independence movement is active.

Due to its strategic position and commercial potential, the island has been coveted, invaded, and dominated by different powers throughout history – Greece, Rome, the Saracens, Pisa, Genoa, and for the last 200 years, France. The Greeks introduced sheep, wine, and olives to the island, and the Saracens their goats.

Most of Corsica has a Mediterranean climate, but above 4,500 ft, it gets colder and more Alpine. The range of climates has permitted around 2,000 species of plant to become established, all of which are resistant to fierce heat, arid conditions, strong winds, and intense cold. Of these, species, 78 are unknown elsewhere. The *maquis*, which is the rocky landscape where many of these bushy and herby plants grow wild, shows an explosion of colors in spring, and provides excellent grazing for goats and sheep.

The mixed climate, varied terrain, robust vegetation, and semi-wild sheep and goats are ideal ingredients for a rich variety of cheeses that are quite different from those of the mainland. Corsican cheeses are generally small or medium-sized and marked by the *faisselle* (colander) when molded. They tend to be salty and highly flavored, with a pronounced smell.

AERIAL VIEW OF THE PLATEAU DU NIOLO
The mountainous Niolo region (right) in the centre of Haute Corse is home to many herds of semi-wild goats and sheep whose milk is used for making a vast range of Corsican cheeses.

FROMAGE CORSE

M. Manenti's home and cheese-making *atelier*, where this *fermier* cheese is made, lie some 1,181 ft up Col San Bastiano in Calcatoggio, which is itself 1,348 ft high. The herds of ewes and goats are taken into the mountains at the end of June or beginning of July, and down again in October. The ewes stay outdoors all year. The rennet (p. 15) that makes the milk coagulate is homemade from an enzyme called chymosin found in the stomach of a young goat. The stomach is dried indoors for at least 40 days, thinly cut, and soaked in a quart of warm water for two days. In the past, the reed colander used to strain the cheese was also homemade. After 100 days, the cheese is covered with mold. It is salty, with a fine texture. Affinage takes at least two months.

❢ Patrimonio

ESSENTIAL FACTS

◒ 5.1 in diameter
   1.6 in high
⚖ 1.1 lbs
◸ 48%
✔ Spring to autumn

 Corse-du-Sud (2A)

 Raw

Affinage of four months

Soft pâte, slightly elastic to finger pressure; uncooked, unpressed

Affinage of ten hours

Affinage of eight days

Affinage of five months

Washed rind

Dried kid's stomach containing cheese

BROCCIU / FROMAGE DE LACTOSÉRUM (AOC)

Fresh, white pâte

Very fresh Brocciu, still hot and steaming

The Corsican name for this cheese is Brocciu, while in French it is called Broccio. The origin of the name may be *brousse* which is another word for *fromage frais* made from goat or ewe's milk. Brocciu is an unusual cheese since it is the first AOC cheese to be made from *lactosérum* or whey, which is usually discarded during cheese production. Since some of the proteins and other nutritional elements remain in it, whey makes an excellent by-product. Brocciu, which is similar to Italian ricotta, is popular with Corsicans and is sold at local markets in returnable baskets.

Production
First the whey is heated to 95°F and salted, then whole milk (10 to 15% of its volume) is added. This blend is mixed while being further heated to194°F. Solid white particles floating on the surface are skimmed, transferred to a colander, and drained. Production may be *fermier*, *artisanal*, or *coopérative*.

How to eat Brocciu
Brocciu is usually eaten fresh, hot or cold, within 48 hours of production, although if drained and salted it can be ripened like other cheeses. The pâte is soft, sweet, smells of milk, and feels liquid in the throat. Brocciu is excellent eaten for breakfast with jam or salt and pepper. It can also be served with local *marc* poured on it, or as a filling for omelettes or cannelloni. *Fiadone* is a tasty, lemon-flavored sponge cake made with brocciu, eggs, sugar, and grated lemon rind.

The AOC was granted in 1983.

❑ *Marc de Corse*

ESSENTIAL FACTS

🝾 Colander-shaped, in different formats
⚖ Generally 1.1 lbs (as shown) to 2.2 lbs
🝛 40–51%
✓ Spring to autumn (fresh goat cheeses); winter to early summer (fresh ewe's cheeses); all year, if matured

Corsica

Raw, whole

DIFFERENT TYPES OF BROCCIU

1. Brocciu in its traditional Corsican basket, from the Domaine de la Porette, near Corte.

2. Brocciu from a *fromager* in Paris.

3. Brocciu from the market at Ajaccio.

4. Brocciu from the market in Lyon.

5. Brocciu *poivré* – pepper Brocciu from a market at Sainte-Maure.

Soft pâte;
uncooked,
unpressed

CALENZANA (LE NIOLO)

This is a well-known *fermier* cheese from the Niolo plateau in the northern part of Corsica. It has an affinage of at least three months. The cheese shown here is somewhat white. The rind is wet, and the pâte is heavy, crumbles like clay, and has a strong taste.

♀ Patrimonio

ESSENTIAL FACTS

◈ 3.9 in square
  1.6 in high
⚖ 1.3 lbs
↻ Not defined
✓ Spring to autumn

Natural rind

Haute-Corse
(2B)

Raw

LE FIUM'ORBO

This *artisanal* cheese, named after a small river in the north of Corsica, has a sticky rind, marked by the colander in which it was molded. It has a concentrated flavor, and the pâte sinks under light finger pressure, with no elasticity. Affinage takes at least two months, during which time the cheese is turned every two days.

♀ Vin de Corse

Soft pâte with no
elasticity; uncooked,
unpressed

ESSENTIAL FACTS

◔ 3.9 in diameter
  1.6 in high
⚖ 16 oz
↻ 50%
✓ November to end June
  (ewe's); January to
  end June (goat's)

Natural
mold rind

Haute-Corse
(2B)

Raw

FLEUR DU MAQUIS

This *artisanal* cheese is covered with juniper berries, chili pepper, savory, and rosemary.

Chilis, juniper berries,

Fleur du Maquis

ESSENTIAL FACTS

◈ 3.9 in square
  2.4 in high
⚖ 1.5 lbs
◫ Fleur du Maquis: 45%;
  Brin d'Amour: not defined
✓ Winter to summer

Soft pâte, with no elasticity; uncooked, unpressed

Natural rind, covered with savory and rosemary

Brin d'Amour

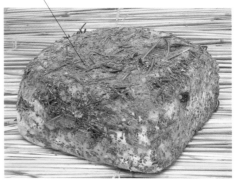

BRIN D'AMOUR

Both this cheese and the Fleur du Maquis above have a strong scent of dried herbs that bites on the tongue. Their pâte is fine-textured and ivory in color, and tastes slightly sour. Both types are occasionally made in France, where they are more popular than in their native Corsica. They are both *artisanal* cheeses with an affinage of at least one month.

♟ Vin de Corse, Côtes de Provence

Haute-Corse
(2B)

Raw

A Filetta (La Fougère)

A filetta means "the fern" in Corsican. This *artisanal* cheese, decorated with a sprig of fern, comes from Isolaccio, which lies 28 miles south of the town of Bastia. It has a faint smell of the cellar and fern leaves. Young cheeses may be exported to the mainland. Affinage takes three to four weeks, during which time the cheese is turned.

♀ Patrimonio

Soft *pâte* with no elasticity; uncooked, unpressed

Rind of natural mold with colander marks and decorated with fern

ESSENTIAL FACTS

⊖ 3.9 in diameter
   1.6 in high
⚖ 12.6 oz
🗅 45%
✔ December to June (ewe's); March to November (goat)

Haute-Corse (2B)

Raw

Fromage de Brebis

The *fermier* cheese shown here was made in November in Santa-Maria-Siché with milk from the farm of M. Cianfarani. This photograph was taken only a week after it was made. The white rind looks fresh, but the pâte is elastic. The first milk from the morning's milking makes it slightly bitter. Affinage usually takes at least three months.

♀ Patrimonio

ESSENTIAL FACTS

⊖ 5.1 in diameter
   2.8 in high
⚖ 2.2 lbs
🗅 50%
✔ Spring to autumn

Soft, elastic, rubbery *pâte*; uncooked, unpressed

Washed rind

Corse-du-Sud (2A)

Raw

FROMAGE FERMIER BREBIS

This *fermier* sheep cheese has a wet rind and sticky pâte and belongs to the same family as Venaco (p.130). It is best eaten from spring to autumn. Production starts at the beginning of winter and continues until summer. Cheesemaking commences as soon as the ewes on the farm begin to produce milk on December 7. Every day of the 45 days of affinage, the cheeses are all washed with a little water and turned. At the beginning of affinage, the cheese has almost no smell.

♀ Patrimonio

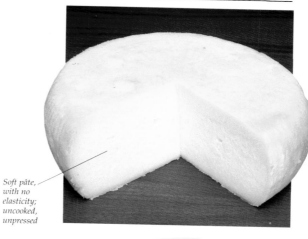

Soft pâte, with no elasticity; uncooked, unpressed

ESSENTIAL FACTS

- ⊖ 4.3 in diameter
  1.6 in high
- ⚖ 14 oz
- ◻ 45%
- ✓ Spring to autumn

Washed rind

 Haute-Corse (2B)

 Raw

HANDMADE CHEESES Although this looks like a washed-rind cheese, it is merely rubbed with a moistened hand and turned several times.

Fresh cheese

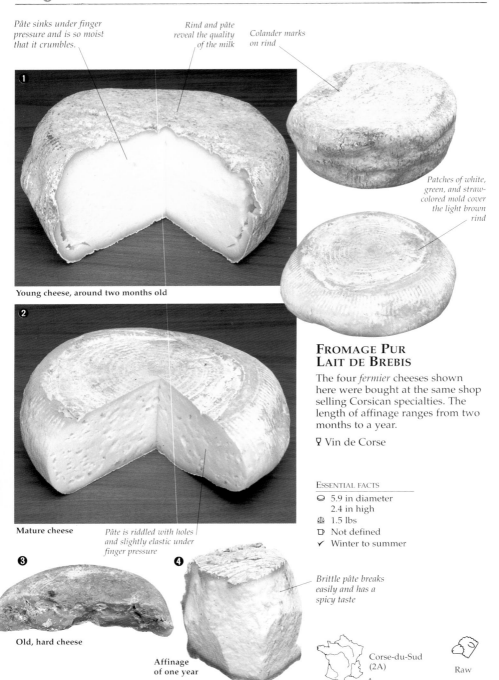

Pâte sinks under finger pressure and is so moist that it crumbles.

Rind and pâte reveal the quality of the milk

Colander marks on rind

Patches of white, green, and straw-colored mold cover the light brown rind

① Young cheese, around two months old

② Mature cheese

Pâte is riddled with holes and slightly elastic under finger pressure

FROMAGE PUR LAIT DE BREBIS

The four *fermier* cheeses shown here were bought at the same shop selling Corsican specialties. The length of affinage ranges from two months to a year.

♀ Vin de Corse

ESSENTIAL FACTS

- ⊖ 5.9 in diameter
  2.4 in high
- ⊕ 1.5 lbs
- ↻ Not defined
- ✓ Winter to summer

③ Old, hard cheese

④ Affinage of one year

Brittle pâte breaks easily and has a spicy taste

Corse-du-Sud (2A)

Raw

FROMAGE CORSE

There are few cheese shops in
Corsica; people usually buy cheese
at the morning market.
Cheesemakers also sell their own
cheeses, which become known by
the maker's name – for example,
Mme. Nicole's cheese. The *fermier*
cheese shown is so young that it is
still exuding whey; pâte and salt
are not yet integrated. It was
bought at the supermarket in
Calacuccia.

🍷 Ajaccio

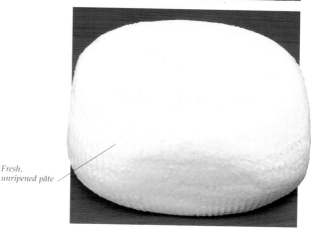

*Fresh,
unripened pâte*

ESSENTIAL FACTS
- ◈ 4.3 in square
  2 in high
- ⚖ 1.3 lbs
- 🗓 Not defined
- ✔ Winter to early
  summer

Haute-Corse
(2B)

Raw

FROMAGE CORSE NIOLO

The *fermier* cheese shown was
bought at a market in Lyon. It was
sold under the name of "Niolo"
but according to Corsican cheese
experts it is of the *bastelicaccia* type
made in the Ajaccio area. The mold
is blue and reddish-brown and the
rind is moist. The pâte sinks under
finger pressure. It is a little young
for a Corsican cheese, but it has
flavor. Affinage takes at least three
months.

🍷 Patrimonio *rosé*

*Soft pâte;
uncooked,
unpressed*

*Washed rind,
marked by colander*

ESSENTIAL FACTS
- ◒ 4.7 in diameter
  1.8 in high
- ⚖ 1 lb
- 🗓 45%
- ✔ Winter to early
  summer

Haute-Corse
(2 B)

Raw

123

ESSENTIAL FACTS

◈ 3.9 in wide
   4.3 in long
   1.6 in high
⚖ 14 oz
🗗 45%
✔ All year

*Soft pâte;
uncooked,
unpressed*

*Natural
rind*

FROMAGE FERMIER DE CHÈVRE DE LA TAVAGNA

The Giancoli family's house lies on the coast in a mountainous area about an hour's drive south of Bastia. For eight months of the year they make some 70 *fermier* cheeses per day. When the airtight package in which the cheese is packed is opened, a pungent smell fills the air and you can see the paper wrapper bearing the marks of the colander. The cheese itself looks moist and is hard, like soap. It has been ripened for seven months.
Affinage usually takes two months during which time the cheese is regularly wiped with a moist cloth.

♀ Château Chalon (*jaune*), Arbois *jaune*, ◻ Marc de Corse,

 Haute-Corse
(2B)

 Raw

LE NIOLO

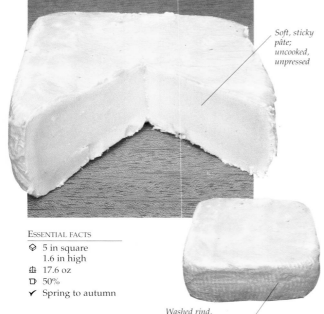

*Soft, sticky
pâte;
uncooked,
unpressed*

The Corsican village of Casamaccioli has only 140 inhabitants. It is here, deep in the mountains, that the Santini brothers produce Le Niolo cheese. It is a *fermier* cheese with a strong smell, a sticky consistency, and a taste that tingles on the tongue. The smell grows with time. In Paris, when people think of Corsican cheeses, this is what comes to their minds. Affinage takes at least three months.

♀ Château Chalon (*jaune*), Arbois *jaune*, ◻ Marc de Corse

ESSENTIAL FACTS

◈ 5 in square
   1.6 in high
⚖ 17.6 oz
🗗 50%
✔ Spring to autumn

*Washed rind,
marked by the colander*

 Haute-Corse
(2B)

 Raw

Le Mouflon

This *fermier* cheese is made from raw goat's milk in Calgèse in southern Corsica. Affinage, which usually lasts for three months, takes place in the mountain town of Calacuccia in northern Corsica.

♈ Patrimonio

ESSENTIAL FACTS

◈ 4.7 in square
    1.2 in high
⚖ 17.6 oz
⊓ 50%
✔ Best in summer

Washed rind

Corse-du-Sud (2A)

Raw

Pâte breaks like hard clay, with no elasticity; uncooked, unpressed

Mouflon

Although cheesemakers think of it as a goat, the *mouflon* is a wild mountain sheep, the ancestor of domestic European sheep, with curved horns but no beard. *Mouflons* are still found today, mainly in Sardinia and Corsica, where they are known as *muflone* and *mufoli*. They are now an endangered species, but they used to be eaten roasted or stewed in much the same way as mutton or venison.

Pâte de Fromage

Pâte de fromage, meaning cheese paste (p. 140), is a Corsican specialty. Ripened cheese is milled, put into a container, and ripened again. Some locals say that it is best when it is infested with the *ciron* or cheese mite. It is an *artisanal* cheese with an affinage of five to six months in vats.

♈ Château Chalon (*jaune*), Arbois *jaune*, ☐ *Marc de Corse*

Essential Facts
- In a pot
- 7 oz net
- 50%
- All year

Haute-Corse (2B)

Raw, whole

A Filetta

It is said that this cheese – a *pâte de fromage* (cheese paste) – was formerly made in all Corsican homes. The smell of A Filetta is so strong that it stings the eyes. It is an *artisanal* cheese with an affinage of five to six months.

♈ Château Chalon (*jaune*), Arbois *jaune*, ☐ *Marc de Corse*

Essential Facts
- Pot shaped
- 8 oz net
- 45%
- All year

Haute-Corse (2B)

Raw

SAN PETRONE

This is another *pâte de fromage* made from mature milled cheese, shaped without any further additives, and ripened for seven to eight months. There is no rind. The pâte looks like dough that has been kneaded. It is sticky, with a strong salty, sharp, and tingling taste, which resembles that of *fromage fort*. Production is *artisanal*.

♀ Château Chalon (*jaune*), Arbois *jaune*, ◻ *Marc de Corse*,

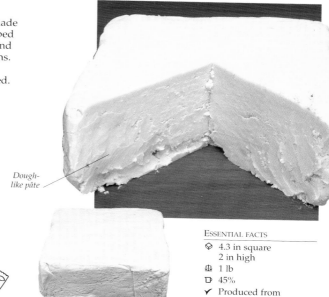

Dough-like pâte

Haute-Corse (2B)

Raw

LE VIEUX CORSE

This *pâte de fromage* is wrapped in three layers of wax paper. The pâte is stained with blue mold. It is salty, spicy, and tasty. The Corsicans eat it thickly spread on bread like butter. This is an *artisanal* cheese with an affinage of at least three months.

♀ Château Chalon (*jaune*), Arbois *jaune*, ◻ *Marc de Corse*

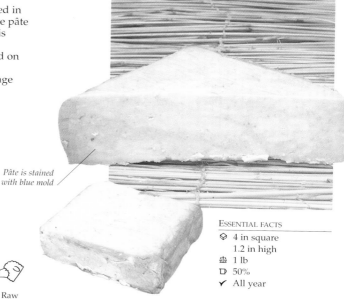

Pâte is stained with blue mold

Haute-Corse (2B)

Raw

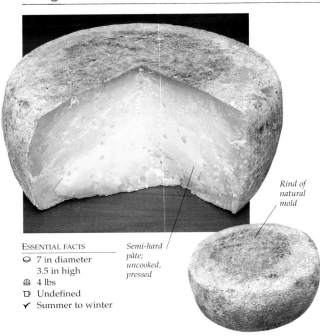

ESSENTIAL FACTS

- 7 in diameter
  3.5 in high
- 4 lbs
- Undefined
- Summer to winter

Semi-hard pâte; uncooked, pressed

Rind of natural mold

TOME CHÈVRE

This is an excellent *fermier* cheese made by M. Andreani from the village of Piaggiola near Sartène. According to the cashier at the local supermarket he sometimes comes to sell his cheeses himself. This cheese is very different from the goat cheeses of the mainland. The mold looks like a dry stone covered with reddish lichen, and the pâte is so shiny that it resembles candle wax and has to be broken with a hammer and chisel.

It smells slightly of the cellar in which it is matured. Affinage takes at least three months. This cheese is probably related to a Sardinian cheese called *Fleur de Sardaigne* (flower of Sardinia), which is said to date from Roman times.

♀ Patrimonio

Corse-du-Sud (2A)

Raw

TOME DE CHÈVRE

This very dry *fermier* cheese smells of hay. Perhaps it is the smell of the flowers that grow in the *maquis* (mountain scrub) on which the goats feed. It has an affinage of at least three months. The origin of the cheese shown here is unknown.

♀ Patrimonio

Semi-hard pâte; uncooked, pressed

Rind of natural mold

ESSENTIAL FACTS

- 6.3 in diameter
  2.4 in high
- 3.3 lbs
- Undefined
- All year

Throughout Corse

Raw

TOMME CORSE

Bite into the hard pâte of this *artisanal* cheese and an almost coppery flavor of salt, sweetness, red pepper, and sourness explodes in the mouth. It goes particularly well with a bottle of old Corsican wine. Compare Ossau *fermier* (p. 54) or Salers (p. 71) with this Corsican cheese.

♀ Vin de Corse (vintage)

Semi-hard pâte; uncooked, pressed

Haute-Corse (2B)

Raw

Rind of natural mold

ESSENTIAL FACTS
- ⬭ 8 in diameter 3 in high
- ⚖ 5.5 lbs
- ▯ 47%
- ✔ All year

TOMME CORSE

The *coopérative* A. Pecurella, where this cheese is made, was founded in 1975. A *pecurella* is the Corsican name for the small ewe that produces the rich, strongly aromatic milk used to make this cheese. The piece shown here is a year old and very crumbly. It has an affinage of three months to one year at 53.6°F and 85% humidity. The locals are very partial to it.

♀ Vin de Corse (vintage)

Semi-hard pâte becomes granular with age; uncooked, pressed

Corse-du-Sud (2A)

Raw

Rind of natural mold

ESSENTIAL FACTS
- ⬭ 8 in diameter 4 in high
- ⚖ 5.5 lbs
- ▯ 48%
- ✔ All year

Affinage of one year

U RUSTINU

Corsican cheeses do not usually have specific names and are simply called cheese or *brocciu*. Sometimes the wholesaler will name them himself. This one was made by Joseph Guidicelli. His cheeses are known by two names: U Rustinu, which is a geographical name, or U Muntanacciu, which is Corsican for a mountain. U Rustinu is an *artisanal* cheese with an affinage of at least three months, during which time it is turned regularly.

♀ Patrimonio

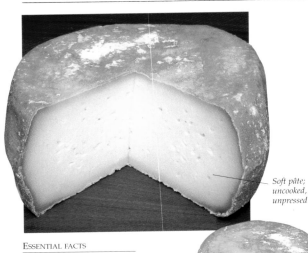

Soft pâte; uncooked, unpressed

ESSENTIAL FACTS
- ⊖ 4 in diameter
  2 in high
- ⚖ 1 lb
- ▯ 45%
- ✔ Produced from December to late June; best in spring

Moist red rind of white and red mold

 Haute-Corse (2B)

Raw

LE VENACO

With Niolo (p. 124), Calenzana (p. 118), and Brocciu (p. 116), Venaco is one of the most typical Corsican cheeses. The name originally derived from the place of production, Venaco, a town in the center of Corsica, but it is no longer made there. It is a *fermier* cheese made from ewe's or goat's milk with an affinage of at least two months.

🍷 Ajaccio

Soft, sticky pâte; uncooked, unpressed

ESSENTIAL FACTS
- ⊖ 3.5 in diameter
  1.6 in high
- ⚖ 12.6 oz
- ▯ 45%
- ✔ Produced from winter to early summer; best from spring to autumn

Washed rind

 Haute-Corse (2B)

Raw, whole

DREUX À LA FEUILLE / FEUILLE DE DREUX

The ancient town of Dreux lies in a cereal-producing region to the north of Chartres, some 50 miles from Paris. The flat, thin cheeses produced there ripen gently under the cover of chestnut leaves, which stop them from sticking to each other. A faint smell of the chestnut leaf mingles with a pleasant scent of mold. The patchy white mold turns to a reddish-brown late in the cheese's affinage, which lasts two to three weeks. This *artisanal* cheese used to be eaten as a snack by workers in the fields.

❢ Touraine

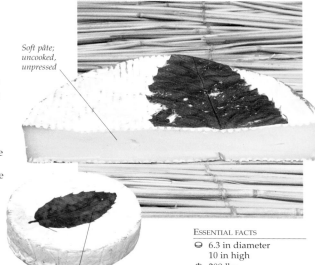

Soft pâte; uncooked, unpressed

Centre
(28)

Raw or pasteurized

Rind of white mold decorated with a chestnut leaf

ESSENTIAL FACTS

- ◯ 6.3 in diameter
  10 in high
- ⚖ 280 lbs
- ▯ 30–40%
- ✔ All year

EMMENTAL GRAND CRU

This cheese has a red *casein* label, which is a guarantee of its quality. This label gives details of the place of production, fat content, and licence number of the maker. Emmental Grand Cru is a large *coopérative* or *industriel* cheese with a cooked and pressed pâte like that of Beaufort (p. 26) and Comté (p. 112). It is produced using raw milk in the Franche-Comté, and parts of Rhône-Alpes, Champagne-Ardenne, Bourgogne, and Lorraine (see map below for specific departments). The pâte is smooth; its aroma and taste are sweet. Affinage takes ten weeks.

❢ Vin de Savoie, Givry, Rully, Mercurey

(01, 69, 73, 74, 52, 21, 71, 88)

Raw

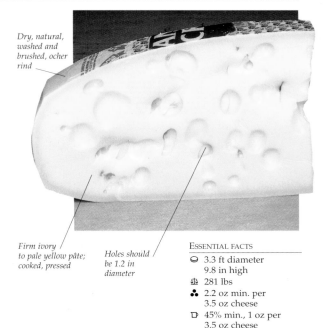

Dry, natural, washed and brushed, ocher rind

Firm ivory to pale yellow pâte; cooked, pressed

Holes should be 1.2 in diameter

ESSENTIAL FACTS

- ◯ 3.3 ft diameter
  9.8 in high
- ⚖ 281 lbs
- ⚬ 2.2 oz min. per 3.5 oz cheese
- ▯ 45% min., 1 oz per 3.5 oz cheese
- ✔ All year

Hard, ivory to pale yellow pâte, with cherry-to walnut-sized holes; cooked, pressed

Hard, dry ocher to light-brown rind

EMMENTAL

This *industriel* cheese is almost identical to Emmental Grand Cru but is made with pasteurized milk.

❢ Vin de Savoie, Givry, Rully, Mercurey

ESSENTIAL FACTS

- ◒ 3.3 ft diameter
  10 in high
- ⚖ 5 oz
- ⁂ 2 oz per 3.5 oz cheese
- ☋ 45% min., 1 oz per 3.5 oz cheese
- ✔ All year

HOW EMMENTAL GRAND CRU IS MADE

The whole process of making this Emmental takes at least 10 weeks.

Coagulation

It takes 238 gallons of milk to make a 54-lb Emmental. The milk is heated to 90°F at the renneting stage and coagulates within 30 minutes. The curd is milled to help the whey separate, and then heated and cooked for 90 minutes at a maximum of 127°F.

Molding

The curd is put into molds and pressed for 24 hours. The *fromage blanc* is then floated in brine for 48 hours. The brine salts the cheese and forms the rind.

Affinage

The cheese rests in a cellar at 55°F for four to five days, then the temperature is raised to 64°F. After a week, the cheese is transferred to a cellar, at 77°F and 60% humidity, where it stays for a month. Natural bacteria in the cheese transform oxygen into carbon dioxide that forms holes, while the pâte becomes more elastic, fine-textured, and tasty. When the surface of the cheese bulges, it is moved back to a cellar at 64°F, then to another cellar at 55°F.

Fromage blanc **is floated in brine to salt the cheese and form the rind**   M. Boujon, the *fromager*, **guillotining his giant cheese**

All regions of France

Pasteurized

EPOISSES DE BOURGOGNE, (AOC)

Napoleon is said to have been partial to this cheese and ate it with Chambertin wine. Although the cheese was very popular at the beginning of the 20th century, production did not survive World War II. M. Berthaut of the village of Epoisses revived it in 1956. A single farm in Bourgogne currently makes all the cheeses of the *fermier* category. There are also *artisanal* versions and both a large and a small version are produced.

This is a strong-smelling, washed-rind cheese, with an aroma of *marc*. The fine-textured pâte melts in the mouth, with mixture of salt, sweet, metallic, and milky flavors. Affinage takes place in specified areas and lasts for at least four weeks; the cheese is first washed in water or brine, then *marc* is added to the liquid. The cheese is washed one to three times a week, with gradually increasing quantities of *marc*.

Ϋ Pouilly-Fuissé, Sauternes (*moelleux*), ☐ *Marc* de Bourgogne

Bourgogne (21, 89); Champagne-Ardenne (52)

Whole

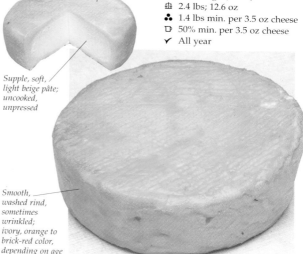

Cheese ripens from outside in

Supple, soft, light beige pâte; uncooked, unpressed

Smooth, washed rind, sometimes wrinkled; ivory, orange to brick-red color, depending on age

ESSENTIAL FACTS
- ◴ 7.5 in diameter
  - 1.8 in high (large)
  - 4.5 in diameter
  - 1.8 in high (small)
- ⚖ 2.4 lbs; 12.6 oz
- ∴ 1.4 lbs min. per 3.5 oz cheese
- ⛉ 50% min. per 3.5 oz cheese
- ✓ All year

AOC REGULATIONS: EPOISSES DE BOURGOGNE

1. The coagulation of the milk must be caused mainly by lactic acid, for a period of 16 hours.

2. The curd is roughly cut. It must not be broken.

3. After spontaneous drainage, the cheese is salted.

AOC GRANTED 1991

L'AMI DU CHAMBERTIN

This *artisanal* cheese is made in the village of Gevrey-Chambertin in Bourgogne. Affinage takes at least four weeks.

☐ *Marc* de Chambertin

ESSENTIAL FACTS
- ◴ 3.5 in diameter, 1.6 in high
- ⚖ 8.8 oz
- ⛉ 50%
- ✓ All year

Bourgogne (21)

Pasteurized

Moist, red rind, washed with water and Marc de Bourgogne

Fourme d'Ambert

Natural
rind of red
or white
mold

Fourme de Montbrison

Pâte of blue
mold;
uncooked,
unpressed

FOURME D'AMBERT / FOURME DE MONTBRISON (AOC)

These two cheeses are made in two regions around the towns of Ambert and Montbrison, now joined by the AOC, which has streamlined methods of production. The word *fourme* comes from the Latin *forma,* meaning form or shape; it is thought that the word *fromage* may have the same roots.

As with Roquefort (p. 178), the blue mold is introduced first, then air is injected into the pâte through a syringe to help it develop (p. 181). This is one of the mildest of all the blue cheeses. Its rind is rather dry, the pâte creamy and firm, with a smell of the cellar. Production is *coopérative* or *artisanal*; there is no *fermier* version. Affinage within AOC specified areas takes a minimum of 28 days from the date of production, but is usually about two months.

♈ Sauternes *moelleux,* Rivesaltes (VDN)

ESSENTIAL FACTS

- ⊖ 5 in diameter
  7.5 in high
- ⚖ 4.4 lbs
- ♣ 1.8 oz min. per 3.5 oz cheese
- ▷ 50% min., 1 oz min. per 3.5 oz cheese
- ✓ All year

Rhône-Alpes
(42);
Auvergne
(63, 15)

Pasteurized

Frinault

In any good ash-covered cheese, the pâte dries slowly under its extra coating and compacts without growing hard. The ancient method of applying ashes to the moist surface of cheese to protect it comes from the Orléanais region of Central France. Originally, only the ash of grapevine shoots was used. The cut cheese shown here is less ripe than the uncut cheese. Frinault reveals its quality in the mouth and has a mild aftertaste. It is an *industriel* cheese, with an affinage of three to four weeks.

🍷 Touraine

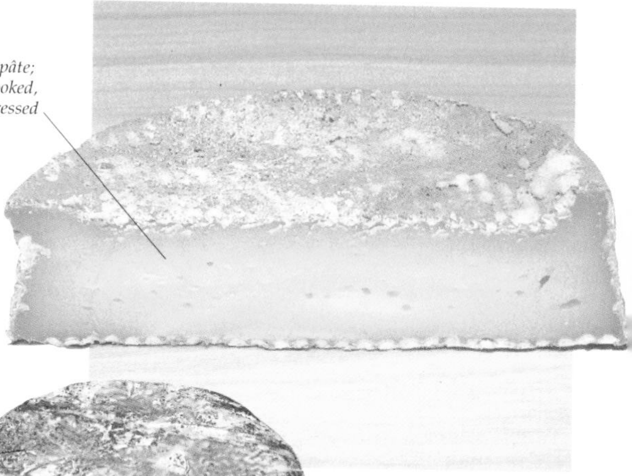
Soft pâte; uncooked, unpressed

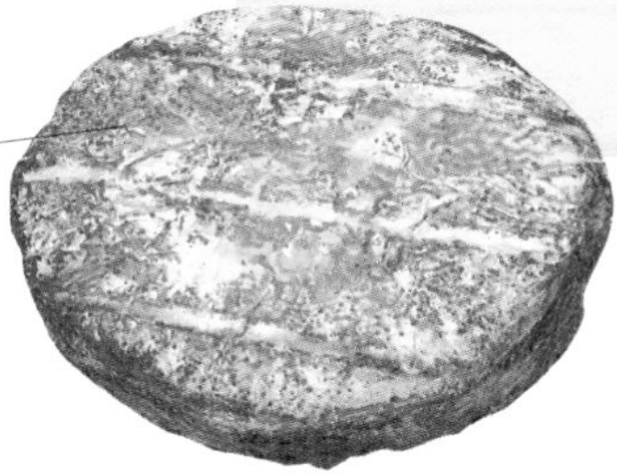
Natural rind covered with ashes

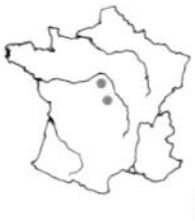
Centre (18, 45)

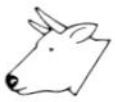
Pasteurized

Essential facts

- 4 in diameter, 1 in high
- 5.3 oz
- 50%
- ✓ Summer to autumn

Types of milk used in cheese production

French cheeses are made from cow, goat, and sheep's milk. The type of milk used to make a cheese determines its taste. The most highly concentrated milk of all is ewe's milk, which gives strong, robust, full-flavored cheeses, with a lingering aftertaste.

The annual quantity of milk produced by one cow over 305 days of milking is 6.7 tons; a goat produces 1,420 lbs over 240 days; and a ewe produces 440 lbs over 180 days.

Cheese may be made from either pasteurized or raw milk. Raw milk is not heat-treated prior to cheesemaking and usually used shortly after milking or within 12 hours; if chilled immediately to 39°F, it may be stored for up to 24 hours. Raw milk contains natural bacteria and is considered to produce cheese with complex taste and flavor. All *fermier* cheeses belong to this category. Raw milk is compulsory for some AOCs.

Pasteurized milk is treated at low or high temperatures. Pasteurization at low temperatures usually means heating the milk to 162°F for 15 seconds and immediately chilling it to 39°F. This process reduces the level of bacteria, allowing the milk to be stored for a long time, and is widely used in factory-produced cheeses. Mass-produced cheeses made from pasteurized milk are simple in appearance and taste.

Weight and Composition of Different Types of Milk

	Cow's Milk	Goat's Milk	Sheep's Milk
Fats	1.6 oz	1.5 oz	2.6 oz
Proteins	1.2 oz	1.3 oz	2.3 oz
Sugars	2 oz	1.8 oz	1.8 oz
Minerals	0.8 oz	0.8 oz	0.4 oz
Water	2 lbs	2 lbs	2 lbs
Approx. net weight:	2.3 lbs	2.3 lbs	2.3 lbs

(From *Les Productions Laitières*, Vol. 1, Tableaux des Calories, 1993)

Fromage allégé

Allégé, meaning light, is a fashionable term used to refer to foods that are low in fat, such as certain kinds of yogurt, butter, margarine, and *fromage blanc*. A cheese may be described as *allégé* when the fat content shown on the label is between 20–30%. The classification for fat content of cheeses is as follows:

- *Maigre* – less than 20%
- *Allégé* – 20 to 30%
- *Normal* – 40 to 50%
- *Double crème* – 60 to 75%
- *Triple crème* – more than 75%
- Some *fermier* cheeses have no clearly defined fat content. This is due to the slight daily variations in their milk.
- Processed cheese (*fromage fondu*, p. 230) has a minimum 40% fat content; light processed cheese (*fromage fondu allégé*) has 20 to 30% fat.

According to the regulations of the *Journal Officiel* governing cheese production, a product must contain more than 0.8 oz dry matter per 3.5 oz to qualify as cheese; 1.5 oz for processed cheese; and 1 oz for light processed cheese.

There is a close link between fat content and taste. Cheeses with a fat content of 40–50% are generally firm, with a rounded flavor. High-fat cheeses tend to be soft and spread easily on bread, rather like butter.

Low-fat cheeses have neither the flavor of a cheese with a *normal* fat content, nor do they have the melting, smooth texture, of the latter. They do, however, offer an alternative for people who may be following a low-fat diet or watching their cholesterol intake, but who do not wish to forgo the pleasure of eating cheese.

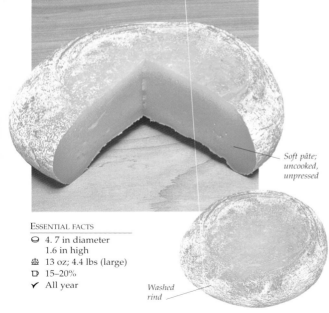

Soft pâte; uncooked, unpressed

Washed rind

ESSENTIAL FACTS
- ⊖ 4.7 in diameter
  1.6 in high
- ⚖ 13 oz; 4.4 lbs (large)
- ▯ 15–20%
- ✓ All year

BERGUES

The town of Bergues in Flandres lies 7 miles from the Belgian border. The cheese shown is untypically thin and may have lost its shape during transportation. Bergues is a *fermier* or *artisanal* cheese with an affinage of three weeks to two months, sometimes longer, during which the cheese is repeatedly washed with brine or beer.

Ⅱ Local beer, ❢ Beaujolais

Nord-Pas-de-Calais (59)

Skimmed

LE BOURRICOT

This cheese from Cantal in the Auvergne is produced in an *industriel* dairy and has a slight smell of the straw in which it was ripened. Affinage takes eight weeks on straw.

♦ St. Pourçain

Natural rind

Semi-hard pâte; uncooked, pressed

ESSENTIAL FACTS
- ⊖ 4.7 in diameter
  1.6 in high
- ⚖ 1 lb
- Ɗ 30%
- ✔ All year

Auvergne (15)

Skimmed

FROMAGE CENDRÉ

Locally, this *artisanal* cheese is also known as Cendré de Champagne and is a specialty of the time of the grape harvest. The white wood ash on the rind keeps the flies away out in the vineyards, but is removed with a wet brush before the cheese is eaten. The smell is musty, and cellar like. During affinage the cheeses are left to cure in ashes for more than two months.

♦ Bouzy, Coteaux Champenois

Soft pâte; uncooked, unpressed

Rind of ashes

ESSENTIAL FACTS
- ⊖ 5.5 in diameter
  1 in high
- ⚖ 14 oz
- Ɗ 20–30%
- ✔ All year

Champagne-Ardenne (51)

Skimmed

137

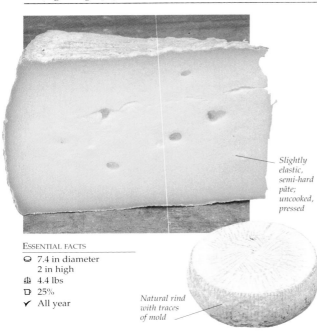

LOU MAGRÉ

This *artisanal* cheese comes from the village of Terraube in the Lomagne region of Gascogne in southwest France. It has a slight smell of the cellar. Affinage takes three to ten weeks.

❢ Madiran

Slightly elastic, semi-hard pâte; uncooked, pressed

ESSENTIAL FACTS

⊖ 7.4 in diameter
   2 in high
⏚ 4.4 lbs
⛒ 25%
✔ All year

Natural rind with traces of mold

Midi-Pyrénées (32)

Raw, skimmed

SOURIRE LOZÉRIEN

This is an *artisanal* cheese from the village of Luc in the Cévennes region of Languedoc. It has a slight smell, a faint blend of the musty cellar in which it was ripened, and mold. Affinage takes at least ten days.

❢ Corbiéres, Fitou

Semi-soft, elastic pâte; uncooked, unpressed

ESSENTIAL FACTS

⊖ 4.3 in diameter
   2 in high
⏚ 1 lb
⛒ 25%
✔ All year

Natural rind

Languedoc-Roussillon (48)

Skimmed

TOMME DE LOMAGNE

This *artisanal* cheese, with a slight smell of the cellar, is produced in the Lomagne region of Gascogne. Affinage takes two months.

♟ Madiran

Semi-hard pâte; uncooked, pressed

 Midi-Pyrénées (32)

 Raw, skimmed

Natural rind, traces of mold

ESSENTIAL FACTS
- 8 in diameter 2.8 in high
- 4.4 lbs
- 30%
- All year

LE VACHARD

This slightly musty-smelling *artisanal* cheese comes from the village of Saint-Bonnet-le-Courreau in the hilly Forez region of the Auvergne. Affinage takes one month.

♟ Côtes d'Auvergne, Châteaugay

Semi-hard pâte; uncooked, pressed

 Rhône-Alpes (42)

 Raw, skimmed

 Rind of natural mold

ESSENTIAL FACTS
- 5 in diameter 1 in high
- 1.3 lbs
- 30%
- All year

Fromage fort

Originally *fromage fort* was made at home by grating and breaking leftover bits of cheese, and mixing them with and letting them ferment in one or more liquids such as whey, milk, or vegetable broth. Oil, *eau-de-vie* or wine was added to stabilize the mixture, and herbs, spices, salt, and wine, or cider to season it. It was then left for months, to be served when finished with wine. *Fromage fort* is a local product, especially in wine-producing regions where each area has its own tradition. The names too are individual – for example, Cachat or Cacheilla, from areas of goat or half-goat-milk cheeses. The Lyonnais, Mâconnais, Beaujolais, Dauphiné, and the Massif du Ventoux are the main areas where *fromage fort* continues to be made under a variety of names.

M. Voy, chief *fromager* and proprietor of the Ferme Saint-Hubert cheesemongers in Paris says: "Our *fromage fort* is strong. We put it in a covered stoneware pot. If the pot did not have its lid on and you took it down the Metro, people would avoid you like the plague."

Cheeses with a strong smell and taste, such as Epoisses (p. 133), Langres (p. 151), and Maroilles (p. 154) are used to make the *fromage fort du Lyonnais* sold in the Ferme Saint-Hubert. The mixture is soaked in *Marc de Bourgogne* until the pâte is completely smooth. Depending on the season, if the smell of cheese in the shop is not strong enough, the pot is stirred every now and then and left open to "scent" the air.

Fromage fort is sold by the ladleful. It tingles on the tongue and is good on toasted garlic bread or accompanying an apéritif. A variety of flavors open in the mouth, leaving a complex aftertaste. It goes well with *Marc de Bourgogne*.

Stoneware pot

FROMAGE FORT DU LYONNAIS

This is a Lyonnais specialty made with hardened cow or goat cheeses left to ferment in a covered stoneware pot at home or in a cheese shop. The strong, piquant smell and flavor go better with *marc* than with wine.

❑ *Marc*, ♀ Château Chalon (*jaune*) or Arbois Jaune

Rhône-Alpes (69)

Not defined

CACHAT

Both Cachat and the Confit d'Epoisses shown below are made by Georges Carbonel and his wife at their Restaurant in Aix-en-Provence. Cachat is made with young goat cheeses (Banon, p. 24) soaked in *marc*.
The cheese turns creamy from the fifteenth day onward.

Provence-Alpes-Côte d'Azur (13)

Not defined

Cachat is made in an earthenware dish

CONFIT D'EPOISSES

Originally from the village of Epoisses, the Confit is made with a young Epoisses cheese, which is soaked in white Burgundy and a little *marc* for a week; then the liquid is discarded and replaced with more white wine. Epoisses de Bourgogne (p. 133) is one of the strongest washed-crust cheeses. Its smell is pungent and the taste of salt is pronounced. After a week in *marc*, it tingles on the tongue, and tastes sharp and copperish. Two weeks later, it turns creamy. The salt appears to be well integrated and there is a sweetness that might be called metallic. It should be eaten with bread.

M. Carbonel says that in the past, there used to be many flavored cheeses made with salt, pepper, saffron, garlic, rosemary, thyme, and mustard. Meat was expensive, so people would eat a lot of bread with a little cheese. The cheeses had such a strong flavor that they made the bread taste better.

❏ *Marc* de Bourgogne

Provence-Alpes-Côte d'Azur (13)

Not defined

Confit d'Epoisses

CACHAILLE

ESSENTIAL FACTS

🍯 Sold in a pot
⚖ 7 oz net
🎨 Not defined
✓ All year

This *fromage fort* comes from the village of Puimichel. It is made by grating dry cheese into an earthenware pot, and adding *eau-de-vie*, pepper, olive oil, and fresh cheese up to three days old. It must be stirred well. Cachaille will keep for up to 20 years, if periodically topped off with new cheese. Affinage takes two to three months.

♥ Coteaux Varois *rosé*

 Provence-Alpes-Côte d'Azur (04)

 Raw

FROMAGÉE DU LARZAC

ESSENTIAL FACTS

🍯 Sold in an earthenware pot
⚖ 5.6 oz net
🎨 50%
✓ All year

Like Roquefort (p. 178) this sweet-tasting *fromage fort* comes from the Causse du Larzac in Rouergue. It is an *artisanal* cheese, made in an earthenware pot.

♥ Sainte Croix du Mont *moelleux*, Rivesaltes (VDN)

 Midi-Pyrénées (12)

 Not defined

PATEFINE FORT

ESSENTIAL FACTS

🍯 Sold in a plastic pot
⚖ 7 oz net
🎨 Not defined
✓ All year

This *artisanal* cheese from Saint-Georges-d'Espéranche in the department of Isère is sold in a plastic pot. The ingredients are 90% cow's milk cheese, white wine, spices, salt, and pepper. It is served spread on country bread and toast. The flavor is slightly sour.

♥ St. Joseph

 Rhône-Alpes (38)

 Not defined

Fromage frais

Fromage frais (fresh cheese) has to be made in the following way:
- It must be unripened and made from milk coagulated by lactic fermentation.
- Bacteria, such as lactic ferment, must be active in the cheese when sold.
- It must contain 0.5 oz dry matter per 3.5 oz of cheese.
- It should be eaten soon after production. The best-eaten-by date must be clearly indicated.
- Pasteurized milk is usually used. There are some *fermier*, raw-milk *fromages frais*.
- Depending on the fat content, *maigre, allégé, double*, and *triple-crème* versions (p. 213) are produced.

COMPARISONS BETWEEN THE COMPOSITION OF FROMAGE FRAIS AND OTHER CHEESES PER 3.5 OZ

	WATER	DRY MATTER	FAT CONTENT
Fromage frais	3 oz	0.5 oz	45%
Camembert	2 oz	1.6 oz	45%
Cantal	1.5 oz	2 oz	45%
Comté	1.3 oz	2.2 oz	45%
Roquefort	1.6 oz	2 oz	52%

BROUSSE DU ROVE

The word *brousser* means to beat or stir in Provençal. This *artisanal* cheese is called Brousse because its curd is beaten before being drained. It was also known as *fromage frais de corne*, meaning fresh cheese in a horn, because it used to be poured into sheep's horns. It is liquid, light, sweet, and mild, with a slight smell of milk.

♀ Côtes de Provence *blanc* or *rosé*

 Provence-Alpes-Côtes d'Azur (13)

 Not defined

ESSENTIAL FACTS

▣ 3.5 in high plastic cones

⬚ 45%

✔ All year; December to June for ewe's-milk cheese

CERVELLE DE CANUT / CLAQUERET LYONNAIS

This is the traditional way of eating *fromage frais* in the Lyonnais region. Shallots, garlic, parsley, chervil, chives, and other herbs are mixed with well-drained, fresh white, *fromage blanc* (p. 145). The cool, sour flavor goes well with toasted bread. The cheese is occasionally served chilled at the end of a meal.

♀ St. Véran, Mâcon

 Rhône-Alpes (69)

 Not defined

CHÈVRE FRAIS

ESSENTIAL FACTS

⊖ 2.4 in
   diameter
   2 in high
🏋 4.4 oz
🗋 45%
✔ All year

This *artisanal* cheese is made in the same region as Selles-sur-Cher AOC (p. 83) in the province of Berry. It has a gentle, sweet smell of goat's milk.

Ÿ Quincy

Centre
(41)

Not defined

FAISSELLE DE CHÈVRE

ESSENTIAL FACTS

⊖ In a pot
🗋 Not defined
✔ Spring to
   autumn

The name of this *fermier* cheese from Rouergue comes from the word *faisselle*, meaning the basket in which the curd is drained. The *industriel* version of Faisselle, made with cow's milk can be found anywhere in France. It is sold in plastic pots and is usually eaten with a spoon.

❢ Côtes d'Auvergne

Midi-Pyrénées
(12)

Raw

*Shaped in a
gauze-lined container*

FONTAINEBLEAU

ESSENTIAL FACTS

🗋 60%
✔ All year

This creamy *fromage frais* is thought to originate from a village near the Forêt de Fontainebleau. It is an *artisanal* blend of whipped cream and *fromage frais* that may be made by the *fromager*. The flavor is mild, sweet, and light, more like a cream cake than a cheese. Try it with crystallized fruit.

Ÿ Maury, Banyuls (VDN);
❢ Bordeaux (with crystallized fruit)

Ile-de-France
(77)

Pasteurized

FROMAGE BLANC

There are two kinds of *fromage blanc*. The first is young cheese which has been drained and shaped in a mold. The second (shown here) is cheese that has undergone lactic fermentation only. It is slightly drained and sold by weight. *Fromage blanc* makes a refreshing, milky dish with a slightly sweet and sour taste.

🍷 Beaujolais, 🍷 Coteaux du Layon *moelleux*, Vouvray *moelleux* (dessert)

ESSENTIAL FACTS
- 🥣 In a pot
- 🗓 40%
- ✔ All year

Throughout France

Pasteurized

May be served with salt, pepper, and chives, or as a dessert with sugar, jam, honey or fruit.

FROMAGE BLANC FERMIER

This *fromage blanc* is a *fermier* cheese made in the small town of Marciac in the department of Gers in Gascogne. Like the Fromage blanc shown above, it makes a refreshing, milky dish and has a slightly sweet and sour taste.

🍷 Tursan

ESSENTIAL FACTS
- 🥣 3.5 in wide
  4 in long
  1.4 in high
- ⚖ 7 oz
- 🗓 Not defined
- ✔ Spring to autumn

Midi-Pyrénées (32)

Raw

FROMAGE FRAIS DE NÎMES

This *artisanal*-produced *fromage frais* comes from Languedoc. It is decorated with a bay leaf, the aroma of which blends with the milk of the cheese. It has a smooth texture and a mildly acidic flavor with a hint of sweetness.

🍷 Faugères

ESSENTIAL FACTS
- 🥣 3.2 in diameter
  0.8 in high
- ⚖ 5.3 oz
- 🗓 Not defined
- ✔ All year

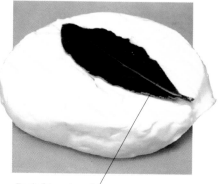

Bay leaf decorates and flavors the cheese

Languedoc-Roussillon (30)

Raw

Bay leaf /   Juniper berry

ESSENTIAL FACTS
- ⊖ 2.8 in diameter
  1.2 in high
- 🔟 8.8 oz
- ☐ 45%
- ✓ December to summer (ewe's-milk cheese); all year (cow's-milk cheese)

GARDIAN

These little *fromage frais* are produced in the Provençal department of Boûches-du-Rhône. They are made with cow or ewe's milk, sprinkled with pepper and *herbes de Provence*, and decorated with a bay leaf. Production is solely *fermier*.

♉ Côtes de Provence *rosé*

Provence-Alpes-Côte d' Azur (13)

Not defined

ESSENTIAL FACTS
- ⊖ Sold in an earthenware pot.
- ☐ 45–50%
- ✓ December to June

GASTANBERRA

Gastanberra means coagulated ewe's milk in the Pays Basque, which is where this *fermier* cheese is produced. One woman makes the cheese, while her daughter-in-law takes it to market. The buyer must return the earthenware pot in which the cheese is sold. It tastes like solidified milk.

♉ Irouléguy

Aquitaine (64)

Raw

ESSENTIAL FACTS
- ⊖ 4 in wide
  4 in long
  1.4 in high
- ☐ 45%
- ✓ All year

GOURNAY FRAIS

This is an *artisanal* cheese from Pays de Bray in the department of Seine-Maritime in Normandie.

♉ Bordeaux, Bourgogne, Côtes du Rhône

Haute-Normandie (76)

Not defined

PETIT-SUISSE

These popular *artisanal* and *industriel* cheeses were invented around 1850 by a Swiss worker a cheese dairy in Normandie. Sold by the half-dozen, they have a sweet-and-sour flavor, with a very soft pâte. These little cheeses are often served with jam or coffee.

❢ Bordeaux, Bourgogne, Côtes du Rhône

ESSENTIAL FACTS

⊖ 1.2 in diameter
  1.6 in high
⚖ 1 oz; 2 oz (large)
♣ 23% min;
⬦ 40% min.(large)
✓ All year

Very soft, fresh, even-textured pâte

 Throughout France

 Pasteurized, with cream

SÉGALOU

The name of this *fermier* cheese comes from the area of production, called Ségala, in the south of the Quercy. Ségala is a poor region in the Tarn, where only rye (*seigle*) can be grown. Although fresh, the cheese shown here has already begun to ripen. It is supple and made from good milk and has a lingering aftertaste.

❢ Gaillac, Cahors

ESSENTIAL FACTS

◇ 1.6 in diameter
  in the middle
  6 in long
⚖ 8.8 oz
⬦ 45%
✓ All year

 Midi-Pyrénées (81)

 Raw

VACHE FRAIS

This unsalted *fermier* cheese is produced in the Béarn by M. A. Penen. Rennet is added to the milk from the evening milking, and one hour later the curd is molded and left to drain overnight. The fresh cheese is taken to market next day.

❢ Tursan

ESSENTIAL FACTS

⊖ 3 in diameter
  1.6 in high
⚖ 10.5 oz
✓ All year

 Aquitaine (64)

 Raw

Fromage de lactosérum

Fromages de lactosérum are obtained by the coagulation or precipitation of *lactosérum,* or whey. These low-fat cheeses may be concentrated, and other dairy products may be added. One of the most famous whey cheeses is Brocciu (p. 116) from Corsica, which is the only whey cheese to have been granted AOC status.

Whey is the liquid extracted when the milk coagulates during cheesemaking. Most of the protein and fat remains in the curd and becomes the main constituent of the cheese, but some of it is lost in the thin, milky whey, which is commonly called *petit-lait.* This liquid still contains a number of nutritious elements, such as protein, fat, and minerals.

Fromage de lactosérum is made from a secondary coagulation (usually by heat) to recoup the residual protein and fat before the whey is finally discarded. It is a useful and profitable by-product of cheese.

Whey cheeses should have a sweet, mild flavor of the milk and may be spread on bread as a savory snack, or eaten as a dessert on their own or with jam.

Fresh, soft pâte – whey is heated, coagulated, and drained

ESSENTIAL FACTS
- ◒ 4 in diameter 2 in high
- ⚖ 13 oz
- ⊡ Not defined
- ✔ All year

BREBIS FRAIS DU CAUSSEDOU

This *fermier* cheese from the Poux Del Mas farm in the department of the Lot, is neither salty nor acid, but mildly sweet. The flavor and strength of the milk produced by ewes grazing on the plateaus of Quercy is pronounced.

♀ Bergerac, Gaillac

 Midi-Pyrénées (46)

 Whey of raw milk

Fresh, soft pâte – whey is heated, coagulated, and drained

 Cheese is shaped by container

ESSENTIAL FACTS
- ⊌ In a pot
- ⊡ 30%
- ✔ December to June

BREUIL / CENBERONA

This low-fat *fermier* cheese from the Pays Basque is called Breuil in French, and Cenberona in Basque. It has a mild milky smell and supple texture. Traditionally it is served as a breakfast dish, with strong coffee spooned over it. The locals claim that its acidity and fat blend well with the coffee. For dessert, it is eaten with sugar and Armagnac.

⊡ Coffee, Armagnac

Aquitaine (64)

 Whey of raw milk

GREUILH

This is a *fermier* cheese from the Vallée d'Ossau in Béarn. Greuilh may be eaten by itself or as dessert with jam. It is light and refreshing and goes especially well with quince jam. Sold in vacuum-packs, this cheese should be eaten within 21 days.

❢ Tursan

ESSENTIAL FACTS

⚖ Vacuum-packs of 4.4–6.6 lbs; also sold by weight

▭ Not defined

✓ December to end of June

Fresh, soft pâte – whey is heated, coagulated, and drained

Aquitaine (64)

Whey of raw milk

SÉRAC

This *fermier* cheese from Savoie is delicious by itself or mixed with herbs and olive oil and spread on toast. A larger version of this cheese is made with whey from Beaufort cheese (p. 26).

⅋ Roussette de Savoie

ESSENTIAL FACTS

Size varies according to container

▭ Not defined

✓ Spring to autumn (goat's cheese); all year (cow's cheese)

Fresh, soft pâte – whey is heated, coagulated, and drained

Rhône-Alpes (73)

Whey of raw ewe or goat's milk

Nutritional values of cheese

Cheese is recommended for children and old people because of its high nutritional value. Compared with milk, it contains the same nutrients although in greater concentration, with quality fats, proteins, minerals (calcium, phosphorus), and vitamins (A, B, and so on), but less water. The proteins change into amino acids and are easy to absorb. Calcium, which is abundant, joins with the amino acids and is equally easily absorbed. Cheese also contains a lot of beta carotene (vitamin A); the only elements lacking are vitamin C and fiber. Eaten with fruit and vegetables, cheese offers an almost complete diet.

NUTRITIONAL VALUES OF CHEESE PER 3.5 OZ

	PROTEINS	FAT CONTENT	CALCIUM	ENERGY
Fromage frais (fresh cheese)	0.3 oz	0.3 oz	75–170 mg	44–160 kcal
Soft cheese (e.g. Camembert)	0.7 oz	0.8 oz	150–380 mg	260–350 kcal
Uncooked, pressed cheese (e.g. Tomme)	0.8 oz	1 oz	657–865 mg	326 384 kcal
Cooked, pressed cheese (e.g. Comté)	1 oz	1 oz	900–1100 mg	390–400 kcal
Blue mold cheese (e.g. Roquefort)	0.7 oz	0.4 oz	722–870 mg	414 kcal
Chicken egg	0.4 oz	1 oz	65 mg	156 kcal

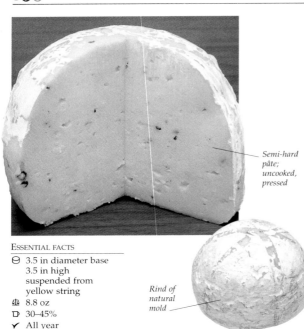

Semi-hard
pâte;
uncooked,
pressed

GAPERON

The name Gaperon may derive from the word *gap* or *gape*, which means buttermilk in the local dialect of the Auvergne. In the past, when butter was made in a butter churn, the liquid left in the churn, called *lait de beurre*, (buttermilk) or *lait battu* (beaten milk); was mixed with fresh milk to make Gaperon.

This *artisanal* cheese has a hard, dry rind, while the pâte, which contains garlic and ground pepper, is elastic. The flavor is tingling and rough. This is a low-fat cheese, cured on a hook by the fire, which explains the tang of smoke. Affinage takes one to two months.

❦ Côtes d'Auvergne

Rind of
natural
mold

ESSENTIAL FACTS

⊖ 3.5 in diameter base
   3.5 in high
   suspended from
   yellow string
⚖ 8.8 oz
♉ 30–45%
✔ All year

Auvergne (63)

Raw, pasteurized, whole, partly skimmed

GRATARON D'ARÈCHES

The *fermier* cheese shown here has been ripened for four weeks. It is salty and sticky, and made from strong milk in a *chalet* in the Beaufort region of Savoie. During the affinage of four weeks, it is rubbed regularly with brine and turned.

❦ Crépy, Seyssel

Soft pâte; uncooked,
slightly pressed

ESSENTIAL FACTS

⊖ 4.3 in diameter
   1.6 in high
⚖ 14 oz
♉ 45%
✔ Spring to autumn

Washed
rind

Rhône-Alpes (73)

Raw

LANGRES (AOC)

As the name indicates, this *artisanal* cheese originates from the high plains of Langres in Champagne. It is shaped like a cylinder and has a deep well on top called a *fontaine*, a kind of basin into which Champagne or *marc* may be poured. This is a pleasant way to eat this cheese and is characteristic of wine-producing regions.

The surface of the cheese is sticky, wet, and shiny, and has a pronounced smell. The pâte is firm and supple, and melts in the mouth, releasing a complex mixture of aromas. The salt too is strong, yet Langres is a milder cheese than Epoisses de Bourgogne (p. 133). The cheeses shown are completely ripe.

Langres is produced in a large and a small version. Affinage usually takes five to six weeks within the areas specified by the AOC. The cheeses are placed in a cellar at a humidity of 95%, where they are regularly rubbed with brine, either using a damp cloth or by hand. The minimum permitted affinage is 21 days for the large cheeses and 15 days for the small ones. A red dye extracted from the seeds of the American annatto tree is applied to color the rind. This is called *rocou* in French and is added to other cheeses and sometimes to butter.

❏ *Marc* de Champagne

White to light-beige pâte, becomes softer toward center; uncooked, unpressed

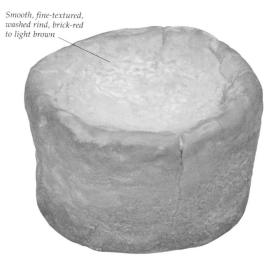

Smooth, fine-textured, washed rind, brick-red to light brown

AOC REGULATIONS: LANGRES

1. The sliced curd must be neither washed nor kneaded. (Concentrated or reconstituted milk is not allowed.)

2. It is permitted to add annatto to the brine applied when rubbing the cheese in order to impart a red colouring to the rind.

AOC GRANTED 1975

Champagne-Ardenne (52); Lorraine (88); Bourgogne (21)   Pasteurized

ESSENTIAL FACTS

- ◯ 10 in diameter, 3 in high (large); 3.5 diameter, 2.4 in high (small)
- ⚖ 1.8 lbs min. (large); 5.3 oz min. (small)
- ⁘ 1.5 oz min. per 3.5 oz cheese
- ⛉ 50% min., 0.8 oz min. per 3.5 oz cheese
- ✓ All year

Livarot (AOC)

This *artisanal* or *industriel* cheese was named after a village in Normandie. Its nickname is the Colonel because it is bound with straps of rush or paper reminiscent of a Colonel's stripes.

Both the smell and taste of Livarot have thinned over the years. Choose a cheese that is very ripe. There should, however, be no smell of ammonia since this indicates that the cheese may be past its best.

Livarot is very strong. The rind is washed and colored with annatto (p. 148), and sticks to the fingers. The ripe pâte has no elasticity and feels heavy and moist on the tongue. The cheese dissolves in the mouth, with a spicy flavor, close to that of hung meat. The sweetness of milk and the smell of butter have gone.

Affinage takes at least three weeks, usually one to two months, during which time the cheese is washed in water or light brine and turned regularly.

♈ Tokay, Pinot Gris d'Alsace *vendage tardive*, ❗ Pomerol *jeune*

Soft pâte, uncooked, unpressed

Moist, washed rind

Essential Facts

◒ 5 in min. diameter
  2 in high
⚖ 1 lb
♣ 8 oz min. per cheese
⛃ 40% min., 3 oz min. per cheese
✓ All year

Basse-Normandie (14, 61)

Raw or pasteurized

MAMIROLLE

The flavor of this brick-shaped
cheese from the village of
Mamirolle in the department of
Doubs is sweet; the consistency
of the pâte is elastic and fine.
Mamirolle is a washed-rind cheese
made by students of the École
Nationale d'Industrie Laitière, a
type of school with a high standard
of learning and a tough admission
policy. It is also made by the Union
Agricole Comtoise at Besançon.
Affinage takes at least 15 days,
during which time the cheese is
washed in brine with annatto.

🍷 Arbois

Semi-hard, elastic pâte; uncooked, pressed

Franche-
Comté (25)

Pasteurized

Moist, brick-red, washed rind

ESSENTIAL FACTS

⬦ 6 in long
  3 in wide
  1.6 in high
⚖ 1.6 lbs
🔲 45%
✓ All year

Buying, storing, and tasting cheese

Buying cheese
• Choose a reputable, well-managed shop with helpful assistants. It should be clean and the cheeses cut in front of you. More important than variety is the quality and condition of the cheeses on sale.
• Learn to choose cheese first by eye and then by taste. With time your eyes and tongue will begin to work together.
• Do not buy more than you can eat. Larger pieces of pressed or cooked pressed cheeses (e.g. Emmental) usually keep well, as do well-ripened goat cheeses. Avoid prepackaged cheeses since they are often inferior to those cut in the shop.

Keeping and storing cheeses
• Cheeses contain living organisms that must not be cut off from air, yet it is important not to let a cheese dry out. As a rule, big pieces of cheese keep well.
• The ideal place for storing cheese is a cool, dark, well-ventilated room, though dark, refrigerators are often too airless.

• Cover the cut sides of a cheese only and let it breathe through its rind or crust. Wrap soft cheeses loosely. Use waxed or greaseproof paper rather than cling film.
• Do not store cheese with strong-smelling foods. As a cheese breathes it will absorb other aromas and may spoil.
• Small quantities of cheese may be stored in a refrigerator for short periods as long as they are wrapped in waxed or parchment paper as described above.

Tasting cheeses
• Let cold cheese warm up for about half an hour before eating to allow the flavor and aroma to develop. Cover it with a damp cheesecloth if the air is very dry.
• Cut the cheese into pieces, with an equal portion of rind as well as the heart and outer bits of the pâte (p. 221).
• Remove hard crusts depending on taste.
• Offer bread and wine with the cheese. There is nothingbeeter than well-matured cheese, crusty fresh bread, and a good wine.

Maroilles

Moist, brick red, washed rind

A Mignon (below and right), the small version of Maroilles

Soft pâte; uncooked, unpressed

MAROILLES (AOC)

This cheese is said to have been created in AD 962 by a monk in the northern town of Maroilles. Maroilles, also called Marolles, is a powerful *fermier* or *industriel* cheese. The pâte is golden, soft, and oily. The sweet taste lingers in the mouth. Affinage takes between two weeks and five months. During this time, the cheese is regularly turned and brushed. Repeated turnings and washings eliminate the natural white mold and promote the development of bacteria (red ferments) that form the distinctive red rind.

♀ Châteauneuf-du-Pape

ESSENTIAL FACTS

- ◈ 5 in square, 2 in high
- ⚖ 1.5 lbs
- ⁂ 13 oz min. per cheese
- ⃝ 45% min., 5.7 oz min. per cheese
- ✓ All year

AOC REGULATIONS: MAROILLES

1. The divided curd must not be washed.

2. Use of fungicides is forbidden.

3. Three sizes are permitted:
Sorbais: 5 in square, 1.6 in high, weight 1 lb with a minimum of 9.5 oz dry matter. Affinage of at least four weeks.
Mignon: 4.5 in square, 1 in high, weight 12.6 oz with a minimum of 6.4 oz dry matter. Affinage of at least three weeks.
Quart: 3.4 in square, 1 in high, weight 12 oz with a minimum of 3 oz dry matter. Affinage of at least two weeks.

AOC GRANTED, 1976

Picardie (02); Nord-Pas-de-Calais (59)

Raw or pasteurized

BAGUETTE LAONNAISE

This is an *industriel* cheese from the ancient city of Laon. It is usually brick-shaped, but baguette-shaped cheeses are available in the Avesnois and Thiérache areas. They are all strong and of the same family as Maroilles. No one seems to know whether the production of this cheese started after World War I or II. Affinage takes two months.

❢ Coteaux Champenois, Bouzy

ESSENTIAL FACTS

◇ 2.4 in wide
  6 in long
  2.4 in high
⚖ 1 lb
▽ 45%
✔ All year

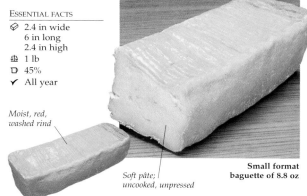

 Picardie (02)

 Pasteurized

Moist, red, washed rind

Soft pâte; uncooked, unpressed

Small format baguette of 8.8 oz

BOULETTE D'AVESNES

This *fermier* or *industriel* cheese is named after Avesnes, an ancient city near the Belgian border. It is made from buttermilk or Maroilles *fromage blanc* flavored with parsley, pepper, tarragon, and cloves, then shaped by hand and dyed with annatto or covered with paprika. Affinage takes two to three months; the *fermier* version is washed with beer.

❢ Bourgogne Passetoutgrains

ESSENTIAL FACTS

◉ 3.2 in diameter at base 3 in high
⚖ 8.8 oz
▽ 45%
✔ All year

 Nord-Pas-de-Calais (59)

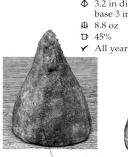

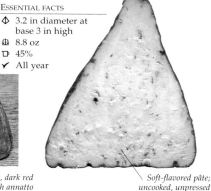

Raw or pasteurized

Moist, dark red colored rind with annatto or covered with paprika

Soft-flavored pâte; uncooked, unpressed

BOULETTE DE CAMBRAI

The region of Cambrai produces cereals and sugar beet, and is known for its *andouillettes* (tripe sausages). The Boulette de Cambrai is made by hand from *fromage frais*, to which salt, pepper, tarragon, parsley, and chives are added. It is only eaten fresh. Production may be *fermier* or *artisanal* with no affinage.

❢ Bourgogne Passetoutgrains, Beaujolais

ESSENTIAL FACTS

◉ 3 in base, 3 in high
⚖ 7 oz
▽ 45%
✔ All year

 Nord-Pas-de-Calais (59)

Raw or pasteurized

No rind

Fresh pâte

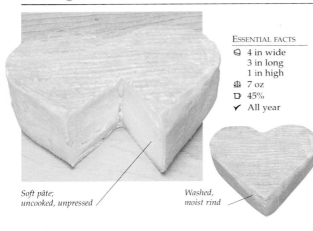

Soft pâte;
uncooked, unpressed

Washed,
moist rind

CŒUR D'ARRAS

ESSENTIAL FACTS
◁ 4 in wide
3 in long
1 in high
⚖ 7 oz
🗇 45%
✔ All year

Do not be put off by the pungent smell of this *artisanal* cheese from the Maroilles family. It has a strong flavor, and the weight of the cheese melts slowly and heavily on the tongue leaving a sweet, lingering aftertaste. Affinage takes three to four weeks, during which time the cheese is washed.

♥ Châteauneuf-du-Pape, Collioure

Nord-Pas-de-Calais (62)

Pasteurized

Soft pâte;
uncooked, unpressed

Washed,
humid rind

CŒUR D'AVESNES

ESSENTIAL FACTS
◁ 4 in wide
3 in long
1.4 in high
⚖ 7 oz
🗇 45%
✔ All year

This *artisanal* cheese is a good introduction to washed-rind cheeses. It has a light smell and flavor, with a lingering sweetness. The pâte is yellow and slightly elastic, with a few small holes. The slightly moist orange rind sticks to the fingers. Affinage takes three to four weeks, during which time the cheese is washed regularly.

❢ Bordeaux *supérieur*

Nord-Pas-de-Calais (59)

Pasteurized

Washed, brick-
red, moist rind

Soft, slightly
sticky pâte;
uncooked, unpressed

DAUPHIN

ESSENTIAL FACTS
⬭ Less than
2 in high
⚖ 10–17 oz
🗇 45%
✔ Spring to
autumn

Legend has it that Louis XIV so enjoyed this cheese when he visited the region that he allowed it to be called Dauphin, the name given to his son, the Crown Prince. It is made with a Maroilles cheese flavored with parsley, tarragon, pepper, and cloves before affinage, which takes two to four months. Both *artisanal* and *industriel* versions are produced.

❢ Côtes du Rhône

Nord-Pas-de-Calais (59),
Picardie (02)

Raw or pas-
teurized

GRIS DE LILLE

Also known as Puant de Lille, Puant Macéré, and Vieux Lille, this cheese is a ripened Maroilles soaked for three months in brine to give a salty taste. *Puant* means strong smelling and this cheese does have a putrefied smell – but the stronger it grows, the more the locals like it. It is said that northern miners ate this *artisanal* or *industriel* cheese down in the pit.

🍺 Local beer, 🍷 Champagne

ESSENTIAL FACTS
◈ 5 in square
  2 in high
⚖ 1.5–2 lbs
🗂 45%
✓ All year

Nord-Pas-de-Calais (62)

Raw or pasteurized

Gray, sweaty, sticky surface – no real rind

Soft, slightly elastic pâte; uncooked, unpressed

GUERBIGNY

This is an *artisanal* cheese produced in the village of the same name in the northern province of Picardy. It has a strong smell and flavor and a moist pâte that sticks to the tongue. It may be a cousin of the heart-shaped Rollot. Affinage takes five weeks.

🍷 Sancerre, Coteaux Champenois

ESSENTIAL FACTS
◔ 4 in wide
  3 in long
  1 in high
⚖ 8.8 oz
🗂 45%
✓ Spring to autumn

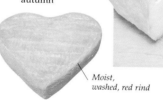

Picardie (80)

Raw, whole

Moist, washed, red rind

Soft pâte; uncooked, unpressed

ROLLOT

The first Rollot was a *fermier* cheese produced in the village of the same name. It has a distinct, salty flavor with a lingering bitterness. The cheese shown here is still young and mild but will be very strong when it ripens. There is also a heart-shaped *industriel* version. Affinage takes four weeks.

🍷 Sancerre, Coteaux Champenois

ESSENTIAL FACTS
◔ 3 in diameter
  1.4 in high
⚖ 10 oz
🗂 45%
✓ Spring to autumn

Picardie (80)

Raw or pasteurized

Washed, brick-red, moist rind

Soft, sticky pâte; uncooked, unpressed

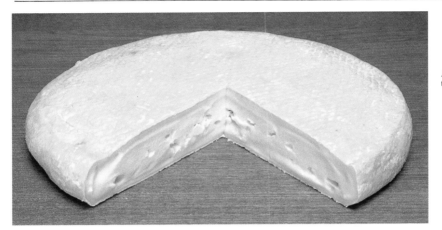

Affinage of
three weeks

Fresh, non-AOC cheese

MUNSTER / MUNSTER-GÉROMÉ (AOC)

This cheese is made under different names on either side of the Vosges mountains, in Alsace to the east and Lorraine to the west. In Alsace it is called Munster while in Lorraine it is known as Géromé. In 1978, the AOC Munster-Géromé united the two cheeses.

Appearance and flavor
The chief characteristics of this cheese are firstly the pungent smell and secondly the soft, smooth pâte, with the consistency of melting chocolate. The rind is brick-red, and the pâte is fine-textured and golden, slightly sticky and sweet, with the flavor of rich milk, as long as the cheese has been properly matured.

When this cheese is young, the rind is orange-yellow, while the pâte is pale cream with the consistency of brittle soap. A ripe Munster smells very strong. Locally, the cheese is eaten with cumin or potatoes boiled with their skins on. Cumin-flavored Munster may be bought ready-made.

Alsace (67, 68);
Lorraine (88,
54, 57);
Franche-Comté
(70, 90)

Raw or
pasteurized

The Munster cows

The milk used to make Munster comes from Vosgiennes cows, a breed that was imported from Scandinavia in the 18th century. The animals are strong and yield good-quality milk that is high in protein.

Production and affinage

Fermier, industriel, and *coopérative* versions of this cheese are produced. Concentrated or reconstituted milk is not permitted. Affinage must take place within the areas specified by the AOC and needs a minimum of three weeks (two weeks for Petit-Munster), although two to three months are more usual. During affinage, the cheeses are stored in a cellar at 59°F and 95–96% humidity, where they are rubbed with a light brine by cloth or by hand every two to three days. This causes the characteristic yellow to reddish-orange rind to develop.

Ɏ Gewürztraminer, Tokay, Pinot gris d'Alsace

Munster flavored with cumin

Rind is a yellow to reddish-orange in color due to red ferments (Bacterium linens)

Affinage of one week

Soft pâte; uncooked, unpressed

AOC Regulations: Munster

1. The divided curd must be neither washed nor kneaded before molding.

2. If the cheese is ripened in a region other than the place of production, the label must indicate the place of production and the place of affinage.

AOC GRANTED 1978

<small>ESSENTIAL FACTS</small>

- ⊖ 7.5 in diameter, 1–3 in high
  3–5 in diameter
  2–6 in high (Petit-Munster)
- ⚖ 1 lb min; 4 oz min. (Petit-Munster)
- ⁝ 1.6 oz per 3.5 oz cheese
- ⛁ 45% min., 0.7 oz per 3.5 oz cheese
- ✓ All year; summer to winter (*fermier*)

Natural, moist, beige rind

ESSENTIAL FACTS
- ⊖ 15.8 in diameter
  3.2 in high
- ⊕ 19.8 lbs
- ⁘ 1.8 oz min.
  per 3.5 oz cheese
- ▽ 45% min.
- ✓ All year

Semi-hard, ivory to pale yellow pâte; uncooked, pressed

MORBIER

The rind of Morbier is natural and rubbed, and the pâte supple and sweet. It is a mild cheese, originally made for personal consumption by the cheesemakers of Comté. In the past, soot was sprinkled on the fresh curd to prevent a rind from forming and keep insects away as it rested for the night at the bottom of a barrel. In the morning, leftover pieces of cheese were put on top to make the Morbier. Today, the black layer is a harmless vegetable product and purely decorative. The shape is round, with bulging sides and a horizontal black furrow through the middle. Production may be *artisanal*, *fermier*, *coopérative*, or *industriel*. Affinage takes at least 30 days, usually two months.

♀ Crépy, Seyssel

Franche-Comté (39, 25)

Raw or pasteurized

Moist affinage

Chestnut leaf

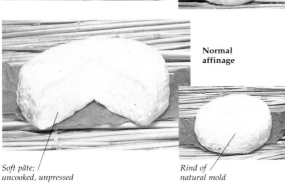

Normal affinage

Soft pâte; uncooked, unpressed

Rind of natural mold

MOTHAIS À LA FEUILLE

This *fermier* goat's cheese has a sticky rind and a melting pâte with a soft flavor. Goat cheeses are usually ripened in drier and better ventilated cellars than other cheeses. This one, however, has an affinage of three to four weeks in a cellar at almost 100% humidity, with no ventilation. The cheese rests on a chestnut or plane leaf to retain as much moisture as possible, and is turned every four to five days.

♥ Fleurie, ♀ Champagne *rosé*, ⌷ Coffee

ESSENTIAL FACTS
- ⊖ 3.9 in diameter, 1.2 in high
- ⊕ 8.8 oz
- ▽ 45%
- ✓ Spring to autumn

Poitou-Charentes (79)

Raw

MUROL

Traces of cloth are visible on the rind of this *industriel* cheese. The pâte is yellow when ripe, fine-textured, and very elastic. Its smell and flavor are mild. Murol is a Saint-Nectaire cheese (p. 184) with a hole in the middle. (The piece cut out makes the Murolait shown below.) Affinage takes one month.

ESSENTIAL FACTS

- 4.7 in diameter, 2 in high
- 1 lb
- 45%
- All year

Washed, orange-red, humid rind

Semi-hard, elastic pâte; uncooked, pressed

MUROLAIT

This cheese is made from the piece cut out of the Murol above.

♥ Fleurie, ♦ Champagne *rosé*

Auvergne (63)

 Pasteurized

ESSENTIAL FACTS

- 1.4 in diameter 1.8 in high
- 1.8 oz
- 45%
- All year

Red paraffin wax

NANTAIS / CURÉ

This is a cheese with many names, including Curé Nantais and Fromage du Pays Nantais dit du Curé, as well as Nantais/Curé. Originally round, and made by the *curé*, or curate of Vendée, it was brought into this region, which previously lacked cheeses, by a monk who was fleeing from the French Revolution. The rind is smooth and wet, the pâte golden and supple, with a few small holes. This is a strong small-scale *industriel* cheese. Affinage takes one month.

♦ Muscadet, Gros Plant

Pays de la Loire (44)

 Pasteurized

Soft, slightly elastic pâte; uncooked, unpressed

Washed, wet, orange-pink rind

ESSENTIAL FACTS

- 3.5 in square 1.2 in high
- 7.1 oz
- 40%
- All year

NEUFCHÂTEL (AOC)

This *fermier, industriel,* or *artisanal* cheese comes from the town of Neufchâtel in the Pays de Bray in northern Normandie. It may date from as far back as AD 1035, when Hugues I of Gournay, a town close to Neufchâtel, offered it as a donation to the Abbey of Sigy. Parisians discovered it through the famous food guide of the time, *Almanach des Gourmands,* (1803–1812). Neufchâtel lies only 182 miles from Paris and the proximity helped increase the popularity of the cheese in the capital.

The rind of the cheese is dry and velvety and crumbles when pinched, while the firm but supple pâte sinks under finger pressure.

Six different versions of Neufchâtel are produced: *bonde* and *double bonde,* which are a small and large cylinder; *carré,* which is square; *briquette,* which is a small brick shape; and a *cœur* and *grand cœur,* a large and small heart.

After a good affinage of at least ten days, usually three weeks, after

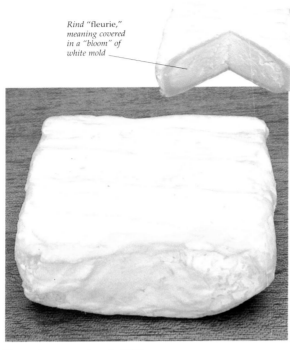

Rind "fleurie," meaning covered in a "bloom" of white mold

The *carré* or square-shaped version

Soft, firm, smooth pâte with no holes; uncooked, slightly pressed

renneting the cheese develops a covering of fine white mold. The mold flavors the cheese and gives it a pronounced moldy smell. The flavor goes well with a good, crusty bread.

❢ Pomerol, St. Emilion

The *bonde,* or cylinder-shaped version

Haute-Normandie (76); Picardie (60)

Raw or pasteurized

ESSENTIAL FACTS

- ◇ *Bonde*: 1.8 in diameter, 2.6 in high
- ⚖ 3.5 oz
- ◇ *Double bonde*: 2.3 in diameter, 3.2 in high
- ⚖ 7.1 oz
- ◇ *Carré*: 2.6 in square, 1 in high
- ⚖ 3.5 oz
- ◇ *Briquette*: 2 × 2.8 in, 1.2 in high
- ⚖ 3.5 oz
- ◙ *Cœur*: 3.9 in wide, 3.4 in long, 3.9 in high
- ⚖ 3.5 oz
- ◙ *Grand cœur*: 5.5 in wide, 4.1 in long, 2 in high
- ⚖ 1.3 lbs.
- ⁘ 1.4 oz min. per 3.5 oz cheese
- ☐ 45% min. 0.6 oz min. per 3.5 oz cheese
- ✓ Summer to winter (raw cheeses); all year (pasteurized cheeses)

> **AOC REGULATIONS: NEUFCHÂTEL**
>
> **1.** The curd, which has been drained beforehand in a cloth, must be kneaded by hand or by machine.
>
> **2.** Pieces of mature, blooming Neufchâtel are then added to it.
>
> AOC GRANTED, 1977

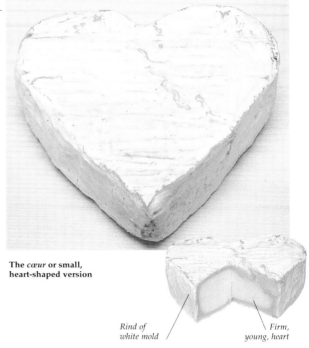

The *cœur* or small, heart-shaped version

Rind of white mold

Firm, young, heart

....

BONDARD / BONDE / BONDON

The point of affinage reached by the cheese shown here is just right. It has a white, velvety mold that forms a thick rind. The fat content is high and the pâte melting. When eaten with the rind, it tingles on the tongue and is rather salty. Production may be *fermier* or *artisanal*, with an affinage of two weeks to two months.

♀ Jasnières

ESSENTIAL FACTS

- ◇ 2 in diameter 3.2 in high
- ⚖ 7.1 oz
- ☐ 50–60%
- ✓ Summer to winter

Rind of white, velvety mold

Soft pâte; uncooked, unpressed

Haute-Normandie (76)

Enriched with cream

Olivet Cendré

This *artisanal* cheese is made in Olivet, a town on the Loire River. In May and June, the milk produced by cows grazing on the lush pastures is very rich, and the cheeses made then are kept for the harvesting season, when there will be more people working in the fields and vineyards. Olivet ripens slowly and used to be preserved in grapevine ashes. The pâte is slightly resistant to the bite and has a slight scent of mold. Affinage in ashes takes at least one month.

Soft pâte; uncooked, unpressed

🍷 Sancerre

ESSENTIAL FACTS
- ⊖ 4.7 in diameter
  1.2 in high
- ⚖ 8.8 oz
- 🜃 40–45%
- ✔ All year

Ash-gray rind

Centre (45)

Pasteurized

Olivet au Foin

This recently introduced cheese is a variation on the Olivet Cendré shown above. The white mold contains a few strands of hay. There is also a version covered in crushed pepper.

🍷 Sancerre

Soft pâte; uncooked, unpressed

Rind of white mold with a few strands of hay

ESSENTIAL FACTS
- ⊖ 3.9 in diameter
  0.8 in high
- ⚖ 8.8 oz
- 🜃 45%
- ✔ All year

Centre (45)

Pasteurized

PALOUSE DES ARAVIS (PUR CHÈVRE D'ALPAGE)

This is a *fermier* cheese from the town of Grand-Bornand in the chain of mountains called the Aravis on the edge of the Alps. In the local dialect, *palouse* means a dry disk, which aptly describes this cheese. The cheeses are made in a *chalet* during the summer, and cured over a long period. The pâte is drained under pressure and the rind washed at the beginning of the affinage, then left for the mold to expand naturally, and dry out. The total affinage takes between five and ten months. The rind is as hard as a rock, and the pâte dry and rough with a concentrated flavor.

♀ Vin Jaune du Jura, Alsace

Semi-hard pâte; uncooked, pressed

Rind of natural mold

Rhône-Alpes (74)

Raw

ESSENTIAL FACTS
- ⊖ 7.5 in diameter
  1.2 in high
- ⚖ 1.8 lbs
- ⮂ Not defined
- ⌄ Summer to winter

PAVÉ D'AUGE

In the center of almost every old French town, there is usually a church in a square of rough paving stones, called *pavés*. This *fermier* or *artisanal* cheese is shaped like one of those stones. It has a mild and supple pâte, with a relatively high fat content. The dry or washed rind bears a slight resemblance to Pont l'Evêque (p. 172). If you can find a Pavé d'Auge *fermier* that has rested long enough in its cellar, you will be able to taste the quality of the Normandie milk used in its production. Affinage takes two to three months.

🍺 Cidre du pays d'Auge,
♀ Champagne

Soft pâte; uncooked, unpressed

Dry or washed rind

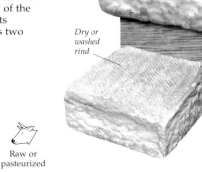

Basse-Normandie (14)

Raw or pasteurized

ESSENTIAL FACTS
- ◈ 4.3 in square
  2.4 in high
- ⚖ 28 oz
- ⮂ 50%
- ⌄ Summer to winter

Le Pavé du Plessis

The pâte of this cheese bounces slightly under finger pressure because it is full of small holes. Its taste is soft, with a flavor of salt. Le Pavé is an *artisanal* cheese from the Fromagerie du Plessis in Normandie, with an affinage of two to three months.

🍷 Haut Médoc, Margaux

Soft, yellow pâte; uncooked, unpressed

Rind of natural dry, white or orange-red mold

Haute-Normandie (27)

Raw

Pavé de Roubaix

Roubaix is a town in the north of France, which grew with the expansion of the textile industry. It is said that this cheese was a permanent fixture on the tables of the weavers and a symbol of wealth. Pavé de Roubaix has a dry, rock-hard rind, and the pâte is of the same carrot-orange color as that of Mimolette (p. 36). It is an *artisanal* cheese with an affinage at 59°F of one or even two years, during which time it is turned and brushed once a month. Sadly, there are only two or three people still making this cheese, and it is in danger of disappearing altogether.

🍷 Banyuls (VDN)

Semi-hard pâte; half-cooked, pressed

Natural, hard, dry rind

Nord-Pas-de-Calais (59)

Pasteurized

PÉLARDON DES CÉVENNES

This young goat cheese comes from the Cévennes region near Alès in Languedoc, where all small goat cheeses are called *pélardon*. It has almost no rind and a compact, nutty pâte. The balance of acidity and salt is just right and there is a full, rich, milky flavor with a lingering aftertaste. Both *fermier* and *artisanal* versions are produced, with an affinage of two to three weeks. It is a candidate for AOC status.

℣ Clairette du Languedoc

Soft pâte; uncooked, unpressed

Rind of natural mold

Languedoc-
Roussillon
(30, 48)

Raw

Affinage of 2 to 3 weeks

ESSENTIAL FACTS

◔ 2.8 in diameter
1.2 in high
⚖ 3.5 oz
🏷 45%
✔ Spring to autumn

PÉLARDON DES CORBIÈRES

This *fermier* goat cheese, another *pélardon*, comes from Lagrasse in the Corbières region on the Mediterranean coast. After one week of ripening, the rind shows a bloom of natural mold, and the pâte is supple. The flavor is slightly acidic, with no sweetness. It is a *fermier* cheese, with an affinage that lasts from one week onward.

℣ Côtes du Roussillon

Soft pâte; uncooked, unpressed

Rind of natural mold

Languedoc-
Roussillon
(11)

Raw

Affinage of more than 3 weeks

ESSENTIAL FACTS

◔ 2.8 in diameter
0.8 in high
⚖ 2.8 oz
🏷 45%
✔ All year

Persillé

The blue goat-milk cheeses that are produced throughout the mountainous Savoie region are called *persillés*. The blue color within the pâte comes from a very subtle natural mold that only becomes visible after a minimum affinage of three months. These cheeses may be made with pure goat's milk, or from a mixture of different milks. Cow's-milk cheeses with internal blue molds are most commonly known as *bleus*, although they may sometimes be called *persillés*, depending on the way the mold is distributed through the pâte. Cheeses in which the pâte is delicately marbled with the blue mold are described as *marbré*. If there are definite veins of blue mold, the cheese is described as *veiné* or *veineux*.

Soft pâte;
uncooked, unpressed

Rind of
natural mold

ESSENTIAL FACTS

⊖ 3.2 in diameter
   3.2 in high
⚖ 8.8–19 oz
🌡 45%
✓ From early
   summer

PERSILLÉ DE LA TARENTAISE

This *fermier* cheese from the Tarentaise area of Savoie has the typically acid tang of a young goat cheese. It has a white, fine-textured pâte, the blue mold is not yet apparent in the cheese shown here. Affinage usually takes one-and-a-half months, but may be shorter.

♀ Crépy

Rhône-
Alpes (73)

Raw

Soft pâte;
uncooked, unpressed

Rind of
natural mold

ESSENTIAL FACTS

⊖ 3.9 in diameter,
   3.2 in high
⚖ 1.3 lbs
🌡 Not defined
✓ Easter to Christmas

PERSILLÉ DE LA HAUTE-TARENTAISE

The Haute-Tarentaise, where this *fermier* cheese is made, lies at the source of the Isère River, which flows just one mile away from the Swiss border. It has an affinage of two to three months.

♀ Crépy

Rhône-
Alpes (73)

Raw

PERSILLÉ DE TIGNES

The original village of Tignes in Savoie, where this cheese was first made, was submerged in 1952 by an artificial lake. These cheeses now come from the new village that was built to replace it. The younger cheese (shown top right), has a raw, salty taste. As the cheese ripens, the crust hardens, and the pâte dries, becomes spicy, and breaks easily. It is said that the mustard-colored crust is a sign that the goats were fed on grass growing on sulphurous soil. This *fermier* cheese has an affinage of at least one-and-a-half months.

♀ Crépy

Affinage of one-and-a-half months

White, blue, natural mold is not visible

Soft pâte; uncooked, unpressed

ESSENTIAL FACTS
- ⊖ 4.3 in diamete, 2.4 in high
- ⚖ 16 oz
- ◻ Not defined
- ✔ From summer onward

Affinage of six months

Slightly bluish pâte

Rhône-Alpes (73)

Raw

PERSILLÉ DU SEMNOZ

The rock-hard crust of this *fermier* cheese is formed by a light brown mold, which peels off easily. The pâte is grayish-yellow, and the blue mold is not yet visible. The sticky consistency is evidence of the high-quality of the milks used in its production – usually equal parts of goat's and cow's milk. Affinage takes one to two months.

♀ Crépy

ESSENTIAL FACTS
- ⊖ 4.3 in diameter 2.4 in high
- ⚖ 16 oz
- ◻ 45%
- ✔ April to December

Rind of natural mold

Semi-hard pâte; uncooked, pressed

Rhône-Alpes (74)

Raw

Picodon

Dry, thin rind of
natural molds;
sometimes no mold

**Picodon de
l'Ardèche**

*Soft, white pâte
cuts cleanly*

❶

**Picodon de
l'Ardèche**

*Smooth, fine-
textured pâte*

❷

**Picodon de
l'Ardèche**

❸

**Picodon de
la Drôme**

❹

PICODON (AOC)

The region of Picodon straddles the Rhône River. The department of the Drôme lies to the east of the river, and the Ardèche to the west. The name of this cheese derives from the ancient language, Langue d'Oc, and means spicy.

The climate of the lower Rhône is dry. Mountain grass and shrubs, with strong aromas and flavors, grow short and thick there. The goats that feed on the mountain devour everything, including the shoots and leaves of trees. Their milk is the basis of this spicy cheese. Its pâte is so dry that the best way of getting all the taste out of it is to suck it.

Pélardon (p. 167) is often mistaken for Picodon. This is not surprising, given the similarity of their names and the fact that both are southern mountain cheeses that look like stones and but weigh less than 3.5 oz. Production may be *fermier*, *artisanal*, or *industriel*, with an affinage of at least twelve days from the day of renneting, although three to four weeks is more usual. AOC regulations forbid the addition of concentrated or powdered milk, lactic protein, and frozen curd.

♀ Rivesaltes (VDN)

ESSENTIAL FACTS

- ⊖ 3.2 in diameter
  1.2 in high
- ⚖ 3.5 oz
- ⁂ 1.4 oz min. per 3.5 oz cheese
- ⟁ 45% min., 0.6 oz min.
  per 3.5 oz cheese
- ✓ All year; spring to autumn (*fermier*)

Rhône-Alpes (07)
Languedoc-
Rousillon (30);
Provence-Alpes-
Côte-d'Azur (84)

Whole

The Picodons shown on these two pages demonstrate the variations in appearance and taste that may be found in these cheeses.

1. Picodon de l'Ardèche
This cheese weighs 1.6 oz.

2. Picodon de l'Ardèche
After an affinage of four weeks, this cheese weighs just 1.4 oz. It has a sticky pâte that smells of dry mold and has good acidity.

3. Picodon de l'Ardèche
This 2.1-oz cheese has an acid, salty flavor. It still needs another week.

4. Picodon de la Drôme
This cheese weighs 1.6 oz. The saltiness and sweetness have blended, and there is little acidity.

5. Picodon de Crest
This cheese is made with rich, high-quality milk, and its flavor has a good blend of salt, sweetness, and acidity. It weighs 2.1 oz.

6. Picodon de Dieulefit
This young cheese weighs 3.2 oz and has white mold and a soft pâte.

7. Picodon de Dieulefit
This cheese has shrunk to half its original size and weighs 1.4 oz. The rind is hard and colored by the mold. The sun of Provence and the aroma of herbs and grass open up in the mouth as the cheese melts.

8. Picodon du Dauphiné
This cheese is well ripened.

9. Picodon à l'huile d'olive
This cheese has been covered and marinated in olive oil flavored with bay leaves.

Picodon de Crest

Picodon de Dieulefit

This is a very young cheese

Pâte becomes hard and brittle as it ripens

Picodon de Dieulefit

Picodon du Dauphiné

Picodon à l'huile d'olive

AOC REGULATIONS: PICODON

1. The milk must be coagulated with a low quantity of rennet. (Concentrated or powdered milk, lactic protein, and frozen curd are not allowed.).

2. The cheese must be salted with dry (fine or semi-coarse) salt.

3. The label may say *affinage méthode Dieulefit*. This method of affinage consists of rubbing the surface of the cheese with water by hand after which the cheese is left to mature and soften for more than a month in covered earthenware jars.

AOC GRANTED 1983

PONT-L'EVÊQUE AOC

ESSENTIAL FACTS

◈ 4.3 in square
   1.2 in high
⚖ 12.6 oz
♣ 4.9 oz min.
   per cheese
Ⴖ 45%, 2.2 oz min.
   per cheese
✓ All year

This washed-rind cheese is probably the oldest Norman cheese still in production. Some people say that Pont-l'Evêque originated in an abbey, but this story has never been substantiated. A document from the 12th century says that "a good table always finishes with a *dessert d'angelot,*" which may be the old name for Pont l'Evêque. During the 17th century, cheeses made in the village of Pont l'Evêque were sent all over France and were very popular.

It takes three quarts of milk to make one Pont l'Evêque of 12.6 oz. After washing, the rind is moist and ocher in color. The pâte is creamy yellow, fine-textured, and smooth. It sinks under finger pressure but has no elasticity. As the cheese ripens, the rind grows sticky and reddens, and small holes spread through the pâte. Further ripening will result in a pâte that glistens with fat when cut. There are lingering traces of sweetness in the taste. Cheeses that are washed and turned during their affinage are strong, but this mature flavor is not present in younger cheeses.

Production of Pont l'Evêque may be *fermier, artisanal, coopérative,* or *industriel.* However, of the 4,100 tons produced in 1991, just over 2% (8.8 tons) were *fermier* cheeses. Affinage takes place within the specified areas at least two weeks from the date of production, although six weeks is more usual. During affinage, the cheeses are washed, brushed, and turned.

♈ Condrieu, ♊ Cider

Soft pâte; uncooked, unpressed

Washed, moist or dry rind

AOC REGULATIONS:
PONT-L'EVÊQUE

1. The curd must be divided, kneaded, and drained.

2. Three different sizes are produced:
Petit-Pont-l'Evêque (small size):
3.7 in square, 3 oz minimum dry matter per cheese.
Demi-Pont-l'Evêque (half-size):
4.5 in x 2.2 in, 2.5 oz minimum dry matter per cheese.
Grand-Pont-l'Evêque large size):
8.3 in square, 1.9 lbs minimum dry matter per cheese.

AOC GRANTED 1976

Basse-Normandie (14, 50, 61); Haute-Normandie (27, 76); Pays-de-la-Loire (53)

Raw or pasteurized

PORT-SALUT

This cheese is related to Port-du-Salut (below) with which it is often confused. It is produced in Entrammes in the department of Mayenne in northwest France.

The rind is slightly moist and uniformly colored, with regular traces of the plasticized cloth used in production. It has a very faint smell. The pâte is elastic under finger pressure and sticks to the knife when cut. It is cream-colored, soft, and supple, with little acidity and a slight aftertaste, the result of successful *industriel* cheesemaking. The development of production from monastery to large industry is proof of the great demand for this cheese. Affinage takes one month.

❢ Chinon, Bourgueil

Pays de la Loire (53)

Pasteurized

Semi-hard pâte; uncooked, pressed

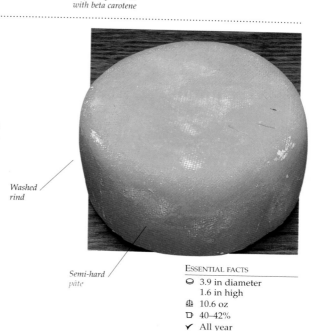

Washed rind artificially colored with beta carotene

ESSENTIAL FACTS

- ◯ 7.9 in diameter 1.6 in high
- ⚖ 3.3 lbs; 13.4 oz (small)
- ▷ 50%
- ✓ All year

PORT-DU-SALUT / ENTRAMMES

This cheese was first made in an abbey in around 1830. The method of production was then passed on to other abbeys. In 1959, the production rights and name were granted to the Société Anonyme des Fermiers Réunis. At this point, Port-Salut (above) began to be produced.

A small number of monks continued to make real Port-du-Salut, naming their cheese Entrammes, after the village where the Abbaye du Port-du-Salut once stood. They were forced to stop, unable to keep up with modernization, but their production method is still followed in abbeys and monasteries across France· it remains therefore, a rare cheese. Affinage takes at least one month.

Pays-de-la-Loire (53)

Pasteurized

Washed rind

Semi-hard pâte

ESSENTIAL FACTS

- ◯ 3.9 in diameter 1.6 in high
- ⚖ 10.6 oz
- ▷ 40–42%
- ✓ All year

PITHIVIERS AU FOIN

This cheese is produced in the small town of Bondaroy, near Pithiviers. It is also call Bondaroy au Foin. Farmers used to make it in summer, when milk was plentiful, and keep it in hay until the autumn or winter. During the grape harvests, when many people were hired, it would be served after meals or as a snack. Today, it is available all year round, but it has lost the pleasant smell of hay of the old *fermier* cheeses. The rind is white, with a slight smell of the mold. This is an *artisanal* cheese with an affinage of three weeks.

❦ Chinon, Bourgueil

Soft pâte; uncooked, unpressed

Rind of white mold sprinkled with hay

ESSENTIAL FACTS
- ⬭ 4.7 in diameter
  1 in high
- ⚖ 10.6 oz
- ◫ 45%
- ✔ All year

Centre
(45)

Pasteurized

White to light yellow pâte, with small holes; supple and firm; uncooked, pressed

RACLETTE

This cheese from Savoie, which may be either round or small, is also called Fromage à Raclette. The name derives from *racler*, meaning to scrape. The cheese is cut and heated so that it melts and can be scraped off with a knife. In the mountains, it is usually eaten with potatoes boiled in their skins and pickles. Its pâte is slightly hard but it melts well, with a light smell of mold when warm, and a full, milky flavor. This is an *artisanal* or *industriel* cheese, with an affinage of at least eight weeks.

❦ Vin de Savoie, Hautes Côtes de Beaune

ESSENTIAL FACTS
- ⬭ 14.2 in diameter, 3 in high
- ◈ 14.2 in square, 3 in high
- ⚖ 15.4 lbs (both formats)
- ⣿ 1.9 oz min. per 3.5 oz cheese
- ◫ 45% min., 0.8 oz min. per 3.5 oz cheese
- ✔ All year

Thin, golden-yellow to light brown rind with uncoated sides

Throughout France

Raw or pasteurized

REBLOCHON DE SAVOIE / REBLOCHON (AOC)

Freshness, youth, and tenderness are the most noticeable features of this mountain cheese from Savoie. The name derives from the verb *reblocher*, which means "to pinch a cow's udder again." This is because Reblochon is made with the thicker, richer milk from the second milking of Abondance, Montbéliard, and Tarine cows.

Reblochon is a well-proportioned cheese with a thin, orange-yellow to pink, tight, velvety rind. Its fresh, clear aroma comes from the mold, and it has a moist, smooth and supple, fatty pâte. The flavor opens in the mouth, leaving a delicately nutty aftertaste.

Production may be *fermier* (sometimes in a *chalet*), *coopérative* (*fruitière*), or *industriel*, with an affinage of at least two (usually three to four) weeks from the date of production. The temperature of the cellar must be kept below 61°F. A regular and a small version (Petit Reblochon) are produced

❢ Vin de Savoie, Pommard

Yellow to orange washed rind with natural white mold

Smooth, soft, ivory pâte; uncooked, slightly pressed

ESSENTIAL FACTS

- ⬯ 1.6 in diameter, 1.4 in high
- ⚖ 1.2 lbs
- ⁂ 1.6 oz min. per 3.5 oz cheese
- ♢ 45% min; 0.7 oz min. per 3.5 oz cheese
- ✔ Best in summer (*fermier* and *chalet*-made cheeses)

AOC REGULATIONS

1. The milk must be brought to the place of production as quickly as possible after each milking.

2. Renneting must be done within 24 hours (36 hours in winter) of the last milking.

3. *Fermier* cheeses must bear a green *casein* label.

AOC GRANTED 1976

Rhône-Alpes (73, 74)

Raw, whole

Rigotte

It is thought that cheeses very similar to *rigotte* may have been produced as early as Roman times.

The name *rigotte* is a local name for cheese in the regions of Isère, Rhône, and the Loire. The word probably derives from the French *recuit* or Italian *ricotta*, both of which mean "re-cooked". Despite the possible origins of the name, however, *rigotte* is not produced by recooking the milky whey, which is the method used to produce most whey

cheeses (see *fromage de lactosérum* on p. 148–149). *Rigotte* used to have a comparatively low fat content, but now it is almost always between 40 and 45%. Made mostly in factories or *artisanal* dairies and almost always of cow's milk, *rigotte* is normally allowed a week to drain before it goes on sale in shops and markets.

Rigottes are usually eaten while firm to the touch but soft inside and slightly sharp in flavor.

ESSENTIAL FACTS	
⊖	2 in diameter 1.6 in high
⚖	3 oz
⛭	50%
✓	All year

Soft pâte, uncooked, unpressed

Rind of natural mold

RIGOTTE D'ECHALAS

This is an *artisanal* cheese from Echalas in the Lyonnais province that is best eaten with toast. The rind on the cheese shown has just formed. The fat content is almost 50%, which accounts for its smoothness. Affinage takes at least two weeks.

🍷 Bourgogne

Rhône-Alpes (69)

Pasteurized

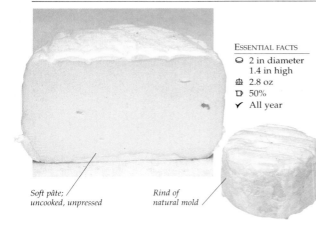

ESSENTIAL FACTS	
⊖	2 in diameter 1.4 in high
⚖	2.8 oz
⛭	50%
✓	All year

Soft pâte; uncooked, unpressed

Rind of natural mold

RIGOTTE DE SAINTE-COLOMBE

This *artisanal* cheese from Saint-Genix-sur-Guiers in Savoie should be eaten young. The rind on the cheese shown has not yet finished developing. The pâte is yellow, rich, fine-textured, and smooth, with a slightly sour flavor. Affinage takes at least 15 days.

🍷 Vin de Savoie, Hautes Côtes de Beaune

Rhône-Alpes (73)

Pasteurized

RIGOTTE DE CONDRIEU

This is a *fermier* cheese from the Lyonnais province. Most *rigottes* are made with cow's milk, but this is a pure goat's-milk cheese and therefore quite rare. The pâte is fine-textured and robust, with a delicate aroma of honey and acacia. Affinage takes up to three weeks, although the cheese can be eaten fresh.

♀ Condrieu

ESSENTIAL FACTS

⊖ 1.6 in diameter
   1.2 in high
⚖ 1.1 oz
🗋 40–45%
✓ Spring to autumn

Soft pâte; uncooked, unpressed

Rind of natural mold

Rhône-Alpes (69)

Raw

RIGOTTE DES ALPES

This *industriel* cheese from the Dauphiné has a slightly sour but pleasant taste. When soaked in white wine for several days, it gains a new flavor. It must be eaten with wine, and perhaps sprinkled with fresh ground pepper. Affinage takes at least ten days.

♀ Crépy, Seyssel

ESSENTIAL FACTS

⊖ 1.6 in diameter
   1.4 in high
⚖ 1.8 oz
🗋 45%
✓ All year

Rhône-Alpes (38, 69)

Pasteurized

Soft pâte; uncooked, unpressed

Almost no rind; reddish-yellow exterior, colored with annatto

Moist, soft, ivory and blue pâte, crumbles under finger pressure; uncooked, unpressed

ESSENTIAL FACTS

⊖ 7.9 in diameter
4.1 in high

⚖ 6.4 lbs

⁛ 1.8 oz min.
per 3.5 oz cheese

↧ 52% min., 1.1 oz
min. per 3.5 oz
cheese

✓ All year

VARIED APPEARANCE
The three Roquefort cheeses shown here were made by different producers. They show the variations in color and texture that can be caused by slight variations in methods of production.

ROQUEFORT (AOC)

A cheese like Roquefort is said to date back to the time of Pliny in ancient Rome and is mentioned in his book of AD 79. In 1411, Charles VI granted the people of Roquefort the monopoly of ripening the cheese in their caves as they had done for hundreds of years. In 1925, they obtained an AOC, the first in France. Very soon, though, there were fakes on the market.

Legal protection

In 1961, the Tribunal de Grande Instance at Millau decreed that although the cheeses could be made in many regions of southern France (see map below for specific departments), they could only be classed as true Roqueforts if they were ripened in the natural caves of Mont Combalou in the commune of Roquefort-sur-Soulzon. This eliminated imitation and the modern monopoly was established.

Appearance and flavor

With Stilton and Gorgonzola, Roquefort is one of the three greatest blue cheeses in the world. It has a clean, forceful flavor with strong salt, very different from the sweetness of milk. The pâte is damp and crumbly and should be cut with a pre-warmed knife. It melts in the mouth, leaving an amazing flavor of mold and salt. When mature, it is very strong. Roquefort goes well with pasta or salad. It is rich and spicy and is best eaten at the end of a dinner, for example, after venison. A young Roquefort might be accompanied by Bandol or Muscat de Rivesaltes, served with raisin bread. Match a ripe, gray-blue-veined Roquefort with Banyuls, a naturally sweet wine from Roussillon.

♀ Sauternes, Banyuls (VDN)

 (12, 81, 82, 31, 46, 33, 47, 64, 24, 40, 2A, 2B, 06, 13, 83, 04, 11, 30, 34, 48) Raw, whole

Production and affinage

Today, some 3.3 million cheeses per year are cured at Roquefort-sur-Soulzon. After Comté (p. 112), Roquefort is France's second most famous cheese. Around 60% of Roquefort cheeses are made by one company, the Société des Caves et des Producteurs Réunis. Roquefort is an *artisanal* or *industriel* cheese – there is no *fermier* version. All the cheeses carrying the name of Roquefort have been ripened for at least three months in natural caves as defined by the AOC. The usual affinage is four months, but may be extended by up to nine months. In a young cheese, the mold is pale and green, becoming bluer and then gray as it ripens, while small, blue-gray holes begin to form. If the cheese is left for a long time, the mold becomes dominant.

Cheese produced by the Société des Caves et des Producteurs Réunis

Affinage of ten days

Affinage of one month

Affinage of three months

Affinage of six months

AOC REGULATIONS: ROQUEFORT

1. The milk may not be delivered by the producers fewer than 20 days after lambing.

2. The renneting must take place within 48 hours at the latest after the last milking.

3. The powders and cultures of *Penicillium roqueforti* used must be prepared in France from traditional sources in the micro-climate of the natural caves in the specified area of the commune.

4. Dry salt must be used for salting.

5. The producers must keep a register available to the agents of control in which the quantities of milk delivered by the producers as well as the weight and number of cheeses made are entered every day.

6. The whole process of making and packing Roquefort cheeses from the moment they enter the caves until they are sold, must take place in the commune of Roquefort.

FULL AOC GRANTED 1979,
FOLLOWING THE ORIGINAL LAW OF 1924

KEY TO CROSS-SECTION OF MOUNTAIN AND CAVE FORMATION
ⓐ the mountain, worn down by water erosion many thousands of
years ago; ⓑ ancient cliff; ⓒ *fleurines*; ⓓ caves; ⓔ scree; ⓕ layers
of mud, which keep the humidity level at 95%; ⓖ the Combalou
mountain; ⓗ the River Soulzon, which flows down the mountain.

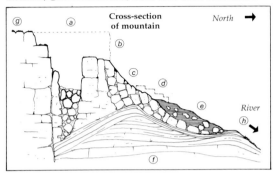

ⓖ ⓐ   **Cross-section**   *North* ➜
              of mountain
        ⓑ
               ⓒ
                ⓓ
                  ⓔ   *River*
                              ⓗ ➨
                  ⓕ

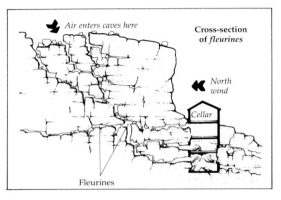

➤ *Air enters caves here*   **Cross-section**
                              of *fleurines*

                              ◀◀ *North*
                                    wind

                                  Cellar

              Fleurines

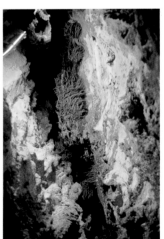

THE CAVES
This underground
labyrinth of tunnels has
changed little since the
17th century, and
extends over a depth of
11 levels. Electricity was
installed about
100 years ago. The
inside of the caves is
dark and cold. Except
in the main alley, the
rock along the walls is
damp, if not wet. There
is a constant draft of
moist air.

FLEURINES
The *fleurines* are similar
to chimneys, providing a
sophisticated ventilation
system through the caves.

The home of Roquefort

The birthplace of Roquefort lies
on a chalky mountain, called the
Combalou or Cambalou. It has a
flattish top, with slightly elevated
sides, and resembles a saddle. The
village of Roquefort hangs on a cliff
to the north. Some two-thirds of the
village is built into its side.

The mountain's partial collapse
was caused by water erosion in
prehistoric times. This geological
accident occurred three times; the
third collapse opened a series of
caves in the debris. Vertical faults
and fissures in these caves provide
natural ventilation and are known
as *fleurines*. These chimneys or wind
holes may be up to 328 ft high and
connect the caves to the outside
world. They serve as an immense
storage area that maintains a
constant temperature of 48°F and
humidity of 95%.

Temperature and ventilation

In winter, when the outside
temperature is low, warm air from
the caves is expelled through the
fleurines. The greater the number
of fresh cheeses being ripened, the
higher the temperature in the caves.
In summer, the temperature outside
is higher than that within. Hot air is
cooled at the shaded northern
surface of the cliff and then falls
to the muddy scree, where it is
humidified, and the draft from the
caves can suck it in. In this way, the
fleurines provide a highly
sophisticated system of ventilation.
A process of self-seeding also occurs
naturally, thanks to the minuscule
cheese particles attached to the
walls of the caves. These serve as a
kind of culture pool for *Penicillium
roqueforti* and yeasts. When wind
blows through the *fleurine*, the air
becomes laden with their spores.
From *Rocailleux Royaume de
Roquefort*, by Robert Aussibal, 1985.)

Penicillium roqueforti

The blue mold that is found only in
the caves of Roquefort is called
Penicillium roqueforti. It lives in
the soil and ferments the cheeses.
Bread is used to extract it from its

environment. Round rye and wheat loaves are specially baked and left where the airflow is strong. After six to eight weeks, they are covered with mold, inside and out. The crust is discarded and the inside is dried. Any bad mold is discarded.

Eight days after production, the white cheeses are taken to the caves, where they are pierced with needles. Carbon dioxide caused by fermentation in the pâte escapes, and spore-laden air is introduced. The mold multiplies until it spreads more or less evenly throughout. Then the cheese is wrapped in aluminum foil in order to eliminate contact with the air and prevent bad mold. It is thus an artificial environment that encourages the development of mold. The cheese is wrapped four weeks after its arrival in the cave.

The ewes of Roquefort

A law of July 1925 decreed that Roquefort must be made from ewe's milk only. Before then, small proportions of cow or goat's milk were allowed. It takes 4.8 quarts of milk to make 2.2 lbs of Roquefort. The ewes are Lacaune, Manechs, Basco-Béarnaise, and four Corsican breeds. A good ewe produces some 53 gallons of milk over six or seven months, equivalent to 99 lbs of Roquefort.

With the increase in demand for Roquefort at the beginning of the 20th century, the milk-producing regions were extended to the Pyrénées and Corsica. In 1930, producers of ewe's milk united with the makers of Roquefort to register the Label de la Brebis Rouge. This meant that minimum standards regarding such things as the fodder and quality of milk were laid down. The first milking machine appeared in 1932, and the maximum number of ewes milked by hand rose from 20 to 40 per day per farmer. Today, 300 ewes can be milked by one person in a single hour. Hygienic conditions have also been improved, with the milk being transferred automatically into vats.

The main cellar

Sheep eat while being milked by a milking machine.

SAINT-MARCELLIN

This small cheese from the Dauphiné region is mild, acidic, and salty. As it matures from a fresh to a dry, ripe cheese, the flavors develop. Saint-Marcellin is often made with cow's milk, but originally it was a goat's-milk cheese. Production may be *fermier*, *artisanal*, or *industriel*, with an affinage of two to six weeks.

❚ Côtes de Ventoux, Gigondas, Châteauneuf-du-Pape

ESSENTIAL FACTS

- ⊖ 2.8 in diameter
  0.8 in high
- ⚖ 2.8 oz min.
- ⋮ 1.8 oz min. per 3.5 oz cheese
- ♉ 40% min., 0.7 oz min. per
  3.5 oz cheese
- ✓ All year

Raw or pasteurized

Rhône-Alpes (38, 26)

Rind of natural mold

Soft pâte; uncooked, unpressed

This cheese has had a long and careful affinage. It should be chewed for a long time to extract all the flavors.

Dry, old cheese with a robust, ripe flavor

Fresh Saint-Marcellin

Ripe Saint-Marcellin with a fine flavor

LE PITCHOU

This is an *artisanal* specialty made by marinating Saint-Marcellin cheeses in grapeseed oil with ample amounts of *herbes de Provence*. The cheese has a strong, salty flavor with some sourness. It is particularly good eaten with bread.

🍷 Côtes du Rhône

Rhône-Alpes (38)

Pasteurized

Ripe Saint-Marcellin can be transported in pairs, tied together with a raffia band

Young Saint-Marcellin may be cut now or left to rest for two or three days.

le Pitchou

Le Pitchou

ESSENTIAL FACTS

- Sold in a plastic pot
- 50%
- ✓ All year

Typically fine, pure-white texture.

Goat-milk Saint-Marcellin

Rind of white yellow or red natural molds, according to level of ripening

Semi-hard pâte; uncooked, pressed

Affinage of just over six weeks

ESSENTIAL FACTS

⊖ 8.3 in diameter, 2 in high

⚖ 3.8 lbs

⊖ Petit Saint-Nectaire: 5 in diameter
   1.4 in high

⚖ 1.4 in min. for 3.5 oz of ripened cheese
   1.7 oz min for 3.5 oz of *fromage blanc*

⊅ 45% min., 0.8 oz min. for 3.5 oz

✓ Best in summer (*fermier*); all year
   (*industriel*)

MARK OF QUALITY
Casein label of Saint-Nectaire
fermier, indicating number of
the department (63), and
the codes of the maker (RG)
and commune (Y).

SAINT-NECTAIRE (AOC)

Like Cantal (p. 68) and Salers
(p. 70), this cheese, which is typical
of the Auvergne, was brought to
the table of Louis XIV by the
Maréchal de Sennecterre. It has a
grayish-purple rind, with dots and
stains of white, yellow, and red
molds. The pâte is supple with a
silky texture, heavy on the tongue,
and resistant to the bite. It melts in
the mouth to reveal a slight acidity.
It also tastes of well-marinated salt,
walnut, copper, and spices.

The soil, wild grass, and rich
raw milk produced by Salers cows
all contribute to this complex taste.
Saint-Nectaire made with
pasteurized milk does not have the
same interesting combination of
flavors. This cheese must be fully
ripe before eating. If the affinage
is too short, the smell and the taste
do not develop sufficiently.

One of the characteristics of
Saint-Nectaire is its distinctive
smell, which could be described as
old, the smell of a dark and humid
cellar, of rye straw on which it
ripened, and of mold. It is very
different from the sweet smell of
milk, and yet it smells delightful.

🍷 St. Estèphe

AOC REGULATIONS:
SAINT-NECTAIRE

1. The *fromages blancs* may be frozen
before they enter the *cave d'affinage*.
They must be thawed at below 54°F.

2. The rind may be colored by E153,
E160, E172, E180).

3. The green elliptic *casein* label must
indicate Saint-Nectaire *fermier* and
the registration number of the place
of production for *fermier* cheeses.
The label for *industriel* cheese
is square.

4. All *affineurs* of Saint-Nectaire must
declare themselves to the AOC.

AOC GRANTED 1979

Auvergne
(15, 63)

Raw or
pasteurized

How Saint-Nectaire is Made

Production on the farms of Saint-Nectaire starts immediately after the morning and evening milkings. Around 4 gallons of milk are needed for one cheese.

Affinage of one week

Coagulation

The milk is heated to 88–99°F. After renneting, it is left to rest for about one hour. The temperature and resting period depend on the weather and the amount of milk used. The curd is milled to the size of wheat grains. The whey is discarded. Finally, the curd is gathered into a big mass, called the *tomme*.

Molding and pressing

Affinage of just under a month

The *tomme* is cut into small cubes of less than 1 inch that are pressed into the mold by hand. Four to six molds are stacked, then pressed. The whey is discarded. The cheeses are taken out of the molds and the *casein* labels are applied. Next, the cheeses are salted, returned to the molds, and pressed for 12 hours, then turned and pressed again for another 12 hours. The cheeses are taken out of the molds and transferred to the drying room, at 48–54°F, for two to three days.

Affinage

The cheeses go into the *cave d'affinage* – at 48–52°F and 90–95% humidity – and are placed on rye straw. Ater two to three days they are washed in brine. Eight days later, they are washed for the second time. After one to two weeks of ripening, they are taken to the *affineur*. Only 5% of Saint-Nectaire cheeses are ripened at the farm.

Affinage of ten weeks on straw

Saint-Nectaire is a *fermier*, *coopérative*, or *industriel* cheese from the Auvergne. Affinage takes a minimum of three weeks, until the cheese is covered in red or yellow mold. It must take place in specified areas (departments of Cantal and Puy-de-Dôme) at a temperature of 42–54°F and almost 100% humidity.

White, yellow and, red mold

Saint-Nectaire *fermier*

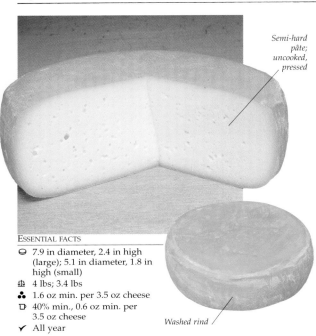

Semi-hard pâte; uncooked, pressed

SAINT-PAULIN

This is one of many cheeses modeled on Port-du-Salut (p. 173). Once made exclusively in monasteries, it is now produced by private companies, both *artisanal* and *industriel*, in Bretagne and Maine. Saint-Paulin was the first cheese to be made with pasteurized milk, in about 1930. Production of the raw-milk version, shown here, did not begin until 1990. The rind is thin and moist, the pâte tender with a sweet and discreetly salty taste. Affinage takes two to three weeks.

❢ Bordeaux *jeune fruité*

ESSENTIAL FACTS

- ◎ 7.9 in diameter, 2.4 in high (large); 5.1 in diameter, 1.8 in high (small)
- ⚖ 4 lbs; 3.4 lbs
- ♣ 1.6 oz min. per 3.5 oz cheese
- ☂ 40% min., 0.6 oz min. per 3.5 oz cheese
- ✓ All year

Washed rind

Throughout France

Pasteurized

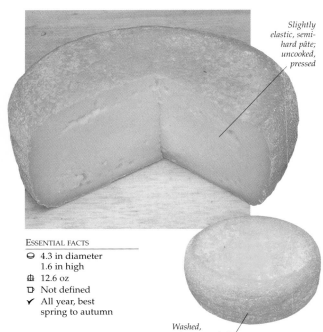

Slightly elastic, semi-hard pâte; uncooked, pressed

LE SAINT-WINOC

The name of this *fermier* cheese derives from the Abbey of Saint-Winoc in the extreme north of France, where it used to be made. Today, Mme. Degraeve is probably the only person to continue its production there. Its beer-washed rind is slightly moist, and the pâte sinks under finger pressure but springs back gently. The cheese shown here is extremely young. With further ripening, the taste and smell will become pungent, a characteristic of beer-washed rind cheeses. Affinage takes at least three weeks.

🍺 Local beer, ♟ Crémant d'Alsace

ESSENTIAL FACTS

- ◎ 4.3 in diameter 1.6 in high
- ⚖ 12.6 oz
- ☂ Not defined
- ✓ All year, best spring to autumn

Washed, pale orange rind

Nord-Pas-de-Calais (59)

Raw, skimmed

Soumaintrain

This *fermier*, *artisanal*, or *industriel* cheese from Bourgogne has a light, creamy pâte and is generally eaten young. The method of affinage is similar to Epoisses (p. 133) and Langres (p. 151) and usually takes six to eight weeks, during which time it is washed in brine.

❑ *Marc* de Bourgogne

Affinage of seven to eight weeks

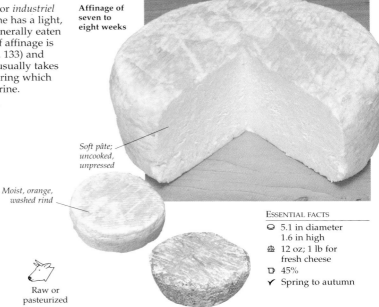

Soft pâte; uncooked, unpressed

Moist, orange, washed rind

Bourgogne (89, 21)

Raw or pasteurized

Essential facts

⊖ 5.1 in diameter
  1.6 in high
⚖ 12 oz; 1 lb for fresh cheese
◻ 45%
✓ Spring to autumn

Tamié

The Abbey of Tamié was founded in 1131 in the Bauges area of Savoie. It is an old monastery where cheese is made now by Trappist monks. Tamié is wrapped in blue paper, which is decorated with the white cross of Malta. It is a mild cheese from the same family as Reblochon (p. 175). Production is solely *artisanal*, with an affinage of at least one month, during which time the cheeses are washed in brine twice a week.

Ⴤ Roussette de Savoie

Semi-hard pâte; uncooked, pressed

Rhône-Alpes (73)

Raw, whole

Moist, pink, washed rind

Essential facts

⊖ 7.9 in diameter
  1.6 in high
⚖ 2.9 lbs
◻ 50%
✓ All year

Tomme

Tommes may be found in all regions of France. The name probably derives from Greek *tomos* and Latin *tomus*, meaning a slice or piece. Small cheeses made on small farms are generally called *tommes* or *tomes*; both spellings are used.

These cheeses require little milk and do not keep for long, but are easy to sell. *Tommes* may be made from cow, goat, or ewe's milk, or a mixture of milks. They are usually small to medium in size and rounded in shape. The pâte may be unheated and pressed and therefore elastic or soft and fresh as in Aligot (p. 74)). The best known *tomme* is probably Tomme de Savoie, made from cow's milk. There are goat *tommes* in Savoie as well as in the Pyrénées. The following pages give details of the great variety of *tommes* to be found in France.

Tomme de Savoie

The name Tomme de Savoie is a generic term, usually combined with the name of the village of production. It is said that there are nearly as many *tommes* in Savoie as there are mountains and valleys. Their rinds are hard and gray, with patches of yellow or red mold. The pâte has a sticky texture, with a smell of cellar and mold and a softer, more gentle taste than might be expected. *Tommes* made in the mountains are pressed to eliminate as much water as possible, so that they keep for longer. This also makes the pâte firm, hard, and elastic, with small holes. If there is not enough milk to make a very large cheese such as Beaufort (p. 26), then *tomme* is made instead. Butter is made with the cream and the remaining skimmed milk is used to make cheese. This is why *tommes* are traditionally low in fat (20–40%), although today whole-milk *tommes* are not uncommon. Some Tommes de Savoie have a regional quality guarantee – the "label Savoie" – indicated by a label showing four red hearts. Tomme de Savoie is currently a candidate for AOC status.

Tomme
de Savoie

TOMME DE SAVOIE

The cheeses shown here are all types of Tomme de Savoie. Production may be *fermier* (sometimes made in a *chalet*), *artisanal, coopérative,* or *industriel,* and affinage takes at least four weeks. Although most Tommes de Savoie are low in fat, a very low-fat version, Tomme de Savoie *maigre,* is also produced with a fat content of as little as 5%. The Vieille Tomme à la Pièce, shown below, is a Tomme de Savoie that has been given a very long affinage. The rind and pâte are riddled with holes, and the cheese has partially disintegrated.

Besides the Tommes de Savoie shown here, there is also the Tomme Label Savoie (see Tomme de Lullin on pages 194–195), which is produced according to regulations that are as strict and precise as those of the AOC. Affinage of this cheese takes at least six weeks.

🍷 Vin de Savoie, Hautes Côtes de Beaune

Tomme de Savoie *maigre:* 5% fat content

Rind of dry, hard, gray natural mold with patches of red and yellow

Tomme de Savoie *maigre:* **30% fat content**

Semi-hard pâte; uncooked, pressed

Rind of gray natural mold, with patches of red and yellow

ESSENTIAL FACTS

- ⬭ 11.8 in diameter
  3.2 in high
- ⚖ 6.6 lbs
- ▯ 40% min.
- ✓ All year (pasteurized); end of spring (raw milk); summer to winter (*chalet*)

Rhône-Alpes (73, 74)

Raw or pasteurized; whole or skimmed

Rind of
natural
mold

TOMME DE SAVOIE AU CUMIN

This cheese has a slightly viscous pâte containing cumin seeds, which grows wild in the Savoie region. The cloth in which it was wrapped during pressing has marked the rind. The cheese shown here has been ripened to perfection. Production of the cheese may be *fermier* or *artisanal*, with an affinage of three to four months.

♀ Condrieu

ESSENTIAL FACTS

- ⊖ 7.5 in diameter
  2.4 in high
- ⚖ 3.3 lbs
- ⧄ 30–40%
- ✔ All year depending on affinage

Semi-hard pâte; uncooked, pressed

Rhône-Alpes (74)

Raw or pasteurized

Rind of
natural
mold or
washed
rind

TOME ALPAGE DE LA VANOISE

The naturally red, mimosa-yellow and violet-gray mold of this cheese is reminiscent of a meadow full of wild flowers. The variety of colors in the rind is said to be due to the high level of carotene in the milk produced by cows grazing on Alpine meadows in the mountains of the Vanoise. This is a mild, full-flavored *fermier* cheese made in summer in a chalet. Affinage takes two to three months.

♀ Crozes Hermitage

ESSENTIAL FACTS

- ⊖ 7 in diameter
  2.4 in high
- ⚖ 4.4 lbs
- ⧄ 45%
- ✔ End of summer to winter

Semi-hard pâte; uncooked, pressed

Rhône-Alpes (73)

Raw, whole

TOMME GRASSE
FERMIÈRE DES BAUGES

This is a *fermier* cheese from the
Bauges mountains in the French
Alps. The cheese shown has been
made from whole milk and ripened
for three months. It has a thick
crust and a strong pâte. Affinage
takes 40 days to three months.

♀ Hermitage

Semi-hard
pâte;
uncooked,
pressed

Rhône-Alpes
(73)

Raw,
whole

Rind forms
naturally

ESSENTIAL FACTS

◯ 6.7 in diameter
   2 in high
⚖ 2.7 lb
▭ 45%
✓ Best from summer
   to winter

TOMME DU FAUCIGNY

The Faucigny region where this
artisanal cheese is made lies on the
edge of the Alps near the Swiss
border. The Tomme du Faucigny
has a reddish-brown rind covered
with natural gray and white mold.
The pâte, which is yellow when
ripe, is full of small holes and sinks
under finger pressure. It has a salty
flavor. Affinage takes four to five
months.

♀ Côtes du Jura

Pâte is
semi-hard;
uncooked,
pressed

Rhône-Alpes
(74)

Raw

Rind of
natural mold

ESSENTIAL FACTS

◯ 8 in diameter
   2.4 in high
⚖ 3.3 lbs
▭ 40%
✓ All year

TOMME DE LA FRASSE FERMIÈRE

This *fermier* cheese originates in the town of Cluses in the Faucigny region on the edge of the Alps. It has a solid crust covered with patches of natural red and white mold. The pâte is firm with holes throughout, yet the texture is supple in the mouth. The flavor is distinctly acid. Since the milk used in production varies in richness, the fat content is not defined. Affinage takes four to six months.

Ÿ Crépy

ESSENTIAL FACTS
- ⊖ 8 in diameter
  2.8 in high
- ⚖ 4.4 lbs
- ⊅ Not defined
- ✓ All year, especially summer to winter

Semi-hard pâte; uncooked, unpressed

Natural rind

Rhône-Alpes (74)

Raw

TOMME GRISE DE SEYSSEL

Semi-hard pâte; uncooked, pressed

This *artisanal* cheese is produced in the town of Seyssel on the Rhône River. The cheese shown weighs 3.5 lbs and is rather large for a tomme. It is still young but already has a strong smell. The gray mold on the rind is called *poils de chat*, meaning cat's fur. During the affinage of two to six months, the cheese is rubbed by hand until the "fur" shortens to form the crust, which then hardens and thickens.

Ÿ St. Péray

ESSENTIAL FACTS
- ⊖ 8 in diameter
  2.8 in high
- ⚖ 3.5 lbs
- ⊅ 40%
- ✓ All year

Rind forms naturally during affinage

Rhône-Alpes (74)

Raw

TOMME FERMIÈRE DES LINDARETS

The village of Lindarets where this *fermier* cheese is made lies close to the Swiss border at an altitude of 4,921 ft. The dry, brown, burned-looking crust is broken by patches of white mold and has a rough, uneven surface from a long affinage of six to eight months. The pâte, which is suffused with holes, is neither too dry nor too salty. The flavor opens as the cheese is chewed.

♈ Châteauneuf-du-Pape

Semi-hard pâte; uncooked, pressed

Rind of natural mold

Savoie (74)

Raw

ESSENTIAL FACTS
- ⊖ 7.5 in diameter 2.4 in high
- ⚖ 3.3 lbs
- ⛃ Not defined
- ✔ Spring to autumn

TOMME AU MARC DE RAISIN

This *fermier* cheese is made by soaking a ripened tomme in *marc* for a month in an airtight container. The heat caused by the fermentation heats the inside of the container, making the pâte tighten and become viscous. The taste of the *marc* permeates through to the heart of the cheese.

⛃ *Marc* de Savoie

Semi-hard pâte; uncooked, pressed

Rind appears naturally, covered with marc de raisins

Rhône-Alpes (73)

Raw

ESSENTIAL FACTS
- ⊖ 8.3 in diameter 2.4 in high
- ⚖ 3.75 lbs
- ⛃ 40%
- ✔ End of autumn to winter

ESSENTIAL FACTS

- ⬭ 7.1 in diameter
  3.2 in high
- ⚖ 4.4 lbs
- ⬭ 40% min.; 0.7 oz per
  3.5 oz cheese
- ✓ All year

*Rind of
natural mold*

*Semi-hard pâte;
uncooked, pressed*

*Rind of white
mold*

TOMME DE LULLIN

The village of Lullin, where this *coopérative* cheese is made lies high in the Alps. Tomme de Lullin is a Tomme Label Savoie (see p. 189), which is a regional guarantee of quality granted by the Association Marque Collective Savoie. Strict guidelines control the place of production of the milk, as well as the quality of the rennet, the animal fodder, the size and weight of the cheese, and the period of affinage. This label, which is specific to the Savoie region, is also applied to hams, sausages, and fruit.

Tomme de Lullin has a soft, mild-flavored pâte that has small holes throughout. It feels thick on the tongue, and melts in the mouth.

♀ Côtes du Rhône

HOW TOMME DE LULLIN IS MADE

Some 15 farms share the same place of production and hire a *fromager* to produce both Abondance and Tomme (p. 20) from the milk of 200 cows. A Tomme of 3.3 lbs needs 33 lbs cow's milk, while the much larger Abondance of 21 lbs requires 227 lbs of milk.

Coagulation

The morning milk is heated to 91°F and coagulated with rennet. The curd is cut then mixed while being heated to 98°F. After 30 minutes, it changes into rubbery grains.

Molding

The curd is put into cloth-lined molds. Once the whey has drained off, the "cheeses" are taken out of the molds and turned. The cloths are removed and replaced by plastic net and red *casein* labels bearing the fat content, department number, and place of production. The cheeses are returned to the molds.

Rhône-
Alpes
(74)

Raw

AFTER 48 HOURS
The cheese is still fresh and shows no signs of mold.

SEVEN OR EIGHT DAYS LATER
The characteristic "cat's fur" mold appears. This is brushed off.

AFTER 20 MORE DAYS
The hairs of the "fur" are soft and beginning to shorten and turn gray.

AFFINAGE OF FOUR WEEKS
After an affinage of four weeks, the gray rind is starting to form.

Pressing and salting

The molds are stacked to create gentle pressure on the cheeses and enable drainage to continue. About ten hours after coagulation, the cheeses are taken out of their molds and soaked in brine for 24 hours.

Affinage

Total affinage takes at least one-and-a-half months. Once salted, the cheeses are transferred to a cellar at 90–95% humidity and 54°F. Seven or eight days later, a mold resembling cat's fur forms on the cheeses. The mold is brushed. Its texture is like fine powder and its spores fill the air. This gray mold, also called *tomme grise*, is characteristic of the *tommes* of Savoie. It tastes of the soil and is the reason why the regions of production and location of the

ripening cellars are specifically defined. Cheeses from other areas are brought to Savoie for this graying process. After four weeks, the cheese is given to an *affineur* or a *fromager*, who will ripen it in a cellar.

MOLDING
Cloth-lined molds are filled with curds.

TURNING
The cheese is turned quickly by hand.

195

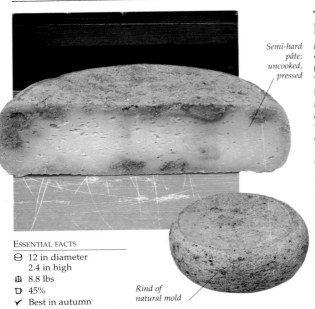

TOME DE MÉNAGE / BOUDANE

Semi-hard pâte; uncooked, pressed

De ménage means "household," which is an exact description of this homemade *fermier* cheese. The cheese's local name, *boudane*, is simply the dialect word for *tome*. The cheese shown has had an affinage of four months and is very mature with a smell of the cellar. Its pâte has a good, strong, fatty, consistency and is the color of egg yolk. Affinage usually takes two to three months.

♈ St. Joseph

ESSENTIAL FACTS
- ⊖ 12 in diameter
  2.4 in high
- ⚖ 8.8 lbs
- ◻ 45%
- ✔ Best in autumn

Rind of natural mold

Affinage of four months

Rhône-Alpes (73)

Raw

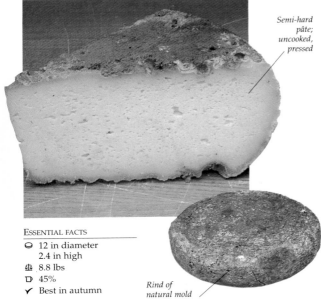

TOMME DU MONT CENIS

Semi-hard pâte; uncooked, pressed

This *fermier* cheese is produced in the area around Mont Cenis in the Alps, close to the Italian border. The pâte has small holes spread all over, and is moist, soft, and pleasantly sticky in the mouth. The taste of sweetness may be due to the alpine flowers on which the cows graze.

The cheese shown has the appearance of a typical alpine *tome*, with shades of gray, brown, red, and white mold. It was made in the month of September, just before the cows came down from the mountains at the end of the summer, making it one of the last *alpage* cheeses of the season. Affinage takes at least three months.

♈ Vinsobres

ESSENTIAL FACTS
- ⊖ 12 in diameter
  2.4 in high
- ⚖ 8.8 lbs
- ◻ 45%
- ✔ Best in autumn

Rind of natural mold

Rhône-Alpes (73)

Raw

TOMME DE THÔNES

This *fermier* cheese comes from the village of Thônes in the Aravis chain of mountains in the Alps. It has a hard, gray-brown crust covered with white mold. The pâte is soft and yellow. Affinage takes at least six weeks.

♀ Vin de pays de l'Ardéche

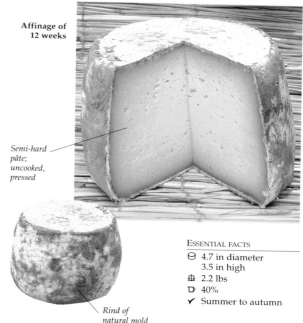

Affinage of 12 weeks

Semi-hard pâte; uncooked, pressed

Rind of natural mold

Rhône-Alpes (74)

Raw

ESSENTIAL FACTS
- ⊖ 4.7 in diameter 3.5 in high
- ⚖ 2.2 lbs
- ◻ 40%
- ✔ Summer to autumn

Tomme de Chèvre, Savoie

TOME DE CHÈVRE, BELLEVILLE

This mountain goat cheese is produced in the Vallée de Belleville in the Tarentaise region of Savoie. It is a pressed *fermier* cheese, with a thick, rubbery pâte riddled with holes. The cheese shown was made in September and kept in the cellar for 14 weeks, which is the usual period of affinage. This cheese is best eaten from autumn onward.

♀ Condrieu, Château Grillet

Semi-hard pâte; uncooked, pressed

Rind of natural mold

Rhône-Alpes (73)

Raw

ESSENTIAL FACTS
- ⊖ 6.7 in diameter, 2.8 in high
- ⚖ 4 lbs
- ◻ 45%
- ✔ All year; best in autumn

197

TOMME DE CHÈVRE D'ALPAGE, MORZINE

Semi-hard pâte; uncooked, pressed

Morzine, where this *fermier* cheese is made, is a well-known ski resort in northern Savoie, about six miles from the Swiss border. In summer, the region becomes a good grazing ground of Alpine pastures and is well known for its cow's- and goat's-milk tommes.

The cheese shown is a *tomme d'alpage* made in an alpine *chalet*. It has a dry rind, covered with a gray to pale blue mold with red dots. When the cheese is young, the pâte has a light, flowery smell that becomes stronger as it matures. Affinage takes from two to 12 months.

♀ Vin de Savoie, Bourgogne Aligoté

ESSENTIAL FACTS
- ⊖ 7.5 in diameter
  2. 8 in high
- 🔥 4.4 lbs
- 🄳 45%
- ✔ Best from autumn

Rind of natural mold

Rhône-Alpes (74)

Raw

TOMME DE CHÈVRE, VALLÉE DE MORZINE

Semi-hard pâte; uncooked, pressed

This is another *fermier* cheese produced from the milk of goats grazing in the alpine pastures of the Vallée de Morzine in northern Savoie. It has a moist and supple, reddish-brown rind and a heavy, cream-colored pâte that sticks to the knife. The pâte melts in the mouth and has a surprisingly full aftertaste. Affinage takes between one and two months, during which time the cheese is washed.

♀ Graves *sec*

ESSENTIAL FACTS
- ⊖ 8 in diameter
  1.6 in high
- 🔥 3 lbs
- 🄳 45%
- ✔ Spring to autumn

Washed, moist rind

Rhône-Alpes (74)

Raw

TOMME DE CHÈVRE, VALLÉE DE NOVEL

This *fermier* cheese comes from the area around Novel, a small village beside Lake Geneva, near the Swiss border. It is an attractive, moist cheese with a firm, mimosa-yellow pâte that slightly resists cutting. This cheese smells of the cellar and is very different from the goat cheeses of the Loire (p. 78). Affinage takes from four to five months.

❢ Vin de Savoie

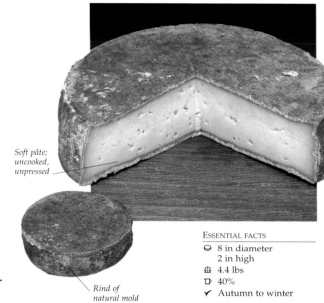

Soft pâte; uncooked, unpressed

Rind of natural mold

 Rhône-Alpes (74)

 Raw

ESSENTIAL FACTS
- ⊖ 8 in diameter 2 in high
- ⚖ 4.4 lbs
- Ⴃ 40%
- ✔ Autumn to winter

TOMME DE COURCHEVEL

This *fermier* goat cheese is produced in mountain *chalets* in the area around the town of Courchevel in the Alps. In the winter, the area is a famous Olympic sports center, but during the summer, the Alpine slopes provide excellent grazing for herds of goats. The cheese shown has a hard crust and a soft pâte, with a rich flavor. Affinage usually takes around two months.

♀ Condrieu

Semi-hard pâte; uncooked, pressed

Rind of natural mold

 Languedoc-Rousillon (48)

 Raw

ESSENTIAL FACTS
- ⊖ 10 in diameter 3 in high
- ⚖ 4.4 lbs
- Ⴃ 45%
- ✔ Summer to winter

*Semi-hard,
gray-yellow
pâte;
uncooked,
pressed*

TOME MI-CHÈVRE DU LÈCHERON

This *fermier* cheese, which is named after a local mountain called the Lècheron, was made in a *chalet* in the Massif de la Vanoise. A decree of 1988 defines *mi-chèvre*, meaning half-goat, as a cheese containing 50% goat's milk. The other half, made up of cow's milk, softens the flavor. The cheese shown was washed with brine at the beginning of its affinage, but after four or five months the crust was quite dry.

♈ Crépy

- ◯ 9.5 in diameter
  2 in high
- ⚖ 4.4 lbs
- 🌡 45%
- ✔ Summer to autumn

*Washed, dry,
white, brown,
and orange rind*

**Affinage of
four or five months**

Rhône-Alpes
(73)

Raw

TOMMETTE MI-CHÈVRE DES BAUGES

Tommette is a diminutive term, meaning a small *tomme*. The crust of this *fermier* cheese from the Massif des Bauges in Savoie is hard and dry, while the pâte is slightly moist, soft, and sticky. Affinage takes two to three months.

♈ Crépy

*Semi-hard pâte;
uncooked, pressed*

- ◯ 4.3 in diameter
  2 in high
- ⚖ 14 oz
- 🌡 45%
- ✔ Best in autumn

*Rind of natural
gray-brown mold*

Rhône-Alpes
(73)

Raw

Tome and Tomme

TOMME D'ARLES

This *fermier* cheese was originally produced in the village of Montlaux in the Alpes d'Haute Provence, but it disappeared some time ago. Production resumed in 1988; the cheese is made by two women with the milk from their small herd of 60 ewes. Their cheese has a soft, white pâte, which is barely ripened, and has a distinct flavor. Affinage is short, lasting only about 10 days.

♈ Cassis, Palette

Soft pâte; uncooked, unpressed

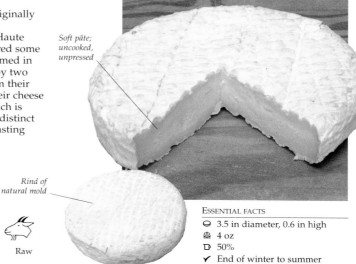

Rind of natural mold

Provence-Alpes-Côte d'Azur (04)

Raw

ESSENTIAL FACTS
- ⬭ 3.5 in diameter, 0.6 in high
- ⚖ 4 oz
- ⌷ 50%
- ☇ End of winter to summer

TOMME DE L'AVEYRON (PETITE)

This dry *fermier* cheese comes from the high plateaus of the Causse du Larzac in the department of Aveyron, from which it takes its name. The pâte is ivory-colored, moist, and filled with small holes. It has a very slight acidity and a fairly strong flavor considering its low fat content of only 20%. It is an ideal choice for people who love cheese but who have to count calories. Affinage takes from one to three-and-a-half months.

♟ Cahors

Soft pâte; uncooked, unpressed

Rind of natural mold

Midi-Pyrénées (12)

Raw

ESSENTIAL FACTS
- ⬭ 4.7 in diameter
  1 in high
- ⚖ 10–12 oz
- ⌷ 20% or 40%
- ☇ Spring to autumn

201

TOME DE BANON

This *artisanal* cheese takes its name from the town of Banon in Provence. A blue and white natural mold has just appeared on the golden rind of the cheese shown here. The sprig of savory on top is not merely decorative but adds the scent of Provence. Its pâte is fine in texture with a light smell of goat's milk and savory. Affinage lasts from five days to three weeks.

♀ Cassis

Soft pâte; uncooked, unpressed

ESSENTIAL FACTS
- 2.4 in diameter
  0.8 in high
- 2.7 oz
- 45%
- All year

Rind of blue and white, natural mold

 Provence-Alpes-Côte d'Azur (04)

 Raw

TOMME DU BOUGNAT

A *bougnat* is a native of the Auvergne. When one asks the cheesemaker where his cheese comes from, all he will say is, "From the mountains of Auvergne." The maker's name and location are commercial secrets.

The pale yellow pâte of this cheese tastes cool on the tongue, and has a concentrated flavor. Production is *artisanal,* with an affinage of two months.

♥ St. Pourçain.

Semi-hard pâte; uncooked, slightly pressed

ESSENTIAL FACTS
- 11.8 in diameter
  2 in high
- 8.8 lbs
- 45%
- All year

Natural rind

Auvergne

 Raw

TOMME CAPRA

This simple goat cheese comes from the village of St. Bardou in the Drôme. Its name comes from the Italian word *capra*, which means goat. The rind is thin and the pâte is firm, even when fresh, with a light flavor of goat's milk. This *fermier* cheese is produced by F. Pozin and has an affinage of at least 12 days.

♉ St. Joseph

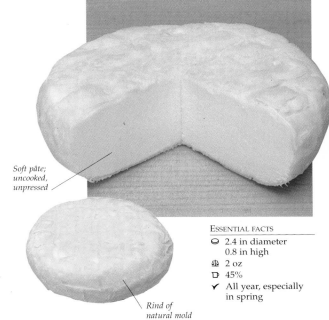

Soft pâte;
uncooked,
unpressed

Rind of
natural mold

Rhône-Alpes
(29)

Raw

ESSENTIAL FACTS

◎ 2.4 in diameter
0.8 in high

⚖ 2 oz

🜄 45%

✓ All year, especially
in spring

TOMME DE CHÈVRE PAYS NANTAIS

The Pays Nantais, from which this medium-size *artisanal* cheese takes its name, lies at the mouth of the Loire River, a region famous for its white wine. The cheese shown has a moist, orange rind. The pâte is the color of cream with a fine texture, firm with no elasticity. The flavor is an unusual combination of goat and wine. Affinage takes three to six weeks during which time the cheese is rubbed with a cloth soaked in Muscadet wine.

♉ Muscadet sur Lie

Semi-hard pâte;
uncooked,
pressed

Washed,
moist rind

Pays de la
Loire (44)

Raw

ESSENTIAL FACTS

◎ 8 in diameter
1.6 in high

⚖ 3.3 lbs

🜄 45%

✓ All year

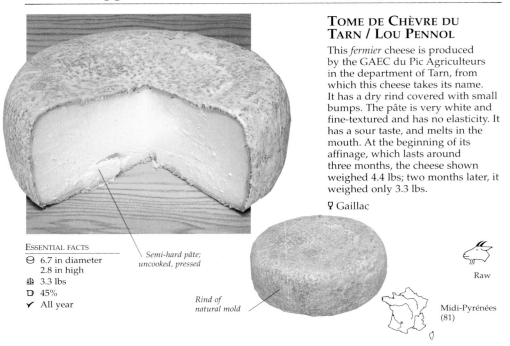

TOME DE CHÈVRE DU TARN / LOU PENNOL

This *fermier* cheese is produced by the GAEC du Pic Agriculteurs in the department of Tarn, from which this cheese takes its name. It has a dry rind covered with small bumps. The pâte is very white and fine-textured and has no elasticity. It has a sour taste, and melts in the mouth. At the beginning of its affinage, which lasts around three months, the cheese shown weighed 4.4 lbs; two months later, it weighed only 3.3 lbs.

♈ Gaillac

ESSENTIAL FACTS

⊖ 6.7 in diameter
  2.8 in high
⚖ 3.3 lbs
🗔 45%
✓ All year

Semi-hard pâte; uncooked, pressed

Rind of natural mold

Raw

Midi-Pyrénées (81)

TOMME LE GASCON

This *artisanal* cheese comes from the Lomagne region of Gascogne, which is well known for its *pâté de foie gras*. It has a dry rind that bounces back under finger pressure. The pâte is yellow and supple, with many holes and a rich, milky flavour. Affinage lasts four to five weeks.

♈ Tursan

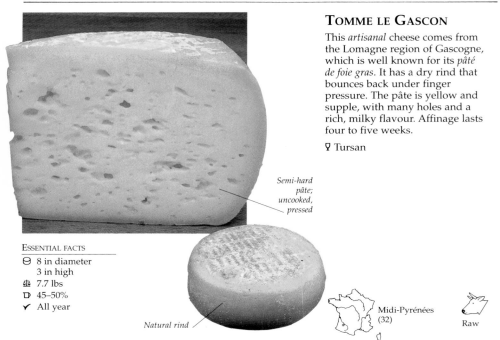

Semi-hard pâte; uncooked, pressed

ESSENTIAL FACTS

⊖ 8 in diameter
  3 in high
⚖ 7.7 lbs
🗔 45–50%
✓ All year

Natural rind

Midi-Pyrénées (32)

Raw

TOMME DE HUIT LITRES

A couple originally from Paris makes this *fermier* cheese in the village of Puimichel in Provence. They raise 45 goats in the Alps of Provence and make several kinds of goat cheese that are distinctive by their methods of production, flavor, and aroma, but alike in the superior quality of their milk. The Tomme de Huit Litres, which is made following an ancient method, has almost no smell and a light flavor of rich goat's milk. Affinage takes from two weeks to six months.

Ŷ Cassis

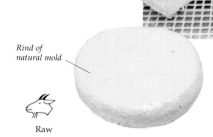

Semi-hard pâte; uncooked, pressed

Rind of natural mold

Provence-Alpes-Côte d'Azur (04)

Raw

ESSENTIAL FACTS
- 7 in diameter
  1. 4 in high
- 2.7 lbs
- Not defined
- Spring to autumn

TOMME DE MONTAGNE

This *fermier* cheese was made by couple of farmers who also make a fine Munster (p. 158) in the Vosges Mountains of eastern France. The rind is golden with red and white stains. The pâte is the color of butter and firm, with a subtle flavor. Affinage takes two months, during which time the cheese is washed and brushed.

Ŷ Sylvaner (good vintage)

Semi-hard pâte; uncooked, pressed

Moist, natural rind

Alsace (68)

Raw

ESSENTIAL FACTS
- 8 in diameter
  3.2 in high
- 5.5 lbs.– size and weight vary according to the quantity of milk produced each day
- Not defined
- All year, best in autumn and winter

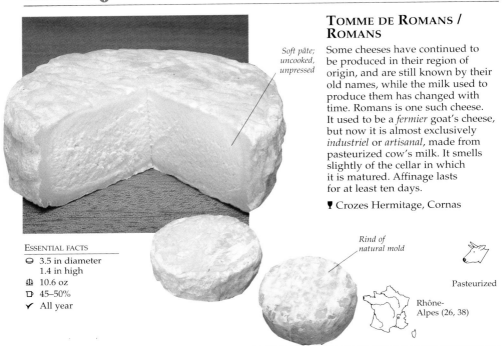

TOMME DE ROMANS / ROMANS

Soft pâte; uncooked, unpressed

Some cheeses have continued to be produced in their region of origin, and are still known by their old names, while the milk used to produce them has changed with time. Romans is one such cheese. It used to be a *fermier* goat's cheese, but now it is almost exclusively *industriel* or *artisanal*, made from pasteurized cow's milk. It smells slightly of the cellar in which it is matured. Affinage lasts for at least ten days.

❢ Crozes Hermitage, Cornas

Rind of natural mold

ESSENTIAL FACTS
- ⊖ 3.5 in diameter
  1.4 in high
- ⚖ 10.6 oz
- ⬥ 45–50%
- ✔ All year

Pasteurized

Rhône-Alpes (26, 38)

TOMME DE SÉRANON

Soft pâte; uncooked, unpressed

The town of Séranon lies at an altitude of 3,281 ft just north of Grasse. The sea breezes blow in to the area and spread the scent of flowers. Even the cheeses produced here have a delicious, lingering aroma of flowers. Summer is the best season for Tomme de Séranon. The rind is thin and almost pink. The pâte is very supple and fragile. This is a *fermier* cheese with a short affinage of about two weeks.

♀ *Rosé* de Provence

ESSENTIAL FACTS
- ⊖ 3.5 in diameter
  1.6 in high
- ⚖ 10.6 oz
- ⬥ 45%
- ✔ All year, best
  spring to summer

Rind of natural mold

Provence-Alpes-Côte d'Azur (06)

Raw

Tomme de Vendée

The pâte and rind of this large *artisanal* cheese from the Atlantic Coast show that the methods of production are different from those of the AOC goat cheeses of the Loire Valley. The taste of salt is quite strong, and the flavor is partly due to the careful affinage of one-and-a-half months.

Semi-hard pâte; uncooked, pressed

ᵧ Fiefs Vendéens *rosé*

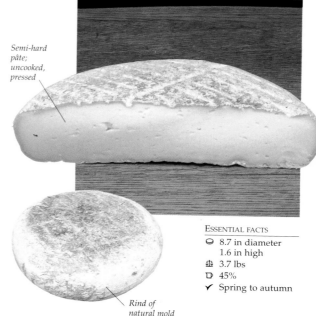

Pays de la Loire (85)

Raw

Rind of natural mold

ESSENTIAL FACTS
- ⊜ 8.7 in diameter 1.6 in high
- ⚖ 3.7 lbs
- ⊐ 45%
- ✓ Spring to autumn

Tommette de l'Aveyron

This *fermier* cheese comes from the Causse du Larzac, which is the home of the famous Roquefort (p. 178). It is named after the Aveyron, the department in which it is produced. This cheese is made with rich milk and has a dry rind with a white, gray, and reddish-brown mold. The pâte is firm and elastic under finger pressure and melts in the mouth with a strong, salty taste. Affinage takes two to six weeks.

Soft, yellow or clear pâte; uncooked, slightly pressed

❢ Gaillac, Cahors

Midi-Pyrénées (12)

Raw

Rind of natural mold

ESSENTIAL FACTS
- ⊜ 3.2 in diameter 2.4 in high
- ⚖ 10.6 oz
- ⊐ Not defined
- ✓ Made from December to 15 August

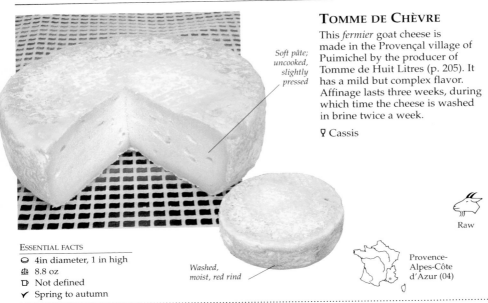

TOMME DE CHÈVRE

This *fermier* goat cheese is made in the Provençal village of Puimichel by the producer of Tomme de Huit Litres (p. 205). It has a mild but complex flavor. Affinage lasts three weeks, during which time the cheese is washed in brine twice a week.

♀ Cassis

Soft pâte; uncooked, slightly pressed

Raw

ESSENTIAL FACTS
- ⊖ 4in diameter, 1 in high
- ⚖ 8.8 oz
- ▱ Not defined
- ✔ Spring to autumn

Washed, moist, red rind

Provence-Alpes-Côte d'Azur (04)

Tomme de Chèvre, les Pyrénées

FROMAGE DE CHÈVRE FERMIER

Sheep cheeses have been produced in the Pyrénées for centuries, but goat cheeses like this one are rare. The curd of the goat's milk is wrapped in a cloth, drained, and lightly pressed to discard the whey. This insures that the cheese will keep for longer. The ripened cheese is large, heavy, and solid, with a firm, white, dry, compact pâte that occasionally splits. The flavor is rich. The maker's mark – a heart – is embossed on the rind. Affinage of this *fermier* cheese takes one-and-a-half months.

♀ Jurançon

Semi-hard pâte; uncooked, pressed

ESSENTIAL FACTS
- ⊖ 7.3 in diameter
  3.2 in high
- ⚖ 5 lbs
- ▱ 45%
- ✔ Summer to autumn

Natural rind, marked by the cloth; stamped with a heart

Midi-Pyrénées (65)

Raw

TOMME DE CHÈVRE/ LOUBIÈRES / CABRIOULET

This *fermier* goat cheese is produced at the Ferme du Col del Fach in Loubières, near the town of Foix in southern France. The cheese shown has had an affinage of five months and the surface seems as dry as stone. The pâte is yellow-gray, with holes, and has little elasticity. This is a strong cheese with a smell of mold and the cellar. It is salty but well balanced, with rich flavors. During the affinage of at least two months, the cheese is washed in brine.

♈ Limoux

Semi-hard pâte; uncooked, pressed

Washed, moist rind

Midi-Pyrénées (09)

Raw

TOME PAYS BASQUE

This *fermier* cheese is produced by the Basque shepherd who makes Ardi-Gasna (p. 44) near the town of St.-Jean-Pied-de Port, close to the Spanish border in southwest France. It is also ripened by the same *fromager*. The rind of the cheese shown here is dry and shows traces of the cloth used during pressing. The pâte is firm, with no elasticity, and breaks easily. Although it is dry, it contains a good balance of salt and fat and melts in the mouth to a sticky consistency. Affinage lasts for two months.

♈ Irouléguy

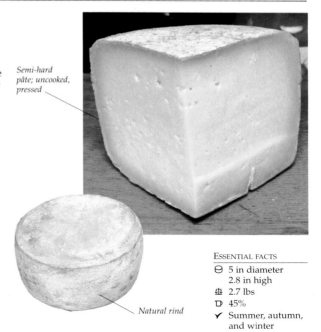

Semi-hard pâte; uncooked, pressed

Natural rind

Aquitaine (64)

Raw

ESSENTIAL FACTS
⊖ 5 in diameter 2.8 in high
⚖ 2.7 lbs
🗓 45%
✔ Summer, autumn, and winter

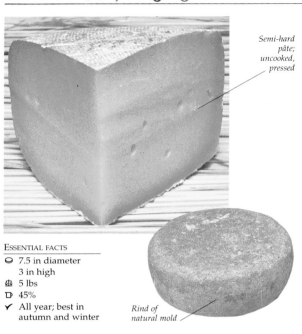

TOMME DE CHÈVRE DE PAYS

Semi-hard pâte; uncooked, pressed

This *fermier* cheese is produced in Les Barronies in the department of Gascogne. It has a dry rind with light brown and red mold showing traces of the cloth used in the production. The flavor has a balanced sweetness and no acidity. Affinage takes two months.

Ⴤ Tursan

ESSENTIAL FACTS

- ⊖ 7.5 in diameter
  3 in high
- ⚖ 5 lbs
- ⅀ 45%
- ✔ All year; best in autumn and winter

Rind of natural mold

Midi-Pyrénées (65)

Raw

TRAPPE (VÉRITABLE)

The name of this *artisanal* cheese means "real Trappist" – it is made in the Trappist Abbaye de la Coudre close to the town of Laval in the province of Maine. It is a mild cheese with a slight smell of mold. Affinage lasts at least three weeks, during which time the cheese is washed in brine.

Ⴤ Chinon

Semi-hard, elastic pâte; uncooked, pressed

ESSENTIAL FACTS

- ⊖ 8 in diameter
  2 in high
- ⚖ 4 lb; 10 oz or
  14 oz (small)
- ⅀ 40%
- ✔ All year

Washed rind

Pays de la Loire (53)

Pasteurized

TRAPPE DE BELVAL

This *artisanal* cheese is produced in a convent called the Abbaye de Belval in the province of Artois. Every year, 40 nuns make about 40 tons. The nuns orginally came from Laval and started to make the cheese in 1892. Its wrapper is tangerine-colored, with six blue crosses and a picture of the abbey in dark blue. The cheese has a soft, pink rind the color of coral. Its pâte is ivory, with a cool, elastic texture and a slight scent. Affinage takes at least six weeks.

❦ Bordeaux, Médoc

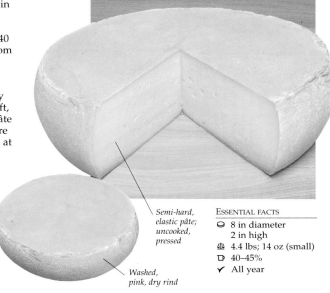

Nord-Pas-de-Calais (62)

Raw

Semi-hard, elastic pâte; uncooked, pressed

Washed, pink, dry rind

ESSENTIAL FACTS

◉ 8 in diameter
2 in high

⚖ 4.4 lbs; 14 oz (small)

🌡 40–45%

✔ All year

FROMAGE D'HESDIN

This *artisanal* cheese is named after the town of Hesdin, which lies just 12 miles from the village where Trappe de Belval is made. The cheese was probably modeled on a similar monastery cheese. Production of Fromage d'Hesdin began around 1960. The smell is soft and light and the aftertaste is slightly sweet. Affinage takes two months, during which time the cheese is washed occasionally in white wine.

❦ Haut Médoc

Semi-hard pâte; uncooked, slightly pressed

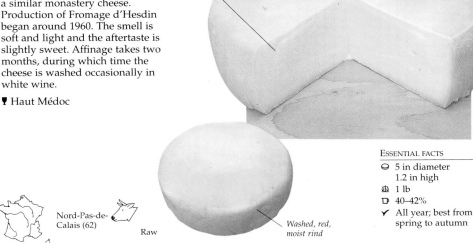

Nord-Pas-de-Calais (62)

Raw

Washed, red, moist rind

ESSENTIAL FACTS

◉ 5 in diameter
1.2 in high

⚖ 1 lb

🌡 40–42%

✔ All year; best from spring to autumn

211

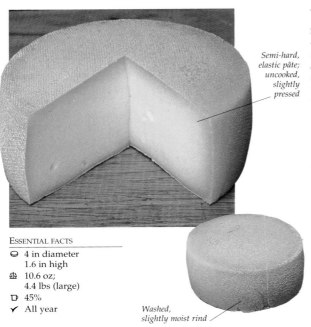

TRAPPE ECHOURGNAC

Semi-hard, elastic pâte; uncooked, slightly pressed

Since 1868, Trappist nuns have collected milk from neighboring farms to make and ripen this *artisanal* cheese in l'Abbaye d'Echourgnac, in Périgord. They use the same methods of production as for Port-du-Salut (p. 173) and succeed in producing 57 tons each year.

The rind of the cheese is very slightly moist and bounces under finger pressure. The flavor is balanced and simple. Affinage takes two months in the abbey cellars, plus another month at the cheese shop.

❦ Cahors

ESSENTIAL FACTS
- ◔ 4 in diameter
  1.6 in high
- ⚖ 10.6 oz;
  4.4 lbs (large)
- ◔ 45%
- ✔ All year

Washed, slightly moist rind

Aquitaine (24)

Pasteurized

TRAPPISTE DE CHAMBARAN

Semi-hard pâte; uncooked, slightly pressed

This *artisanal* cheese comes from the town of Roybon on the Plateau de Chambaran, in the province of the Dauphiné. It has a moist, pale pink rind and a mild flavor. Production, which is modeled on that of Reblochon (p. 175) and Port-du-Salut (p. 173), began in 1932. The milk is bought from neighboring farms, then pasteurized. Around 88 tons of cheese are produced each year.

During the affinage, the cheeses are washed in brine for two weeks in the natural cellars of the abbey. Large cheeses need at least four weeks.

❦ Côtes Rotie

ESSENTIAL FACTS
- ◔ 3.5 in diameter
  0.8 in high
- ⚖ 5.6 oz; 10.6 oz; 4.4 lbs
- ◔ 45%
- ✔ All year

Washed, pink, moist rind

Rhône-Alpes (38)

Pasteurized

Triple Crème, Double Crème

Triple crème and *double crème* cheeses are popular because of their subtle, creamy flavor. They may be found in most French cheese shops and are often included in a cheese platter to add variety to a selection.

These cheeses are made by adding cream to the milk during production. *Triple crème* has a minimum fat content of 75%, whereas *double crème* contains between 60 and 75% fat. These cheeses generally have no rind at all, or a soft rind

of mold. The pâte is soft, sweet, and tastes pleasant; there may also be a slight sourness. Since these cheeses do not have strong flavors, they are often used in the production of other cheeses (p. 218). The length of affinage is usually short. The cheeses may be eaten fresh and go particularly well with a red wine such as Moulis, which is also known as Moulis-en-Médoc, the smallest of the communities of Haut-Médoc.

LA BOUILLE

This *artisanal* cheese was first produced in Normandie at the end of the 19th century by "Monsieur Fromage." Fromage de Monsieur (p. 216) was also first made by the same man. It is possible that this cheese no longer exists today. Despite its high fat content, this *double-crème* cheese is ripened for two months.

🍷 Médoc

ESSENTIAL FACTS
⊖ 3.2 in diameter
   2 in high
🧀 7.8 oz
🐮 60%
✔ Summer to winter

Rind of white mold

Soft pâte; uncooked, unpressed

Haute-Normandie (76)

Enriched with cream

BOURSAULT

This *industriel* cheese has a mild flavor, reminiscent of Brie (p. 56), and a slight acidity. It was first made after World War II and was named after its creator. It is a soft, creamy cheese with a slight smell of mold. Affinage lasts two months.

🍷 Bordeaux

ESSENTIAL FACTS
⊖ 3.2 in diameter
   2.2 inhigh
🧀 7 oz
🐮 70%
✔ All year

Rind of very light, white mold

Soft pâte; uncooked, unpressed

Ile-de-France (77)

Enriched with cream

Fresh pâte;
uncooked, unpressed

No rind

ESSENTIAL FACTS
⊖ 3 in diameter
1.6 in high
🝡 5.3 oz; 4.4 oz
(in a container)
🝊 70%
✔ All year

BOURSIN

The picture on the near left shows
a Boursin made with garlic and
herbs; the one on the far left has
been made with black pepper.
Boursin is a soft, creamy, *industriel*
cheese from Normandie with no
affinage. It goes well with fresh
bread and dry white wine.

❦ Graves

 Haute-
Normandie
(27)

Enriched
with cream

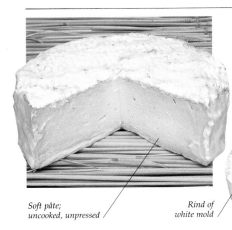

Soft pâte;
uncooked, unpressed

Rind of
white mold

BRILLAT-SAVARIN

ESSENTIAL FACTS
⊖ 5 in diameter
1.6 in high
🝡 1 lb
🝊 75%
✔ All year

This cheese was created in the
1930s by Henri Androuët, father
of French cheese expert Pierre
Androuët. It was named after the
renowned 18th-century French
food writer Brillat-Savarin. This is
an *industriel* cheese with an
affinage of one to two weeeks.

❦ St. Emilion, Fronsac

 Mainly
Normandie

Enriched
with cream

ESSENTIAL FACTS
◈ 5.5 in long,
2.4 in wide,
1.4 in high
🝡 7.4 oz
🝊 60%
✔ All year

CAPRICE DES DIEUX

This *industriel* cheese from the
Bassigny region of Haute-Marne
was first produced commercially
in 1956. In addition to the cheese
shown here, there is a larger
version at 11 oz and a smaller
version of 5 oz. Affinage takes at
least two weeks.

❦ Coteaux Champenois

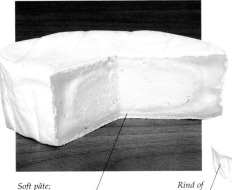

Soft pâte;
uncooked, unpressed

Rind of
white mold

 Champagne-
Ardenne (52)

Enriched
with cream

CROUPET

The name of this cheese derives from a village in the Brie region of the Ile-de-France. It is produced in a small *industriel* dairy. Affinage takes one to two weeks.

🍷 Bourgogne

ESSENTIAL FACTS
⊖ 4.3 in diameter
   2 in high
⚖ 1 lb
🗋 75%
✔ All year

Ile-de-France (77)

Enriched with cream

Rind of white mold

Soft, creamy pâte; uncooked, unpressed

DÉLICE DE SAINT-CYR

This cheese from Saint-Cyr-sur-Morin in the region of Brie is similar to Boursault (p. 213). It is produced in a small *industriel* dairy. Affinage takes four to five weeks.

🍷 Bordeaux

ESSENTIAL FACTS
⊖ 3.5 in diameter
   2.4 in high
⚖ 8.8 oz
🗋 75%
✔ All year

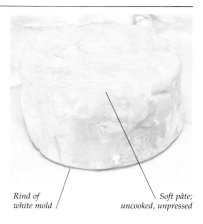

Ile-de-France (77)

Enriched with cream

Rind of white mold

Soft pâte; uncooked, unpressed

EXPLORATEUR

This *industriel* cheese has a slight smell of mold and a creamy texture and taste. Affinage takes two to three weeks. There are also larger versions of 1 lb and 3.5 lbs that are usually sold pre-cut.

🍷 Bordeaux

ESSENTIAL FACTS
⊖ 3.2 in diameter
   2.4 in high
⚖ 8.8 oz; 1 lb;
   3.5 lbs
🗋 75%
✔ All year

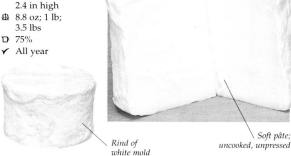

Ile-de-France (77)

Enriched with cream

Rind of white mold

Soft pâte; uncooked, unpressed

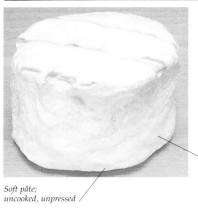

Soft pâte;
uncooked, unpressed

Rind of
white mold

ESSENTIAL FACTS
- ⊖ 3.2 in diameter
  2 in high
- ⚖ 9.5 oz
- ▯ 72%
- ✔ All year

FIN-DE-SIÈCLE

This *artisanal* cheese from the Pays de Bray in Normandie was given its name by cheesemaker Henri Androuët. It is a soft, creamy cheese with a slight smell of mold. Affinage lasts two weeks.

❢ Bordeaux

Haute-
Normandie
(76)

Enriched
with cream

Soft pâte;
uncooked, unpressed

Rind of
white mold

ESSENTIAL FACTS
- ⊖ 3 in diameter
  2 in high
- ⚖ 8.8 oz
- ▯ 60%
- ✔ All year

FROMAGE DE MONSIEUR / MONSIEUR FROMAGE

This *industriel* cheese was created by Monsieur Fromage, as was Bouille (p. 213). Affinage takes three weeks.

❢ Bordeaux

Basse-
Normandie
(14)

Enriched
with cream

Soft pâte;
uncooked, unpressed

Rind of
white mold

ESSENTIAL FACTS
- ⊖ 5 in
  diameter
  1.6 in high
- ⚖ 1 lb
- ▯ 75%
- ✔ All year

GRAND VATEL

This is an *artisanal* cheese from Bourgogne, with an affinage of six weeks. It is a solid cheese with a buttery taste. There is also a Petit Vatel, with an affinage of only four weeks.

❢ Côte de Beaune

Bourgogne
(21)

Enriched
with cream

GRATTE-PAILLE

This is an *artisanal* cheese from
the department of Seine-et-Marne,
with an affinage of three weeks.
It has an oily texture and a rich,
creamy taste.

🍷 Bordeaux

ESSENTIAL FACTS

◈ 4 in long,
   2.8 in wide
   2.4 in high
⚖ 10.6–12.6 oz
🍶 70%
✔ All year

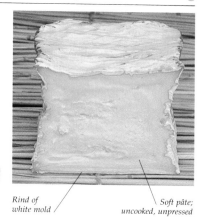

Ile-de-France
(77)

Enriched
with cream

*Rind of
white mold*

*Soft pâte;
uncooked, unpressed*

LUCULLUS

This soft, creamy *industriel* cheese
is named after Lucullus, the Roman
general and gourmand. Affinage
takes three to four weeks.

🍷 Bordeaux

ESSENTIAL FACTS

◔ 3.2 in diameter
   2 in high
⚖ 8.8–10.6 oz
🍶 75%
✔ All year

Ile-de-France
(77)

Enriched
with cream

*Rind of
white mold*

*Soft pâte;
uncooked, unpressed*

PIERRE-ROBERT

This *artisanal* cheese from Seine-
et-Marne was conceived by
cheesemaker Robert Rouzaire,
who named it after himself and
his friend Pierre. His son continues
to make it today. It is a mild cheese
that is popular with children.
Affinage takes three weeks.

🍷 Bordeaux

ESSENTIAL FACTS

◔ 5 in
   diameter
   1.8 in high
⚖ 1 lb
🍶 75%
✔ All year

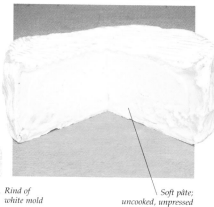

Ile-de-France
(77)

Enriched
with cream

*Rind of
white mold*

*Soft pâte;
uncooked, unpressed*

Imaginative creations
The cheeses shown on this page
are all double crème and triple
crème cheeses that have been
decorated by the fromager with
a variety of herbs and spices.

Cannelle – **covered with cinnamon**

Gargantua à la feuille de sauge **is
decorated with sage leaves**

Paprika – **covered with paprika**

Poivre – **covered with
coarsely ground black pepper**

*Dried grapes marinated
in rum cover the cheese
entirely*

Soleil – **covered with raisins and sultanas**   *Trois-Epis* – **covered with cumin seeds**

Vache des Pyrénées

The Pyrénées are about 250 miles long and extend over five French departments and 11 provinces. At the center of this area, in the departments of Ariève and Haute-Garonne, the cheeses that used to be made from sheep's milk are today being made with cow's milk.

These cheeses are solid and quite large, with a tough rind that protects a firm, fat, and fruity pâte. They bear the names of their villages, although the local people simply call them *fromage de montagne,* meaning mountain cheese. They are nearly all *fermier* cheeses made from raw milk, and have small eyes or holes in the pâte. Affinage develops the full character of a mountain cheese. The cheese becomes meaty and retains none of the softness, mildness, and sweetness of milk. It should be matched with a fruity red wine.

BAROUSSE

Both Barousse and Esbareich (below) are produced by similar methods. The taste varies according to whether they are made with the milk of cows fed on spring and summer grass, or with milk from cows fed dry fodder in their sheds during winter. The cheese shown was made by the Sost family from the village of the same name, where they make five cheeses a day. This one looks homemade. The cheese is named after the Vallée de Barousse de l'Ourse in the Pyrénées. It is a strong-smelling *fermier* cheese, with an affinage of at least one-and-a half months. It is washed, wiped, and turned every day for the first two weeks of its affinage.

❦ Madiran, Côtes du Frontonnais

Semi-hard, elastic pâte, with many small holes; uncooked, pressed

Washed, pink-brown rind

Barousse

ESBAREICH

This cheese is the twin of Barousse. It is a *fermier* cheese from Esbareich, 1 mile from Sost, with an affinage of two-and-a half months.

❦ Madiran, Côtes du Frontonnais

Midi-Pyrénées (65)

Raw

Esbareich

ESSENTIAL FACTS

⊖ 7.5 in diameter, 3 in high
⚖ 5.5 lbs
ⅅ Not defined
✔ All year

ESSENTIAL FACTS

⊖ 7 in diameter 3 in high
⚖ 5.5 lbs
ⅅ Not defined
✔ All year

- ⊖ 10 in diameter
  4 in high
- ⚖ 13 lbs
- 🌡 45–50%
- ✓ All year

Natural rind

BETHMALE

This is the best-known of the traditional cow's-milk cheeses from the Pyrénées. It is named after the village where it is made in the Couserans region of the Comté de Foix. Legend has it that it was favored by King Louis VI, who passed through the area in the 12th century.

Bethmale is probably the mildest of all the cow's-milk cheeses of the Pyrénées. The cheese shown here has a semi-hard, uncooked, pressed pâte and smells of the cellar. Affinage takes two to three months, during which time the cheese is brushed and turned.

🍷 Collioure

Midi-Pyrénées (09)

Raw or pasteurized

Semi-hard pâte; uncooked, pressed

- ⊖ 11.4 in diameter,
  11 in high (large);
- ⊖ 5 in diameter
  3 in high (small)
- ⚖ 13 lbs (large)
  2 lbs (small);
- 🌡 50%
- ✓ All year

Natural reddish-brown rind

E BAMALOU

This *artisanal* cheese is made in two sizes, large and small, in the town of Castillon-en-Couserans in the Comté de Foix. It is probably the strongest of all the cow's-milk cheeses of the Pyrénées. The pâte is supple, greasy, and well-wrapped in its solid rind, which is brownish with red spots. The taste and smell of this cheese blend well with a red wine with good tannin. Affinage takes about six weeks.

🍷 Châteauneuf-du-Pape, Cahors

Midi-Pyrénées (09)

Raw, whole

FROMAGE DE MONTAGNE

The tiny house of the two young cheesemakers who produce this *fermier* cheese lies at an altitude of 4,265 ft in the Pyrénées in Poubeau, close to the town of Luchon. The crust of the cheese is less strong smelling than the pâte, is orange and pinkish-white in color, and soft and moist. The pâte is egg-yolk yellow and suffused with holes. It smells quite strong. The cheese shown here looks young but it is already four months old, which is about the right age for eating. Affinage takes at least three months, during which time the cheese is washed and turned.

❢ Bergerac, Bordeaux, Fitou

Elastic, semi-hard pâte; uncooked, slightly pressed

Supple, natural rind

Midi-Pyrénées (31)

Raw

ESSENTIAL FACTS
- ◎ 8.7 in diameter
  3.5 in high
- ⚖ 6 lbs
- ⅁ Not defined
- ✓ All year

FROMAGE DE MONTAGNE DE LÈGE

This *fermier* cheese is produced by the Ferme Camille Cazaux in the village of Lège. It has a reddish-brown, sticky, and slightly moist rind, and a dense, yellow pâte, which is full of holes. This cheese may be eaten after an affinage of just three months, but true connoisseurs prefer to wait six months until it is completely mature.

❢ Madiran, Cahors, Fitou

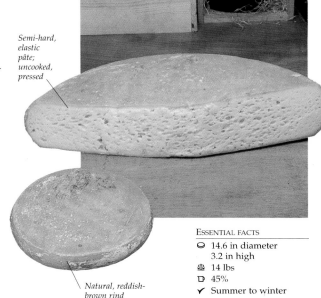

Semi-hard, elastic pâte; uncooked, pressed

Natural, reddish-brown rind

Midi-Pyrénées (31)

Raw

ESSENTIAL FACTS
- ◎ 14.6 in diameter
  3.2 in high
- ⚖ 14 lbs
- ⅁ 45%
- ✓ Summer to winter

Semi-hard,
elastic pâte;
uncooked,
pressed

FROMAGE DE MONTAGNE, LE PIC DE LA CALABASSE

This *artisanal* cheese is made in the village of Saint-Lary at the foot of the 7,250-ft Pic de la Calabasse Mountain. Besides the large cheese shown here, there is also a smaller version. The cheese shown here is ripe and has hints of white, gray, pink, and brown on the rind. The pâte is yellow and brown, and full of holes; it is firm but melts in the mouth. The smell of this sticky cheese is strong and fruity, with a trace of flowers. Affinage takes three months.

❦ Corbières, Minervois, Fitou.

ESSENTIAL FACTS

Natural rind,
marked
by cloth

- ◯ 14.6 in diameter
  3 in high
- ⚖ 13 lbs
- ◫ 45%
- ✓ Best in spring

Midi-Pyrénées
(09)

Raw

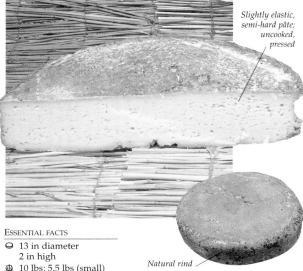

Slightly elastic,
semi-hard pâte;
uncooked,
pressed

FROMAGE DE MONTAGNE / LE ROGALLAIS

This *artisanal* cheese is made by the Fromagerie Coumes in Seix in the Couserans region of Comté de Foix. It has a well-ripened, brown, or pinkish brown rind, and a yellow to light brown pâte with eyes or holes in it. The pâte is thick and greasy and smells of the cellar and mold. The cheesemaker explains: "The eyes form during the affinage of one-and-a-half months and air the pâte. Their quality depends on how the whey is drained. The cellar is at 57°F with a humidity of 95%. This humidity and the board of oak on which the cheese matures cause the mold to form and the pâte to ferment to create the eyes."

❦ Graves, Medoc

ESSENTIAL FACTS

Natural rind

- ◯ 13 in diameter
  2 in high
- ⚖ 10 lbs; 5.5 lbs (small)
- ◫ 50%
- ✓ All year, especially
  spring to autumn

Midi-Pyrénées
(09)

Raw

Le Moulis

This is an *artisanal* cheese made by a long-established family business in Moulis in the province of Comté de Foix. Sixty-six tons are made each year, which amounts to some 17,000 cheeses.

Both young and mature Moulis have strong tastes. At first the pâte is straw-colored, then it turns brown. Despite its many holes, it is moist, fatty, and melts softly in the mouth. The distinct taste of fermentation and decay stings the tongue. The cheese smells strong and is piquant when old. During affinage, it is washed in brine once every two days for the first two weeks, then brushed and turned for one to two months.

♈ Vin du Jura *sec*

Semi-hard, elastic pâte; uncooked, slightly pressed

A young Moulis

Natural, dry, white, brown, and black mold marked by cloth

A Moulis after an affinage of six months

ESSENTIAL FACTS

- ◯ 9.5 in diameter
  3 in high
- ⚖ 7.7 lbs
- ◷ 48%
- ✓ All year

Pâte darkens and becomes harder with age

Midi-Pyrénées
(09)

Raw

Soft, creamlike pâte that smells of spruce wood; uncooked, unpressed

Rhône-Alpes
(74)

Raw

Thin rind with natural white mold

VACHERIN D'ABONDANCE FERMIER

This *fermier* cheese is made in Abondance in Savoie. The unusual feature of this cheese is the strip of spruce bark in which it is wrapped. The bark protects the exterior and the scent of the wood permeates the cheese. The pâte is fine-textured, with a mild, creamy, slightly salty flavor. Affinage lasts three weeks.

Locally, Vacherin d'Abondance fermier is eaten with *patates au barbot*, which means potatoes boiled in their skins in salt water. The cheese is spread on the hot potatoes with a spoon.

♈ Vin de Savoie, Marin

ESSENTIAL FACTS

- ⊖ 5 in diameter, 1 in high
- ⚖ 17.6 oz
- ↻ Not defined (including wood covering)
- ✓ Winter and spring

HOW VACHERIN D'ABONDANCE IS MADE

Cheesemaker Célina Gagneux produces this cheese following traditional methods. The numbers below refer to the photographs.
1. At 6:30 a.m. the cows are milked and the milk is poured into a large copper bowl.
2. The rennet is mixed in with a ladle and coagulation begins. The mixture is left to rest for an hour at 54°F.
3. At 8 a.m. the curd is poured into 15 bowls lined with gauze.
4. The gauze is knotted around the curd to drain off the whey.
5. The whey is discarded and kept to extract the cream.
6. The balls of curd in cloth are bound with a band of spruce bark and left to rest for about three hours, then transferred to the draining board. At 3 p.m. drainage continues.
7. The cloth is removed.
8. The cheeses are laid on the draining board until the next morning. The whey continues to drain off while the cheeses remain sweet, light, and soft.

9

9. At 8 a.m. the following morning, the cheeses are moved to a cellar at a temperature of 54°F, and salted on one side only. After 48 hours, they are taken out of their bands, turned, and salted on the other side. The bands are put back and tightened as the cheeses ripen.

The cheeses are turned every morning for 15 to 20 days and the cloth covering the board is changed, leaving marks on the surface of the cheeses. About 15 to 20 days later, white mold appears on the surfaces. The rind is not yet formed, but a thin, creamy-white skin has appeared. The cheeses are ready for sale.

The cheesemaking year
Célina Gagneux, who is the only person to produce this cheese in Abondance, learned her technique from her mother-in-law soon after she married 30 years ago. Cheesemaking continues for 210 days, beginning in December and ending in July. With nine cows, which give 16 gallons of milk every morning, she makes 15 cheeses. The evening milking is less productive and results in another 12 or 13 cheeses. Each cheese requires one gallon of milk.

In July, the cows go up to the alpine pastures, where they join others in a herd of about 50. The summer milk is used to make the big Abondance cheeses (p. 120) in chalets in the mountains. The herdspeople and the cows return in early October and the cows calve. The female calves are kept and raised for three years before they themselves start to produce milk. Each cow can continue to produce milk for 10 years.

ABONDANCE
The peaceful mountain town of Abondance lies on the river of the same name in the Alps, close to the Swiss border.

VACHERIN DES BAUGES

Two people make this *fermier* cheese in the Massif des Bauges in Savoie. According to a local cheesemaker, although it is generally better to allow the cheese to ripen fully, it can be eaten two weeks after the start of affinage, as long as it is wiped once every two days with water in which cream has been added. This is also done during the full affinage, which should last a month. The cheese shown has been ripened for two weeks and includes patches of a bad gray mold that will impair the flavor.

❦ Vin de Savoie, Arbois

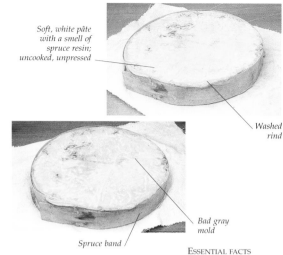

Soft, white pâte with a smell of spruce resin; uncooked, unpressed

Washed rind

Bad gray mold

Spruce band

Rhône-Alpes (73)

Raw

ESSENTIAL FACTS

◔ 8 in diameter
1.8 in high
⚖ 3 lbs in a band of spruce bark
⌁ Not defined
✓ Winter

How to cut a cheese

The most important thing to bear in mind when cutting a cheese is to give everybody a chance to enjoy each part of the cheese, from the rind to the heart. The way a cheese is cut depends largely on its shape and size. The illustrations show typical cuts for some of the cheeses in this book.

Valençay (p. 84)

Emmental (p. 132)

Camembert (p. 66)

Brie (p. 56)

Charolles (p. 92)

Pont l'Évêque (p. 172)

Picodon (p. 170)

Epoisses (p. 133)

Tomme (p. 188)

Band of hoop wood keeps the chees in shape and should not be removed, even when serving

Washed, wrinkled, yellow to light brown crust of natural mold

Soft, creamy, white to ivory pâte; uncooked, very slightly pressed

VACHERIN DU HAUT-DOUBS / MONT D'OR (AOC)

The Massif du Mont d'Or which rises to a height of 4,800 ft, lies near the French border with Switzerland. Although this winter cheese has been made on the French side for two centuries, for many years there was disagreement over its origins, with both the French and the Swiss maintaining that they were the first to make it. The controversy ended when the Swiss eventually conceded to the French.

Mont d'Or is simply called Vacherin in the shops. It is sold in a wooden box where it continues to ripen. The cheese is bound by a band of spruce, which permeates the cheese and gives it a distinct and pleasant aroma. The spruce band also helps the cheese to keep its shape and should not be removed even when serving.

The surface of the cheese is moist and the rind golden and slightly reddish, with imprints of the cloth. The pale yellow pâte is creamy. It can be spread on bread or boiled potatoes.

The AOC permits both *artisanal* and *coopérative* production of this cheese. Affinage must take place within specified areas over three weeks at a maximum temperature of 59°F. After three weeks of ripening, the aroma of spruce is distinct. The cheese is cured on a board of spruce wood and turned and rubbed with a cloth soaked in brine.

❗ Beaujolais Nouveau, Côtes du Jura, ❗ Champagne

ESSENTIAL FACTS

- ◎ 12 in diameter, 2 in high
- ⚖ 22 lbs or 6.6 lbs in a band of spruce bark
- ∴ 1.6 oz min. per 3.5 oz cheese
- ⧖ 45% min. or 0.7 oz per 3.5 oz cheese
- ✔ Best winter, autumn, spring

Franche-Comté (25)

Raw

In the cheese shop, a piece of marble is used to stop the cheese from running

Winter cheesemaking

On the French side of the Massif du Mont d'Or, there are around 40 villages that lie above 2,625 ft, spread roughly from the River Doubs to the Saut du Doubs. They produce 1,870 tons of cheese every year. From August 15 until March 31, milk from Montbéliard and Pie Rouge de l'Est cattle is gathered from farms in the mountains, and the cheese is made at the same 20 *fruitières* where Comté (p. 112) is produced in spring and summer. The AOC does not permit cows to be fed on silage or other fermented fodder, and the milk must be produced in the mountains at 2,297 ft or higher.

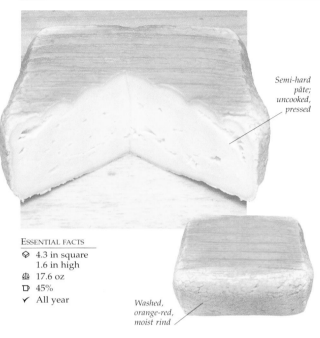

Semi-hard
pâte;
uncooked,
pressed

VIEUX-BOULOGNE

This is a new *pré-salé*, meaning pre-salted, cheese. It is made from the milk of cows raised by the sea near Boulogne. The rind, which is washed with beer, is moist and red. The cheese has a strong odor, although the smell of beer is quite faint. The pâte is elastic. Production is *artisanal*, with a long affinage of seven to nine weeks.

🍺 Local beer, 🍷 Champagne

Washed,
orange-red,
moist rind

Nord-Pas-de-Calais (62)

Raw

Processed cheese

Processed cheese was invented around 1908 by the Swiss, who were looking for a way to use up surplus cheese. In 1911, it was made with Emmental and commercialized by the Swiss firm Gerber. At the same time, processed cheese was being developed in the United States.

The first European factory for the mass production of processed cheese was opened in 1917 in the Jura, France by the Graf brothers, and in 1921 the trademark for La Vache Qui Rit cheese was registered by Léon Bel. In 1953, a French decree laid down strict guidelines as to what exactly a processed

BONJURA
This is a type of canned, processed cheese spread specially produced twice a year for the French Army. It keeps for a long time and is available in plain or ham flavor.

cheese should contain in terms of minimum fat and dry matter, and established a law that was revised at the end of 1988.

Processed cheese has little to do with real cheese. One or several ripened cheeses are heated and mixed, then pasteurized at high temperature (266°F–284°F) after other dairy products, such as liquid or powdered milk, cream, butter, *casein*, whey, and seasoning, have been added. Processed cheese has the advantage of a long shelf life, although the flavor of the original cheeses alters during processing.

Some processed cheeses are made with several ripened cheeses of the same type, others with cheeses of different types. The most often used are Emmental and Cantal, but Saint-Paulin (p. 180) or Roquefort (p. 172) may be used to vary the taste. They are sometimes seasoned with pepper, herbs, ham, onions, mushrooms, or even seafood.

Glossary

AFFINAGE The curing and maturing of cheeses.

AFFINEUR Expert in the curing and maturing of cheeses.

ALPAGE Movement of animals and herdspeople high into the mountains for summer grazing.

AOC Appellation d'Origine Contrôlée. See p. 77

À POINT A cheese that is just at the right point of ripeness.

ARTISANAL Used to describe a cheese that is made by hand rather than by machine.

BREBIS The French word for a ewe, or a sheep's-milk cheese.

BRINE Very salty water.

BRIQUE A rectangular, brick-shaped cheese.

BROUSSE A cheese made from whey or skimmed milk.

BÛCHE A log-shaped cheese.

BURON A simple mountain dairy and cheese store, with a sleeping space (Auvergne).

CABANE Mountain *chalet* where cheese is made in summer (Pyrénées and Corsica).

CAILLÉ Curd.

CARRÉ Adjective used to describe a square cheese.

CASEIN The main protein in milk, precipitated into curd by the use of **rennet**. It is used to make some edible cheese labels, which are embedded in the crust.

CAUSSES Limestone plateau of the Massif Central.

CAVE Natural cave or cellar in which cheeses are ripened and stored until ready to eat.

CENDRÉ A cheese traditionally coated with ash from burned grapevine roots, but today usually covered with a mix of industrially powdered charcoal and salt.

CHEESE IRON A small metal corer for removing a plug from the interior of a cheese to test aroma, flavor, and texture.

CHÈVRE A nanny goat, or a goat-milk cheese.

COAGULATION The clotting of milk, usually by rennet.

COMMUNE The smallest unit of French local government.

CURD The coagulated fats and other solids produced from milk by natural ripening and renneting.

DEPARTMENT (French *département*) Modern administrative division of France, often disregarding old provincial boundaries.

DRY MATTER The remaining solids after all the water in a cheese has been eliminated.

EAU-DE-VIE Spirit, usually made from wine-pressings, e.g., **marc**.

FAT CONTENT Degree of fatness of cheese, expressed as a percentage of fat in total **dry matter**.

FERMIER Adjective used to describe a farm-made cheese.

FOURME The old word for cheese derived from the form or mold in which it was made.

FRAIS, FRAÎCHE Fresh.

FROMAGE Cheese.

FROMAGE BLANC A fresh cheese that has been lightly drained.

FROMAGE FORT Strong preparation usually made in a pot from cheese leftovers with alcohol and herbs added.

FROMAGE FRAIS Cheese that has been salted, but sold unripened.

FROMAGER 1. Cheesemaker. 2. Wholesaler, or retailer of cheese.

FROMAGERIE Cheese dairy. Also used by some cheese shops.

GAEC This stands for *Groupement Agricole pour l'Exploitation en Commun*, which is an agricultural association for common exploitation, that is a kind of cooperative.

HALLE Covered market.

INDUSTRIEL Indicates a large-scale, factory-style creamery with mechanized cheesemaking.

LAIT Milk.

LAURIER Bay leaf.

MAÎTRE FROMAGER Master cheesemaker or cheese expert. Fewer than 100 are listed by the Guilde des Fromagers.

MARC Spirit made from distilled wine pressings.

MOELLEUX Soft and velvety.

MORGE **Brine** enriched with scrapings from old cheeses, used to rub the surfaces of some cheeses during affinage.

MOLD 1. Wood, metal, or plastic container used in cheesemaking to shape the cheese. 2. Fungal species that form on the crust of cheeses or form veins within the pâte. Some molds occur naturally, but many are artificially introduced.

PÂTE Everything within the rind of a cheese.

PAVÉ A thick, square cheese, shaped like a paving stone.

PAYS Village, district, or province.

PELLE Round cutting-edged shovel used to handle curd (Brie).

PERSILLÉ Blue cheese.

PETIT LAIT Whey.

RENNET The enzyme derived from the fourth stomach of a calf or goat, used in cheesemaking to break down the solids in milk into digestible form, helping coagulation. Some plants can have the same effect as rennet.

TOME, TOMME 1. Small, round goat-milk cheeses. 2. Larger pressed cheese of all types of milk.

TRANSHUMANCE The movement of flocks or herds from winter pasture or stabling to high mountain pastures in summer.

VACHE A cow, or a cheese that has been made with cow's milk.

WHEY Residue of milk after most of the fats and other solids have been coagulated into the curd.

VDN *Vin doux naturel* – a naturally sparkling white wine.

List of contributors

The authors wish to thank the following producers and *fromagers*

ABBAYE DE LA JOIE NOTRE-DAME, 56800 Campénéac.
The nuns at this convent produce chocolate as well as cheese.

MME. CAZAUX, 65250 La Barthe-de-Neste.
Based in the region noted for Pyrenean cow's-milk cheeses, Mme Cazaux has a stall at the morning market.

PIERRE ANDROUËT
Formerly head of the Androuët cheese shop in Paris, M. Androuët is the author of several books, including *Le Brie*, *Le Livre d'Or du Fromage*, and *Le Guide du Fromage*.

GILBERT CHEMIN
Crémerie du Couserans, 3 rue de la République, 09200 Saint-Girons.
M. Chemin has a shop in the town, as well as a delivery service to local villages.

ROLAND BARTHELEMY
51 rue de Grenelle, 75007 Paris.
One of the best young *fromagers* in Paris, M. Barthelemy supplies cheese to the Elysées Palace.

EDOUARD CENERI
La Ferme Savoyarde, 22 rue Meynadier, 06400 Cannes.
Known for his brie with truffles, M. Ceneri owns several ripening cellars.

J. BLANC
Crémerie des Halles, 64500 St-Jean-de-Luz.
With his daughter, M. Blanc runs a shop in the town market.

BRIGITTE CORDIER AND FRANÇOISE FLEUTOT, 04230 Montlaux.
These *fromagers* have successfully revived a legendary and once extinct *Tomme d'Arles*.

DANIEL BOUJON, 7 rue Saint-Sébastien, 74200 Thonon-les-Bains.
This second-generation *fromager* has saved the *Vacherin d'Abondance* from extinction.

JACQUES AND JACQUELINE COULAUD, 24 rue Grenouillit, 43000 Le Puy.
From their shop on the eastern edge of Auvergne, M. and Mme. Coulaud offer a wide range of local cheeses.

XAVIER BOURGON, XAVIER, 6 Place Victor-Hugo, 31000 Toulouse.
M. Bourgon is the owner of Xavier, a high-class cheese shop that has become an institution in Toulouse.

M. AND MME. CLAUDE DUPIN, 41 rue Gambetta, 64500 Saint-Jean-de-Luz.
The Dupin's shop on the Spanish border has an excellent selection of Basque cheeses.

MICHEL BOURGUE, La Maison du Fromage, Les Halles Centrales, 84000 Avignon.
This third-generation *fromager* sells an unforgettable *Brousse du Rove*.

HENRI GRILLET, Crémerie du Gravier, 22 Cours Monthyon, 15000 Aurillac.
M. Grillet runs his shop in the region of *Saint Nectaire*, *Cantal*, and *Salers* cheeses.

M. AND MME. CANTIN, 12 rue du Champ-de-Mars, 75007 Paris.
A second-generation *fromager,* Mme. Cantin is the founder of the Association Respect Traditionnel Fromage Français

M. AND MME JACQUES GUERIN, La Fromagerie, 18 rue Saint-Jean 79000 Niort.
The Guerin's distinctive affinage produces unforgettable *Chabichous* and *Mothais*.

RAYMOND LECOMTE / ODETTE JENNY, 76 rue Saint-Louis-en-l'Ile, 75004 Paris.
Although both owners have retired the shop is still open.

A. PENEN AND FAMILY, Préchacq-Navarrenx, 64190 Navarrenx.
These *fromagers* offer a unique cheese from their farm in Navarrenx.

M. AND MME. JEAN-PIERRE LE LOUS, Marché des Grands-Hommes, 33000 Bordeaux.
These *fromagers* can be found at the morning market in Bordeaux.

DENIS PROVENT, Laiterie des Halles, 2 Place de Genève, 73000 Chambéry.
With his knowledge of the mountains, M. Provent, a third-generation *fromager*, travels on foot to small mountain villages.

MICHEL LEPAGE, Conseils-Assistance-Fromagers, 3 Les Prés Claux, 04700 Oraison.
M. Lepage advises on cheesemaking and also participates in reviving extinct cheeses.

JACQUES VERNIER, La Fromagerie Boursault, 71 avenue du Général Leclerc, 75014 Paris.
M. Vernier is well known in Paris for his excellent Beaufort.

GÉRARD LOUP AND FAMILY, Les Provins, 04700 Puimichel.
Preferring to make cheese rather than live in the city, M. Loup and his family left Paris to become *fromagers* in the country.

HENRY VOY, La Ferme Saint-Hubert 21 rue Vignon, 75008 Paris.
M. Voy owns a restaurant adjoining his shop; it specializes in cheese dishes.

M. AND MME. MARIUS MANETTI, Col de San-Bastiano, 20111 Calcatoggio.
M. Manetti is a member of the Chambre d'Agriculture Corse du Sud (Corsican Agricultural Chamber).

FRANÇOIS DURAND, La Heronnière, 61120 Camembert.
M. Durand, a second-generation *fromager*, is one of only two producers of Camembert *fermier*.

ALAIN MARTINET, Halle de Lyon, 102 Cours Lafayette, 69003 Lyon.
This young *fromager* runs a stall in Lyon market, where *fromagers* Mme. Richard and Mme. Maréchal can also be found.

JEAN-PIERRE MOREAU, Elevage Caprin de Bellevue 41400 Pontlevoy.
M. Moreau is an expert producer of goat-milk cheese. His Selles-sur-Cher is excellent.

PHILIPPE OLIVIER, 43-45 rue Thiers, 62200 Boulogne-sur-Mer.
One of the best young *fromagers* in France, M. Olivier belongs to the "short affinage" generation of cheesemakers.

JEAN-MARTIN AND MARGOT KEMPF, 155 Ferme du Saesserlé, 68380 Breitenbach.
The Kempfs produce and sell a very popular Munster cheese, which is matured in their own cellar.

B. ANTONY, 17 rue de la Montagne, 68480 Vieux Ferrette.
R. BOUSQUET, Halles Centrales, 11000 Carcassonne.
LE CAGIBI, 17 allée d'Etigny, 31110 Luchon.
MARECHAL, Halle de Lyon, 102 Cours Lafayette, 69003 Lyon.
E. MILLAT, Halle Brauhauban, 65000 Tarbes.

G. PAUL, 9 rue des Marseillais, 13100 Aix-en-Provence.
RENÉ AND RENÉE RICHARD, Halle de Lyon, 102 Cours Lafayette, 69003 Lyon.
BATUT 22 rue Vieille-du-temple, 75004 Paris.
LE CALENDOS, 11 rue Colbert, 37000 Tours.
FROMAGERIES BEL, 4 rue d'Anjou, 75008 Paris .

List of producers, shops, and markets

The following numbered list of producers, shops, and markets works in conjunction with the index on pages 236–239.

Each cheese in the index is followed by a number in parentheses and a page reference. The number in parentheses refers to the number beside each producer, shop, and market listed here, and shows where the cheese was bought. The list, which is organized by region (see map on p. 16–17), also serves as a quick-reference guide as to where good cheeses can be bought in France.

ALSACE
1. Margot and Jean-Martin Kempf, 155 Ferme du Saesserlé, 68380 **Breitenbach.**

AQUITAINE
2. A.–M. Garat, Halles de Biarritz, 64200 **Biarritz.**

3. Jean-Pierre Le Lous, Marché des Grands-Hommes, 33000 **Bordeaux.**

4. Daniel Casau, 6 rue de Bordeu, 64260 **Izeste.**

5. Etablissement Canonge, 64440 **Laruns.**

6. A. Penen, Préchacq-Navarrenx, 64190 **Navarrenx.**

7. Chez Roger, Halles de Pau, 64000 **Pau.**

8. J. Blanc, Crémerie des Halles, 64500 **Saint-Jean-de-Luz.**

9. Claude Dupin, 41 rue Gambetta, 64500 **Saint-Jean-de-Luz.**

AUVERGNE
10. Henri Grillet, Crémerie du Gravier, 22, Cours Monthyon, 15000 **Aurillac.**

11. Fromageries Morin, Bvd Pavatou, 15000 **Aurillac.**

12. La Maison du Bon Fromage, Marché Saint-Pierre, 63000 **Clermont-Ferrand.**

13. Marché d'**Egliseneuve d'Entraigues** (cheese stall).

14. Jacques Coulaud, 24 rue Grenouillit, 43000 **Le Puy.**

15. G.A.E.C. Louvradou, Margorce, 15140 **Saint-Rémy-de-Salers.**

BOURGOGNE
16. Tast Fromages, 23 rue Carnot, 21200 **Beaune.**

17. Marché de **Dijon** (cheese stall).

CENTRE
18. Halles Châtelet, 45000 **Orléans.**

19. Elevage Caprin de Bellevue, 41400 **Pontlevoy.**

20. Marché de **Sainte-Maure.**

21. Le Calendos, 11 rue Colbert, 37000 **Tours.**

CORSE
22. Marché d'**Ajaccio** (cheese stall).

23. Marché de **Bastia** (cheese stall).

24. Super Viva, 20224 **Calacuccia.**

25. Marius Manenti, Col de San Bastiano, 20111 **Calcatoggio.**

26. Auberge Chez Jacqueline, Pont-de-Castirla, **Corte.**

27. Domaine de Porette, 20250 **Corte.**

28. Coopérative A Pecurella, Route d'Afa, Appietto, 20167 **Mezavia.**

29. Paul Cianfarani (cheesemaker), 20190 **Sainte-Marie-Sicché.**

30. Supermarché Tomy, **Sartène.**

ÎLE-DE-FRANCE AND PARIS
31. Ferme Jehan de Brie, 15 Place du Marché, 77120 **Coulommiers.**

32. Ganot, Marché de **Meaux** (cheese stall).

33. Jacky Boussion, 8 rue Carnot, 77000 **Melun.**

34. Alleosse, 13 rue Poncelet, 75017 **Paris.**

35. Androuët, 41 rue d'Amsterdam, 75008 **Paris.**

36. Restaurant Ambassade d'Auvergne, 22 rue du Grenier Saint-Lazare, 75003 **Paris.**

37. Roland Barthélemy, 51 rue de Grenelle, 75007 **Paris.**

38. Batut, 22 rue Vieille-du-Temple, 75004 **Paris.**

39. Gisèle Cantin, 2 rue de Lourmel, 75015 **Paris.**

40. Marie-Anne Cantin, 12 rue du Champ-de-Mars, 75007 **Paris.**

41. Jean Carmès et fils, 24 rue de Lévis, 75017 **Paris.**

42. A. Dubois, 79 rue de Courcelles, 75017 **Paris.**

43. La Ferme Saint-Aubin, 76 rue Saint-Louis-en-l'Ile, 75004 **Paris.**

44. Fromagerie de Montmartre, 9 rue du Poteau, 75018 **Paris.**

45. Lecomte,
76 rue Saint-Louis-en-l'Ile,
75004 **Paris.**

46. La Maison du Bon Fromage,
35 rue du Marché Saint-Honoré,
75001 **Paris.**

47. Jacques Vernier,
La Fromagerie Boursault,
71 avenue du Général Leclerc,
75014 **Paris.**

48. Henry Voy,
La Ferme Saint-Hubert,
21 rue Vignon, 75008 **Paris.**

49. La Ferme (shop),
Société Brie le Provins (maker,
77160 **Provins.**

50 Société fromagère de la Brie,
19 Avénue du Grand Morin,
77169 **Saint-Siméon.**

LANGUEDOC-ROUSSILLON
51. R. Bousquet,
Halles Centrales,
11000 **Carcassonne.**

52. Fromagerie du Buron,
Le Polygone, Niveau Bas,
Montpellier.

LORRAINE
53. Marché d'**Epinal** (cheese stall).

54. Ferme Marchal,
La Chapelle des Vés,
88160 **Le Thillot.**

MIDI-PYRÉNÉES
55. Marché de Bagnères-de-Bigorre
(cheese stall),
65200 **Bagnères-de-Bigorre.**

56. Le Cagibi,
17 allée d'Etigny, 31110 **Luchon.**

57. G.A.E.C. de Poubeau,
31110 **Luchon.**

58. Fromagerie à Millau,
Millau.

59. Marché de Mirande,
32300 **Mirande** (cheese stall).

60. Marché de Montesquieu-
Volvestre (cheese stall),
31310 **Montesquieu-Volvestre.**

61. Marché de Montréjeau (cheese
stall), 31210 **Montréjeau.**

62. Fête des Fromages,
46500 **Rocamadour.**

63. Gabriel Coulet,
Le Papillon, Société des Caves,
12250 **Roquefort-sur-Soulzon.**

64. Cap del Mail,
Cierp-Gaud,
31440 **Saint-Béat.**

65. Gilbert Chemin,
Crémerie du Couserans,
3 rue de la République,
09200 **Saint-Girons.**

66. E. Millat,
Halle Brauhauban,
65000 **Tarbes.**

67. Xavier Bourgon,
6 Place Victor-Hugo,
31000 **Toulouse.**

NORD-PAS-DE-CALAIS
68. Marché d'**Arras** (cheese stall).

69. Philippe Olivier,
43-45 rue Thiers,
62200 **Boulogne-sur-Mer.**

70. Cave de l'Abbaye de Maroilles,
59550 **Maroilles.**

NORMANDIE (HAUTE-)
71. Marché de Rouen (cheese stall),
76000 **Rouen**.

POITOU-CHARENTES
72. Jacques Guérin,
La Fromagerie,
19 rue Saint-Jean,
79000 **Niort.**

PROVENCE-ALPES-CÔTE-D'AZUR
73. Gérard Paul,
9 rue des Marseillais,
13100 **Aix-en-Provence.**

74. Restaurant de Puyfond,
Lieu-dit-Rigoulon,
13100 **Aix-en-Provence.**

75. Michel Bourgue,
La Maison du Fromage,
Halles Centrales,
84000 **Avignon.**

76. Halles Centrales, **Avignon**
(cheese stall).

77. Fromagerie Ranc,
40 rue Bonneterie,
84000 **Avignon.**

78. Edouard Ceneri,
La Ferme Savoyarde,
22 rue Meynadier,
06400 **Cannes.**

79. Le Fromagerie,
5 rue de l'Oratoire,
06130 **Grasse.**

80. Laiterie du Col Bayard,
Laye,
05500 **St-Bonnet-en-Champsaur.**

81. Bataille,
18 rue Fontange,
13006 **Marseille.**

82. Brigitte Cordier &
Françoise Fleutot,
04230 **Montlaux.**

83. Gérard Loup,
Les Provins,
04700 **Puimichel.**

RHÔNE-ALPES
84. Raymond Gagneux,
Sur le Cret, Richebourg,
74360 **Abondance.**

85. Denis Provent,
Laiterie des Halles,
2, Place de Genève,
73000 **Chambéry.**

86. Maréchal,
Halle de Lyon,
102 Cours Lafayette,
69003 **Lyon.**

87. Alain Martinet,
Halles de Lyon,
102 Cours Lafayette,
69003 **Lyon.**

88. Renée & René Richard,
Halles de Lyon,
102 Cours Lafayette,
69003 **Lyon.**

89. Daniel Boujon,
7 rue Saint-Sébastien,
74200 **Thonon-les-Bains.**

Index

The numbers in parentheses after the cheese names indicate where each cheese was bought and refer to the list of producers, shops, and markets on p. 234–235.

Bibliography

Androuët, Pierre, *Guide du Fromage*, Stock, Paris, 1971 (in French). English translation, Aidan Ellis, 1973; 2nd edition, Aidan Ellis, 1977; revised 1983.

Androuët, Pierre, *Le Livre d'Or du Fromage*, Atlas, Paris 1984

Androuët, Pierre, and Chabot, Yves, *Le Brie*, Presses du Village, Etrepillat, 1985

Annuaire des Industries Laitières, Comindus, Paris, 1991

Atlas Routier France, Michelin, London, 1989

Bon, Colette, *Les Fromages*, Hachette, Paris, 1979

Cart-Tanneur, Philippe, *Fromages et Vins de France*, Trame Way, Paris, 1989

Charron, G. *Les Productions Laitières*

Chast, Michel, and Voy, Henry, *Le Livre de l'Amateur de Fromages*, Robert Laffont, Paris, 1984

Clozier, René, *Géographie de la France*, Collection "Que sais-je?" Presses Universitaires de France, Paris, 1970

Courtine, Robert J., *Grand Livre de la France à Table*, Bordas, Paris, 1982

Courtine, Robert J., *Larousse des Fromages*, Librairie Larousse, Paris, 1987

Eck, André, *Fromages*, Technique et Documentation (Lavoisier), Paris, 1987

Evette, Jean-Luc, *La Fromagerie*, Presses Universitaires de France, Paris, 1975

Foubert, Jean-Marie, *Guide de la Route du Fromage*, Charles Corlet, Condé-sur-Noireu, 1987

Girard, Sylvie, *Fromages*, Editions Hermé, Paris, 1986

Le Jaouen, Jean-Claude, *La Fabrication du Fromage de Chèvre Fermier*, Itovic, Paris, 1982

Journal Officiel de la République Française

Le Liboux, Jean-Luc, *Nouveau Guide des Fromages de France*, Ouest-France, Rennes, 1984

Michelin Guide de Tourisme, Michelin, Paris

Montagne, Prosper, and Gottschalk, Docteur, *Larousse Gastronomique*, Librairie Larousse, Paris, 1938

Petit Robert (I, II), Dictionnaires Le Robert, Paris, 1989

Rance, Patrick, *The French Cheese Book*, Macmillan, London, 1989

Roc, Jean-Claude, *Le Buron de la Croix Blanche*, Editions Watel, Brioude, 1989

Stobbs, William, *Guide to the Cheeses of France*, Apple Press, London, 1984

Viard, Henry, *Fromages de France*, Dargaud, Paris, 1980

Acknowledgments

The authors would like to thank the following for their help in the preparation of this book:

Snow Brand Milk Products Co. Ltd.;
Chesco., Ltd.;
Cheese & Wine Academy, Tokyo;
Maison du Fromage, Valençay;
Fermier S. A;
SOPEXA, Japon;
Katsunori Kobayashi; Yohko Namioka;
Katsushi Kitamura;
Syndicat de Fromages d'Appellation d'Origine;
Institut National des Appellations d'Origine;
Association Nationale des Appellations d'Origine Laitières Françaises;
Association Marque Collective Savoie;
I.N.R.A. (Corte) E. Casalta /I.N.R.A. (Aurillac);
Chambre d'Agriculture;
La Société Fromagère de la Brie;
Société des Caves et des Producteurs Réunis de Roquefort;
INSEE / SOPEXA;

Centre Interprofessionnel de Documentation et d'Information Laitières;
Coopérative A. Pecurella;
A. Franceschi, A. Vinciguerra, J.-E. La-Noir, Crédit Agricole, Corsica;
T. Basset, Paris / D. Pin, Rungis;
Collette and Catherine Faller, Domaine Weinbach;
GAEC Louvradou, Margorce, 15140 Saint-Rémy-de Salers;
Fromageries Manhés, Bvd. Pavatou, 15000 Aurillac;
BATUT, 22 rue Vieille-du-Temple, 75004 Paris;
François Durand, Heronnière, 61120 Camembert (p. 64–65);
Coopérative de Lullin, 74470 Bellevaux (p. 21, 195).

Special thanks are extended to:
Kikuko Inoue, Takayoshi Nakasone, Kozue Tarumi, andReiko Mori.

PAGEOne wishes to thank
Matthew Cook for design assistance;
Neil Kelly for DTP assistance.